Biblical Psychotherapy

Biblical Psychotherapy

Reclaiming Scriptural Narratives for Positive Psychology and Suicide Prevention

Kalman J. Kaplan
Paul Cantz

Foreword by Thomas H. Jobe

LEXINGTON BOOKS
Lanham • Boulder • New York • London

Published by Lexington Books
An imprint of The Rowman & Littlefield Publishing Group, Inc.
4501 Forbes Boulevard, Suite 200, Lanham, Maryland 20706
www.rowman.com

Unit A, Whitacre Mews, 26-34 Stannary Street, London SE11 4AB

British Library Cataloguing in Publication Information Available

Library of Congress Cataloging-in-Publication Data Available

ISBN 978-1-4985-6081-8 (cloth : alk. paper) | ISBN 978-1-4985-6083-2 (pbk. : alk. paper) | ISBN
978-1-4985-6082-5 (electronic)

∞™ The paper used in this publication meets the minimum requirements of American
National Standard for Information Sciences Permanence of Paper for Printed Library
Materials, ANSI/NISO Z39.48-1992.

Printed in the United States of America

The authors dedicate this book to Dr. Erich Wellisch, unsung visionary, who had the depth and courage in 1953 to call for a biblical psychology. Sadly, he died of a sudden illness before his book *Isaac and Oedipus* was published in 1954. Unfortunately this work has been largely ignored over the years. It is truly groundbreaking and breathtaking in its vision. We belatedly honor Dr. Wellisch in this book. He is truly the father of modern biblical psychology, and we are proud and honored to walk in his footsteps.

Contents

Foreword

Biblical Psychotherapy by Kalman Kaplan and Paul Cantz is primarily a book about the psychology of suicide. It is not primarily about biblical theology or about cultural history. That said, the authors needed to deconstruct the texts of Greek drama and the relevant biblical texts that related to the issue of suicide. And, like gutting a building prior to its rehabilitation, they also had to deconstruct the Hellenized interpretation of the Greek translation of the Bible established by Ptolemy II of Egypt that influenced both Hellenized Christianity as well as Hellenized Judaism. It is important to remember that for Hellenized Judaism, Ha-Shem (Yahweh) was construed as an unpredictable and vengeful God, more Zeus on steroids than the actual Jewish conception of God as loving father. Not to mention the first- and second-century Gnostic Christians, who went out of their way to demonize Yahweh as the original source of evil in the world. The Christian fathers also used Latin translations of the *koine* Greek to denigrate the Old Testament for the purpose of highlighting the significance of the New Testament. The positive psychology of the biblical stories really emerged only after the authors exploded some of these negative rhetorical and hermeneutic interpretive distortions. The strong connection between the tradition of positive psychology from Maslow to Seligman, on the one hand, and the deconstructed biblical suicide narratives of the authors, on the other, leads one to suspect that though secular in tenor, positive psychologists have been implicitly influenced by these very biblical narratives.

For Kaplan and Cantz the scholarly preliminaries only serve to make room for the main event which focused on developing the key *psychological* interventions to help persons on the brink of suicide to take the crucial step back from the precipice. They de-center the stories involving suicide in the Bible and Greek literature from their theological, artistic, and cultural contexts, and as a result something quite remarkable happens. Once liberated from these contexts the suicidal personalities at the center of these stories emerge as human, all too human, but a sharp contrast distinguishes the two groups. The figures in ancient Greek drama and literature show resignation and despair and find no substantive mental resources to resist their inevitable suicides. On the other hand, the figures from the Bible stories show hope and resilience within their mental worlds and resist even the most extreme suicidal urges. Why the difference? The answer is complex but decisive and lies in the last eight chapters of this book in which the authors contrast seven Greek suicidal personalities with their biblical counterparts: a novel version of Plutarch's Lives but centering on the *differences* between Athens and Jerusalem. In each of the seven categories of suicidal motivation, the authors articulate what they term a biblical psychological intervention. They leverage these biblical psychological interventions as tools for both secular psychologists and psychiatrists, as well as rabbis, priests, and ministers who are uncomfortable with using biblical narratives in their pastoral counseling for fear that their parishioners might take the biblical text in a negative way. Their findings are demonstrated in actual clinical case reports in which the biblical psychological interventions are actually successfully employed for suicidal patients in their clinical care.

The overall thesis begins by showing that in the much valorized culture of ancient Greece, it was indeed the fates, and the fates alone, who ruled both mortals and gods, but, to the misfortune of mortals, the gods had both cunning and eternal life. The strong ambivalence among mortals to gain an exact knowledge of one's fate was predicated on the terrible certainty that, once discovered as in the Oedipus story, one's fate would more likely than not turn out to be worse than the present desultory moment of willful ignorance. While the gods themselves could not change what the fates had decreed for any given mortal, they could play selfish games with mortal men and women, raising them up at one moment only to cast them down at the next. Even when mortals proudly affirmed their individual freedom to decide their own fate it tragically conformed in precise detail with what the fates had originally decreed. Thus when Iphigenia self-assuredly announced that "I have chosen death, it is my own free choice," the audience knew full well that the fates had decided her sacrifice at the moment of her birth. The essence of the ancient Greek mentality came down to this: the Hobson's choice.

Thomas, or as some say, Tobias Hobson, was a prosperous merchant in early seventeenth-century England who provided horses to carry the mail from Cambridge to London. He had about forty horses in his Cambridge stable at any one time. He decided to rent out his horses to both students and professors at the university when his steeds were not carrying the mail to London. A customer would enter the stable, survey the vast numbers of potential mounts, and inevitably pick out the strongest horse available. Eventually Hobson realized his best horses were being over used so he worked out a profitable system of having his customers first marvel at the number of horses present but restrict the customer's choice to only the horse located next to the stable door: take it or leave it. Of course that steed had been carefully selected by Hobson to be the least worked horse at that moment in his entire stable. The citizen of the Hellenistic world was offered only one choice, a Hobson's choice, either accept the fate you currently suffer, the horse at the door, or freely walk away through suicide.

The Greek aristocracy and merchant elites played the role of Hobson, like the mid-western balloonist who frantically worked the controls behind the curtains in the Emerald City, to produce this masterful ideology, which locked in place the status quo that kept people in their place: take it or die trying to leave it. This is why suicide is glorified in ancient Greek drama and culture. And this ideology fit perfectly with a shrewd understanding of the psychology of the desperate individual who, because of his or her unenviable situation in life, may be contemplating suicide. Because even if desperate persons can still barely perceive other possibilities or other alternatives to suicide, once thrust into their depressed and turbulent state of mind by circumstances, those very possibilities and alternatives to suicide appear subjectively altogether unattainable reinforcing a sense of helplessness. Those very positive alternative possibilities vanish in the rush to self-destruction.

There is nothing, either philosophical or mythical, within the framework of Greek thought, to hold a person back, nor is there anything to enlighten an individual, that would make that person realize that there is a viable alternative to suicide when the urge overwhelms. The most original Greek philosopher, Socrates, served as the paradigm of honor while sipping his drought of hemlock. We are also reminded of the Sirens whose seductive call to destruction would have lured Odysseus had he not been strapped to the mast of his ship. The ancient Greeks also practiced infanticide often by abandonment and exposure of the infant as we see in the story of the Oedipus narrative. Ancient Greek epics and dramas tell tales about a mythical elite whose collective decisions were secondarily manipulated by a conspiracy among the gods. In the end, both gods and heroes were ultimately brought down by the rule of fate despite a valiant moment of grandeur, or a hero's rare elevation from mortality to divinity. The message to non-elites, such as ordinary citizens, traders, farmers, slaves, mercenary soldiers, and captives was clear: if those who rule you and the very gods themselves have suffered *their* terrifying fate then you, more than they, given your low station in life, deserve to suffer your sad fate, there is no alternative but suicide.

The authors brilliantly dissect the large number of suicides that were dramatized in the 26 surviving extant plays of Sophocles and Euripides. They show that whether or not actively entered into, or passively acquiesced to, by their aristocratic victims, those dramatic suicides had been artfully presented in such a way that they must have served as models that had the effect of removing any commonsense alternatives that might have stopped a deeply affected individual in the audience from imitating them. It is of relevance that the ever astute philosopher Aristotle only could find in Greek drama the cathartic emotions of pity and fear. There was no mention of positive emotions, no mention of resilience, and no mention of redemption. The authors are quick to point out that within these ancient Greek dramas and myths, Freud found the Hellenistic inspiration to abandon his early correct conviction that real childhood abuse and real childhood traumas played an important causative role in the origin of the neuroses and the psychoses and to substitute the idea of imaginary forces or fantasy in early childhood as the causative factor. Finally, with his speculative invention of the death instinct and the repetition compulsion after World War I, Freud discredited the role of trauma as the key causative factor in psychopathology and foreshadowed aspects of secular psychotherapy in the twentieth century that unfortunately trended toward blaming the victim.

Within the perspective of this negative turn in theoretical speculation in twentieth-century secular psychotherapy and psychoanalysis the reader must ask the question exactly how do the biblical psychological interventions proposed by the authors actually play a role in reversing this trend and succeed in real clinical cases? In chapters 5 through 11 of this book the reader will experience a breathtaking journey through the emotional peaks and valleys of actual patient experiences. These patients hover between life and death as Kaplan and Cantz use their biblical psychological interventions to thwart the patient's suicidal urges. Each of the evidence-based risk factors for suicide is first presented and a Greek character representing that risk factor interacts with a biblical figure who has had a similar life experience but who has pulled back from the brink of suicide. Each chapter then includes two actual clinical situations with the therapist using the biblical characters' triumph over suicidal urges as a model for clinical intervention.

As the suicidal urge waxes and wanes within a patient's experience the reader senses the unfolding of a general truth that is threaded through the biblical psychological interventions. That general truth comes down to this: the real authentic freedom we mortals are granted is the freedom *to depend* on others in choosing life over death. The biblical psychological interventions constitute new versions of an ancient wisdom that makes operative what is truly human about us, namely, that we all know instinctively that our loneliest moment comes at the moment of our death but none of us is strong enough to face that fact alone. The interventions formulated by the authors are therefore generalizable to both the secular therapeutic setting as well as the pastoral counseling area. This work substantially adds to the techniques of the therapeutic community and is the reason that this work warrants careful study. Think of the lives it might save. Scholars who are not therapists and who do not struggle daily with the exigency of the urge to self-destruction are clueless with regard to the insights of the authors who are both scholars *and* therapists. Scholars who believe that all mythology originates from the same source or that Athens and Jerusalem are somehow linked in some grand scheme of the Western tradition have gotten the picture all wrong. Alexander the Great got it right when he realized how destructive his own Greek culture could be to the vibrant Persian mentality and the peoples who had prospered under Persian rule, notably the lands governed by Jerusalem, as well as the Bactrian provinces he conquered. He may have paid with his life if his physician was indeed poisoning him or he could have simply died because of an infection. I believe in the former but what indeed do I know? Dear reader I leave it to you to judge.

Thomas H. Jobe

Acknowledgments

The authors would like to acknowledge the help of Kasey Beduhn and Becca Rohde, our editors at Lexington who diligently worked with us to bring *Biblical Psychotherapy* to fruition. We would also like to thank Dr. Anand Kumar, Chair of Psychiatry at the University of Illinois College of Medicine (UICCOM) and Drs. Martin Harrow and Thomas Jobe, also in the Department of Psychiatry at UICCOM. The authors would also like to thank Dr. Dean Bell, Provost at Spertus Institute of Jewish Learning and Leadership, and Gerald R. Stapleton, Director for Distance Education, Department of Medical Education at the University of Illinois at Chicago College of Medicine for facilitating an online running of much of the material in this course.

Dr. Kaplan would also like to acknowledge the support of friends and family as well as the International Exchange Program of the Fulbright Foundation and the John Templeton Foundation for providing needed support to develop aspects of this work. Dr. Cantz would like to thank Dr. Eunice Kim, Director of Training at Adler University and Dr. David Katz, former Department Chair of Clinical Psychology at Adler University (currently Dean of the Graduate School of Arts and Social Sciences at Lesley University) for their support while writing this book. Dr. Cantz would also like to acknowledge the unwavering love and support from his wife and three children.

Both authors would like to also express strong support for the Faith-Based Task Force of the National Action Alliance for Suicide Prevention, of which they are both members, for encouraging an atmosphere where religious and spiritual dimensions of life and death are discussed in an open atmosphere of interdisciplinary collegiality.

Introduction

At a certain point in the writing of a book, authors invariably ask themselves (even if only tacitly) the simple question as to why they have embarked on the exercise to begin with. Why have they invested such time and effort into the enterprise? A multitude of answers are possible: promotion, financial reward, peer recognition, a feeling of accomplishment, a sense of mission, an enjoyment of writing per se, or even something as simple as something to do to fill otherwise unoccupied time.

All these answers are reasonable and understandable, but they still beg the question of why the authors have written this particular book. So, we ask ourselves this question, why have we, Drs. Kalman Kaplan and Paul Cantz, written this particular book, *Biblical Psychotherapy: Reclaiming Scriptural Narratives for Positive Psychology and Suicide Prevention*? At one level, the answer is easy. We are both schooled in religious thought and also practicing psychotherapists. On a deeper level, this endeavor seems to bring together two fields which historically have been separate if not antagonistic to each other: religion and mental health. The background of this estrangement is complex and discussed somewhat in the body of the book itself. Yet something is very curious here.

Both fields, religion and mental health, deal with the human condition, often with very complex situations that challenge the very fabric of what it means to be human. Both religion and mental health seem more similar to great literature than to philosophy, focusing on real situations people find themselves in, rather than solutions to abstract issues or problems, which often seems more akin to strictly technical fields, such as mathematics or engineering. The enterprises of both religion and mental health understand full well that a person's arm-chair analysis of a problem is often a distant cousin, at best, of how he/she will actually act when confronted with this problem in a concrete situation.

Let us give a vivid example. Most philosophical systems share the value that lying is morally incorrect. However, our experience tells us that this is not always true. The senior author (Kalman Kaplan) would like to relate a personal story passed down by his late mother Edith Saposnik Kaplan, an author herself, in this regard. As a child fleeing pogroms with her mother and siblings during the upheaval in Russia during the revolution, Edith remembered the following harrowing incident.

Their family was stopped on the road to Chernobyl by a notorious anti-Semitic gangster named Shtrook who was going to rob and kill them. However, Edith's mother, Krana, recognized Shtrook as a man whose various infections she had helped to cure with herbs when he was a child. Krana reminded Shtrook of this and begged him to save their lives. He agreed to let them go on one condition: that she not tell the Bolshevik authorities as to their whereabouts. Krana vowed not to report them and swallowed a piece of earth as a pledge. The bandits shot in the air and let them go. However, news spread that Shtrook and his gang murdered two daughters of the *shochet* (the ritual slaughterer of animals in Judaism) the same day.

Upon arrival in Chernobyl, Krana immediately reported the whereabouts of Shtrook and his gang to the authorities at the commissariat who sent out the army, caught the gang, and hung them in the public square. Krana told my mother that she had done this in the service of preventing other murders (Kaplan, 1995, 13, 14).

This story has stayed with the senior author his entire life. His grandmother lied and broke her oath to a man who did not kill her and her family. Yet he had killed and was going to kill others. Did my grandmother do the right thing in reporting him? To me (Kaplan), the answer is unquestionably "yes"—meaning that it is sometimes morally right to not stand by your word, and conversely, morally wrong to stand by it. Indeed, the philosophical approach of situational ethics is aware of this reality. Moreover, both the fields of religion and mental health are immersed in the belief that abstract mathematical philosophical rules may have very little to do with how real people act in real situations.

Yet, as mentioned above, the fields of religion and mental health, while both dealing with highly emotional, unconscious, and often primitive drives, have, with some exceptions, had very little to do with each other. And when they did, they seemed to be either disparaging each other or talking past each other. This book is aimed at addressing this problem, focusing on a comparison of biblical and Graeco-Roman narratives with regard to seven risk factors for suicide prevention and life promotion. We argue throughout this work that the biblical narratives provide a sense of hope and resiliency to counter the hopelessness and despair so prevalent in comparable Greek and Roman narratives and which have left an indelibly fingerprint on traditional models of mental healthcare treatment.

Over 16 suicides and self-mutilation emerge in the 26 surviving tragedies of the great Greek playwrights Sophocles and Euripides. Countless other suicides occurred in actual Greek and Roman lives. In contrast only six suicides are found in the Hebrew Scriptures, while numerous suicide-prevention narratives exist. To combat the suicide epidemic with narratives implicitly based on ancient Greek narratives and pessimism is akin to treating a patient suffering from influenza with medicine contained on a spoon infected with the virus itself.

This book is unique in developing a suicide-preventive therapy based on these contrasting narratives to real-life patients that the authors have treated. Many of our recommendations are very simple yet rooted in biblical wisdom. We call for *Biblical Psychotherapy* as an in-depth approach to positive psychology, suicide-prevention, and indeed life-promotion. As Tevye proclaims in *Fiddler on the Roof*: "*LaChaim. LaChaim.* To Life!"

Chapter One

The Relevance of Biblical Narratives to Mental Health

The classical Greeks were quarrelsome as friends, treacherous as neighbors, brutal as masters, faithless as servants, shallow as lovers—all of which was in part redeemed by their intelligence and creativity. (Philip Slater, *The Glory of Hera*, 1968, 4)

There are many differences between the American middle-class male, with his elaborate controls, and the impulsive fifth century (B.C.E.) Greek. Yet the important differences are only quantitative—the qualitative differences are merely stylistic. Buried beneath every western man is a Greek—Western man is nothing but Alcibiades with a bad conscience, disguised as a plumber. (Philip Slater, *The Glory of Hera*, 1968, 451)[1]

The very word "psyche" is Greek. The central psychoanalytic concept of the formation of character and neurosis is shaped after the Greek Oedipus myth. . . . There is need for a Biblical psychology. (Erich Wellisch, *Isaac and Oedipus*, 1954, 115)

THE SUICIDE EPIDEMIC

Americans and Westerners generally have been living in recent times in an affluent society with an abundance of choices. Yet many people report feeling that their lives are aimless and without purpose, and moreover spiritually empty. Such people do not consider themselves to be leading fulfilling lives or even having lives worth living. Indeed, an April 22, 2016, article on health by Sabrina Tevernise in the *New York Times* reported that suicide rate in the United States has surged to a 30-year high, according to the National Center of Health Statistics, with increases in every age group except older adults.

1

The rise was particularly steep for women and was substantial among middle-aged Americans. The increase of suicide hit all segments of American society, jumping 63 percent for middle-aged women aged 45 to 64 over the course of the study while it rose 43% for men in that same age range. The overall suicide rate rose by 24% from 1999 to 2014, according to the National Center for Health Statistics, lifting the nation's suicide rate to 13 per 100,000 people, the highest since 1986. In all, 42, 773 died from suicide in 2014, compared with 29,199 in 1999. (Tavernise,April 22, 2016).

Statistics are just statistics, and cannot always be applied to a particular clinical case (i.e., the "ecological fallacy"), though these statistics offer compelling evidence that something has gone terribly wrong in the American society. Why are so many people choosing to take their lives? In this book we will approach this problem from what may seem by some to be an unusual perspective; a contrasting of biblical versus Greek narratives regarding suicide and suicide prevention, and a general promotion of life rather than death.

THE CHANGING ROLE OF RELIGION

In traditional societies, religious leaders have often applied the psychological wisdom implicit in the biblical religious traditions to the problems in living of members of their congregations. The situation in the West seems to be dramatically different where many people see biblical religions as irrelevant or atavistic and may be even be actively antagonistic and indeed hostile to religious ideology and even religious practitioners. This seems to be especially the case in contemporary Western Europe. Mental health professionals are thus left alone to deal with problems of everyday life, demonstrating a shift in the traditional scope of practice of the clergy. Moreover, mental health practitioners have until recently tended to disparage belief in a creator as a delusion (an "illusion" or even a "mass delusion" as Freud famously called it) or immature, and to avoid in therapy any reference to a patient's religious beliefs and their influence on them.

The antagonism towards religion among the general public is considerably less in America, but even here psychotherapists are too often ignorant of if not antagonistic to religion, frequently in a manner incongruent with the patient's own orientation. More than that, the psychotherapist often fails to appreciate or even possess more than a superficial or caricatured understanding of what entails a serious religious approach to life. For example, the current *Diagnostic and Statistical Manual of the American Psychiatric Association* (*DSM-5*) lists "scrupulosity" as a pathological guilt about moral or religious issues. It is typically conceptualized as a moral or religious form of obsessive-compulsive disorder. Although certainly not all religious people would be diagnosed with scrupulosity, the diagnosis itself is a bit disquieting, dove-tailing too closely for comfort with the traditional antipathy towards religion too often exhibited by mental health professionals.

Clergy and Mental Health

However, consider the following actual statistics in America today. On the surface psychologists and psychiatrists seem to service the majority of the population's mental health needs, while clergy are often reduced to purely religious, ceremonial, or social duties. However, is this really true? In a comprehensive review of 10 separate studies Weaver (1995) found that in reality clergy provide a great deal of counseling to their congregants, indeed spending 10% to 20% of their 40- to 60-hour workweek counseling people with emotional or marital problems. Koenig (2005) ingeniously applied this percentage to a 1998 Department of Labor estimate of 353,000 clergy serving congregations in the United States (including 4,000 Jewish rabbis, 49,000 Catholic priests, and 300,000 Protestant pastors) and arrived at the following aggregate statistic: clergy spend approximately 138 million hours delivering what most would categorize as mental health care each year! For the approximately 83,000 members of the American Psychological Association (APA) to reach such a figure would require each member to offer mental health services at an unrealistically high rate of 33.2 hours per week (this is before accounting for the fact that many APA members are not even clinicians but purely researchers!). Koenig goes on to report a study of help-seeking for personal problems from 1957 to 1976. What is significant is that in these years (and this is the important point), more Americans sought help from a clergyman than from a mental health professional.

Yet, many clergy and even practicing pastoral counselors do not have a solid base of knowledge regarding treating moderate to profound psychological distress, and of the various emotional issues that their sermons may provoke. Lafuze et al. (2004) for example, report that 86% of 1,031 mainline Methodist ministers sampled agreed that medication helps people control symptoms and manage their relationships better. However, 47% of these same pastors incorrectly believed that psychiatric patients are "more dangerous than an average citizen," with only 24% in disagreement. Views of more fundamentalist or conservative clergy have yet to be determined, but are assumedly even less encouraging than those just cited.

Secondly, many pastoral counselors put aside their religious instincts when providing counseling, often feeling compelled to wear two hats, neither of which fit to their satisfaction. In their zeal to treat religion as a private as opposed to a public matter, pastoral counselors have often adopted a therapeutic mode which is far from neutral, but based on assumptions and values emerging from an implicit classical Greek framework, in the process creating a hybrid approach that ironically neither satisfies a reasonable benchmark of religious or psychological therapeutic sophistication. Too busy retrofitting biblical pegs into Greek holes, most religious clinicians eschew the very idea of using the Bible as a source-text for the development of an epistemologically sound meta-theory. The privileged position that Greek thought maintains within the ethos of the psychiatric establishment has rendered sterile the potential theoretical contributions of biblical narratives, even for those clinicians already sympathetic to biblical material.

Sermons and Treatment

Let us provide a vivid example of this lacuna. Some number of years ago, the senior author was teaching a class of clergy a course in biblical psychology, and specifically as how to use biblical narratives in helping members of their congregations to live better lives. Clergy were asked to present memorable incidents from their experiences. Some of the stories were fairly commonplace. However, one story stood out. A rabbi from the East Coast told of giving a sermon on the early liaison between King David and Bathsheba (2 Samuel 11); specifically, on how David coveted Bathsheba after seeing her bathing nude and indeed had sexual relations with her even though she was married to Uriah, one of David's generals. To make matters worse, when David realized Bathsheba had become pregnant, David tried to hide his deed by calling Uriah home from the battlefield so as to sleep with his wife and thus hide the fact that David had impregnated her. When Uriah refused to sleep with his wife while his men were fighting in the battlefield, David arranged to abandon Uriah in a most dangerous part of the battlefield, and thus facilitated his death.

The rabbi directly quoted the following two lines from the biblical text: "When Uriah's wife heard that her husband was dead, she mourned for him. After the time of mourning was over, David had her brought to his house, and she became his wife and bore him a son. But the thing David had done displeased the Lord" (2 Samuel 11:26–27).

The rabbi indicated that he drew a moral lesson from this story and concluded it with the prophet Nathan's encounter with David and the parable Nathan presented to him.

There were two men in a certain town, one rich and the other poor. The rich man had a very large number of sheep and cattle, but the poor man had nothing except one little ewe lamb he had bought. He raised it, and it grew up with him and his children. It shared his food, drank from his cup, and even slept in his arms. It was like a daughter to him.

"Now a traveler came to the rich man, but the rich man refrained from taking one of his own sheep or cattle to prepare a meal for the traveler who had come to him. Instead, he took the ewe lamb that belonged to the poor man and prepared it for the one who had come to him." David burned with anger against the man and said to Nathan, "As surely as the Lord lives, the man who did this must die! He must pay for that lamb four times over, because he did such a thing and had no pity."

Then Nathan said to David, "You are the man! This is what the Lord, the God of Israel, says: 'I anointed you king over Israel, and I delivered you from the hand of Saul. I gave your master's house to you, and your master's wives into your arms. I gave you all Israel and Judah. And if all this had been too little, I would have given you even more. Why did you despise the word of the Lord by doing what is evil in his eyes? You struck down Uriah the Hittite with the sword and took his wife to be your own. You killed him with the sword of the Ammonites.

"Now, therefore, the sword will never depart from your house, because you despised me and took the wife of Uriah the Hittite to be your own" (2 Samuel 12:1–10).

After his sermon, according to the rabbi, a member of his congregation came up to him, seemingly upset, and asked if he could speak with him immediately. The rabbi of course agreed and ushered the man into his private office. When the member of the congregation entered the rabbi's office, he broke down in tears, and told the rabbi *that he himself* (the member of the congregation) *was that man*. Although he was married, he has been having an affair with a friend's wife. And that hearing the sermon filled him with guilt. The rabbi reported that he began to talk with the man and offered him some tea and cake. The man then announced that he felt so guilty that he wanted to kill himself.

Does "Suicide" Scare Clergy?

At the mention of the term "suicide," the rabbi reported freezing and wanting to get the man out of his office and off his hands as soon as possible Rather than treat the congregant's statement as hyperbole, and an understandable reaction to the experience of strong guilt, the rabbi honestly confessed that his major goal became to get the man out of his office as quickly as possible and "wash his hands"[2] of the entire matter and go to see an expert in suicide, in other words, a "suicide prevention specialist" (whatever this connoted), who would be better equipped to handle this case who the rabbi thought was too serious a problem for him to deal with. I pointed out that the rabbi had needlessly recused himself from this case under the mistaken belief that this hypothetical "suicide prevention specialist" would better know how to treat this "suicidal" man. All this, even though this "specialist" might have been totally ignorant of or even hostile towards the biblical story, and not able or willing to acknowledge that the man's experience of guilt towards his cuckolding of his friend was actually a healthy response, that he had been repressing. And that the man's statement of "feeling so guilty he wanted to kill himself" was probably hyperbole rather than the statement of a specific plan or even an intent.

I pointed out to the rabbi that he could have gone on with the biblical narrative to help provide a vehicle for the man to attempt to atone for his misdeed, and thus come to a resolution of his morally disruptive and ugly situation.

"This is what the Lord says: 'Out of your own household I am going to bring calamity on you. Before your very eyes, I will take your wives and give them to one who is close to you, and he will sleep with your wives in broad daylight. You did it in secret, but I will do this thing in broad daylight before all Israel.'"

Then David said to Nathan, "I have sinned against the Lord."

Nathan replied, "The Lord has taken away your sin. You are not going to die. But because by doing this you have shown utter contempt for the Lord, the son born to you will die."

After Nathan had gone home, the Lord struck the child that Uriah's wife had borne to David, and he became ill. David pleaded with God for the child. He fasted and spent the nights lying in sackcloth on the ground. The elders of his household stood beside him to get him up from the ground, but he refused, and he would not eat any food with them.

On the seventh day, the child died. David's attendants were afraid to tell him that the child was dead, for they thought, "While the child was still living, he wouldn't listen to us when we spoke to him. How can we now tell him the child is dead? He may do something desperate."

David noticed that his attendants were whispering among themselves, and he realized the child was dead. "Is the child dead?" he asked.

"Yes," they replied, "he is dead."

Then David got up from the ground. After he had washed, put on lotions, and changed his clothes, he went into the house of the Lord and worshipped. Then he went to his own house, and at his request they served him food, and he ate.

His attendants asked him, "Why are you acting this way? While the child was alive, you fasted and wept, but now that the child is dead, you get up and eat!"

He answered, "While the child was still alive, I fasted and wept. I thought, 'Who knows? The Lord may be gracious to me and let the child live.' But now that he is dead, why should I go on fasting? Can I bring him back again? I will go to him, but he will not return to me." Then David comforted his wife Bathsheba, and he went to her and made love to her. She gave birth to a son, and they named him Solomon. The Lord loved him; and because the Lord loved him, he sent word through Nathan the prophet to name him Jedidiah (2 Samuel 12:1–10).

In other words, the continuation of the biblical story provides a vehicle for the member of the congregation to begin to atone for his misdeed and set his conscience at rest. As reprehensible as his behavior was, the congregation member had not impregnated his paramour nor had he arranged to have her husband killed. Yet the rabbi was so frightened by the very mention of suicide that he lost his bearings and cast the man adrift to the care of a suicide-prevention "specialist."

This was most unfortunate and is an all too typical occurrence of therapists in today's world to trust biblical stories and metaphors in a world hostile to biblical religion, in which hopelessness and meaninglessness saturate the emotional life of too many patients/clients. This sense of hopelessness and despair can lead to all kinds of deleterious effects such as a sense of inertia, discontent, and general gloom—basically an unfulfilled life. It can lead one to the feeling that he/she is hopelessly trapped in a repetitive cycle which can provoke sporadic bursts of involvement in dead-end or even self-destructive ventures. These ventures can lead to a range of psychological maladies, from emotional paralysis, eating disorders, aggressive outbursts towards others or oneself, and even suicide or homicide or both. Examination of historical narratives indicates that many of these problems were quite prevalent in the high societies of ancient Greece and Rome.

What Does Jerusalem Have to Say to Athens?

Philip Slater brilliantly illustrated the pathological patterns in Greek family life that we can observe echoes of in contemporary society. Overcoming the rampant idealization of Greek society, Slater describes the classical Greeks as, "quarrelsome as friends, treacherous as neighbors, brutal as masters, faithless as servants, shallow as lovers—all of which was in part redeemed by their intelligence and creativity." Slater goes on to argue that there are many differences between the American middle-class male, with his elaborate controls, and the impulsive fifth-century (B.C.E.) Greek. Yet, for Slater, the important differences are only quantitative—the qualitative differences are merely stylistic. "Buried beneath every western man is a Greek—Western man is nothing but Alcibiades[3] with a bad conscience, disguised as a plumber" (Philip Slater, *The Glory of Hera*, 1968, 451).

In this same vein, Bennett Simon (1978) has pointed to the dependence of psychiatry on Greek thinking highlighting the intellectual heritage that the contemporary mental health establishment has unwittingly bought into. This should not be surprising as so many of our psychological models have been either implicitly or explicitly based on ancient Greek and Roman narratives (e.g., Oedipus, Electra, and Narcissus). Even the word *psyche* derives from the Greek word for soul and implies a dissociation with the *soma* (body). This is very different than the ancient Hebrew word for soul, *nefesh*, which has been classically understood as enjoying an integrated relationship with the body—a true and cooperative synthesis between body and soul which aligns with leading edge neuropsychological and neuro-psychoanalytic research on the mind/body connection.

While it is true that many Greek myths reflect truths regarding core conflicts of the human condition, there must be room to question whether the resolutions promoted by these myths represent the highest ideals of psychological progression, or if they merely represent the best solutions that could be expected from the Greek world view. The rich dynamism of biblical thought conveyed through its narratives remains pregnant with potential contributions to the theoretical edifice and clinical practice of psychology. Yet the freedom presented in the original biblical Hebrew may have itself been compromised through the translation of the Hebrew Scriptures into Greek.

Indeed, the Russian-Jewish philosopher Lev Shestov, in his magnum opus *Athens and Jerusalem* (1937/1966), warned against exactly this—the seductive trend to analyze the Hebrew Bible through Greek optics, posing the question:

> How shall we succeed in reading and understanding Scripture not according to the teaching of the great Greek masters, but as they have transmitted to us, by means of the Books of Books. As long as the Bible was exclusively in the hands of the "chosen people," this question did always find themselves under the dominion of rational principles and of that technique of thought which has somehow become our second nature, which we consider—without even realizing it—as the immutable conditions for the grasping and possession of truth. . . . Is a man educated by the Greeks capable of preserving that freedom which is the condition of the right of understanding what the Bible says? (278)

More recently, Clines (1995) has aptly observed that "the function of commentary on biblical texts has been to familiarize the Bible, to normalize it to our own cultural standards, to render it as undisturbing as possible, to press it into the service of a different worldview," concluding that "it is the task of scholars, taking a step of critical distance as best they can from their own culture and their personal scripts, to bring back into the foreground the otherness of the familiarized" (33).

The Norwegian clergyman and noted linguist Thorlief Boman (1960) has attempted to differentiate Hebrew and Greek ways of thinking. Boman argued that Greek thinking emphasizes the observable, the static, the logical, and the nomothetic, while in contradistinction, Hebrew thought stresses hearing, the dynamic, the psychological, and the ideographic. More recently, Yosef Yersushalmi continued in the same vein, arguing that Freud himself carried the Greek cyclical view of history and sense of hopelessness into the very fabric of psychoanalysis. As a result, Freud's approach was fundamentally constrained by a Greek-based meaning structure that failed to offer practitioners and patients alike an ambitious vision of psychological well-being.

IF FREUD WAS SO ANTI-RELIGIOUS, WHY DID HE EMBRACE GREEK RELIGION?

An interesting pattern emerges. Although Freud clearly dismissed religion as a "mass delusion," his hostility seemed largely focused on biblical legends (which he seems to define as religious) and not on Greek myths such as Oedipus and Narcissus which he seems so enamored of (and which themselves emerge from the Pantheon of Greek gods). A letter from Freud reproduced in a recent work by Rolnik (2007) confirms this impression. A short time after the publication of *The Interpretation of Dreams*, the Jewish historian and folklorist Alter Druyanov (then of Odessa) wrote to Freud to alert him of the considerable similarity between his ideas and those of the early Hebrews. Here is Freud's answer: "I'm happy to learn of a competent reader of my book from so far a place. As far as I'm concerned however the similarity between my ideas and those of the early Greeks strikes me as much more salient." When made aware of the aforementioned work of Shestov by a mutual friend Max Eintington, Freud replies: "You cannot imagine how unaffected I am by these convoluted philosophical discussions" (Rolnik, 2007, 56).

The effects of Freud's anti-biblical bias are still apparent in psychology and psychiatry. Greek narratives leave people trapped, or worse, resulting in unsatisfactory attempts to reach positive psychological accommodations. Greek narratives (e.g., Oedipus, Electra, Narcissus) make abundantly clear that it is impossible to escape one's fate, no matter how hard one tries, in order to achieve constructive accommodations. Sadly, Greek characters find their attempts at resolution to be fruitless, destructive, and sometimes even fatal.

Freud tries his best to bring the unconscious father-son conflict to conscious awareness in order to make it amenable to control. Yet he has no real way of transforming it. Yerushalmi puts it this way: "Like Sisyphus pushing his rock, Oedipus and Laius must contend forever. At one point in the cycle, the father must be slain by the son; at another, the return of the repressed, the father returns; the return is only illusion, for the cycle will begin again" (Yerushalmi, 1991, 95). Freud seems unappreciative if not antagonistic to the biblical tradition. Freud insists that his work is based on Greek legends and thus seems to have had no ultimate faith in the transformative powers of the God of the Hebrew Bible to bring any genuine hope to the human condition. The best that can be hoped for then, is an amelioration of a miserable existence, rather than anything genuinely hopeful. As a case in point, we cite

Freud's response to a question from a patient as to how psychoanalysis will help him.

When I have promised my patients help or relief by means of a cathartic treatment, I have repeatedly had to listen to the following objection: "You yourself tell me that what I am suffering from is probably connected with my circumstances and fate. You can't change anything about that. So how are you going to help me?" And I have been able to answer: "I do not doubt that it would be easier for fate to take away your suffering than it would for me. But you will see for yourself that much has been gained if we succeed in turning your hysterical misery into common unhappiness. Having restored your inner life, you will be better able to arm yourself against that unhappiness" (Freud and Breuer, 1895/2004, 306).

It can be debated what Freud meant by this quote. On the one hand, it can be argued that Freud conveyed a message of hope to his distraught patient, forecasting that after a successful treatment one can expect to address their pathology and begin experiencing a range of sadness that does not risk cascading into a major depressive condition. To fully experience life is to experience the full range of human emotion, and therefore the goal of treatment would not be to abolish the possibility of developing feelings of sadness and sorrow, but rather to help the patient cultivate the resilience to successfully weather these unwelcomed emotions in a psychologically mature manner (c.f., Cyrulnik, 2011). On the other hand, as we will detail below, this quote also speaks to the prognostic limitations of Freud's imagination, choosing only to address negative symptomatology without being concerned for what makes an individual's life fulfilling.

Unfortunately, modern psychology and psychiatry have been dependent, implicitly or explicitly, on this ancient Greek world view. In this tragic Greek view, protagonists are done in by immutable and unchangeable character flaws. In Shakespeare's tragedies, for example, Macbeth is done in by ambition, Othello by jealousy, Hamlet by indecision, Lear by foolish vanity, and Coriolanus by an excessive rigidity. All their attempts at change are for naught, and they wind up spinning their wheels, cycling back and forth. This hardly represents a positive world view or a positive psychology (Seligman and Csíkszentmihályi, 2000).

IS THERE A BIBLICAL MEDICINE?

Despite the importance of ancient biblical civilization and the great involvement of Jews in medical science, it is striking how little biblical and Talmudic ideas seems to have influenced Jewish physicians, who seemed completely under the influence of the Greek physician Galen. Sussman Muntner, a professor of the history of religion at the Hebrew University of Jerusalem makes the following observation.

It is surprising to note that Talmudic pathology seems to have had no impact on medieval medicine, not even on the great Jewish physicians of the Middle Ages, such as Moses Maimonides and Isaac ben Solomon Israeli (I. Judaeus), who were thoroughly familiar with the Talmud. Medieval medicine was so completely under the spell of (the Greek physician) Galen that anything he ever said about medicine was accepted as infallible; while the health rules of the Talmud were ignored. . . . *The Talmud was regarded as a purely religious code and not as a medical treatise of any kind* (emphasis ours; Muntner, 1977).

It was not until 1911 that a systematic presentation was published of Biblical views of anatomy, epidemiology, surgery, dentistry and otology, neurological disorders, obstetrics as well as mental disease (Preuss, 1971)

The Prayer of Maimonides versus the Hippocratic Oath

Perhaps the single most important distinction between a Greek and biblical approach to medicine lies in their different approaches to treating a disease versus a whole person. This difference is dramatically illustrated in the contrast between the Hippocratic Oath (Edelstein, 1943) and the physician's prayer attributed, perhaps incorrectly, to Maimonides (Golden, 1900).

Kaplan, Schwartz, and Jones (2010) have summarized five differences between the approaches of Maimonides and Hippocrates as follows: For Hippocrates, (1) The physician is the servant of the "art" or "nature." (2) The "art" consists of three parties: the disease, the patient, and the physician. (3) The disease is the enemy, something to be combated by the patient along with the physician. (4) With regard to the disease, the physician is exhorted to do good or to do no harm. (5) In the Hippocratic Oath, the physician swears to "give no deadly medicine to any one, if asked, nor suggest any such counsel."

The physician's prayer attributed to Maimonides is fundamentally different: (1) The physician has been chosen by God to watch over the life and health of his creatures. (2) The physician prays for inspiration from God for love for his art and for God's creatures. There are three involved parties: God, the physician, and God's creature (the patient). (3) The disease is a beneficent messenger sent by God to foretell approaching danger and to urge him to avert it. (4) The physician has been chosen by God in his mercy to watch over the life and death of his creatures. (5) The physician specifically prays to remove from his patients "all charlatans and the whole host of officious relatives and know-all nurses, cruel people who arrogantly frustrate the wisest purposes of our art and often lead Thy creatures to their death."

The most important distinction for our purposes is the contrasting view of disease between these two men. In the Hippocratic Oath, the disease is the enemy and the fight of the physician is to eradicate the disease or to cure the symptom. The patient seems secondary to this. In the prayer attributed to Maimonides, in contrast, the physician must treat the person (God's creature) and the disease or symptom can be seen as an ally warning the physician of danger to the patient and as a signal to avert it. This latter view resonates quite well with more modern views of disease, especially with regard to disorders of the immune system. Nevertheless, a Hebrew basis for medicine is far from achieving widespread acceptance or even acknowledgment.

Maimonides called his ideal type of human being—the sage—a rofe nefashot, a "healer of souls." Today we call such a person a psychotherapist, a word coined relatively recently from the Greek word "psyche," meaning "soul," and therapeia, "healing." Although many of the pioneering psychotherapists in modern times have been Jewish, many of them have ignored or actively disparaged the Hebrew Scriptures, thus explicitly or implicitly buying into a Greek view of man (c.f., Slater, 1968; Simon, 1978). A number of interesting thinkers in psychology have begun to develop a more biblical and Jewish approach to psychology in the last few decades. For example, a number of innovative psychologists, sociologists, and political scientists have been developing this topic in the last few decades (e.g., Bakan, 1975; Caspi, 2011; Hazony, 2012; Rottenberg, 1993; 2004; 2005; 2016; Shoham, 2011; Yerushalmi; 1991). Weiss (2000) has specifically published a study of rabbis as mental health professionals.

Enter Erich Wellisch

Perhaps the modern founder of the field of biblical psychology is the psychiatrist Dr. Eric Wellisch, medical director of Grayford Child Guidance Clinic in England, who over 60 years ago called specifically for a biblical psychology, arguing that:

> The very word "psyche" is Greek. The central psychoanalytic concept of the formation of character and neurosis is shaped after the Greek Oedipus myth. It is undoubtedly true that the Greek thinkers possessed an understanding of the human mind which, in some respects, is unsurpassed to the present day, and that the trilogy of Sophocles still presents us with the most challenging problems. But stirring as these problems are, they were not solved in the tragedy of Oedipus. In ancient Greek philosophy, only a heroic fight for the solution but no real solution is possible. Ancient Greek philosophy has not the vision of salvation.
>
> No positive use has been made, so far, of the leading ideas of Biblical belief in the attempts of modern psychology to formulate basic findings and theories. But there is no reason why the Bible should not prove at least if not more fruitful than the concepts of Greek or Eastern religious experience. . . .

Psychology and theology are at the crossroads. The atheistic and pantheistic aspects of modern psychology lead to dangerous conclusions. . . . The non-biological aspect of theology is doomed to lead to frustration. There is need for a Biblical psychology. (Wellisch, 1954, 115)

Wellisch was an unrecognized visionary who tragically died shortly before his book was published. Yet, like many visionaries, he was far ahead of his time and did not receive the recognition he deserved during his lifetime. The field of biblical psychology is slowly emerging at the present time and is absolutely unique in being driven by an intrinsic reading of the Scriptures themselves rather than retrofitting our understanding of these readings to artificially support one current fashionable psychological theory or another.

A genuine biblical psychology, in contrast, has the potential of transcending the limitations of earlier waves of psychology in several ways. First, it differs from both psychodynamic theory and behaviorism in its emphasis on the integration of inner processes and outer behavior. Second, it differs from humanistic psychology, in being open to the spiritual concerns of faith communities. Third, it transcends multicultural psychology by trying to identify the universal processes intrinsic to human life itself as they are manifested in the particular culturally specific yet universal areas of behavior described in the Hebrew Bible.

This book presents a psycho-biblical approach to therapy, which we have developed in response to the Greek bias in mental health that has led to a limited and narrow view of psychological health (e.g., Oedipus, Electra, Narcissus, the mind-body split). Nowhere is the Greek sense of the tragic more dangerous for psychotherapy and counseling than in dealing with suicidal patients or clients. Biblical narratives provide an absolutely necessary alternative world view, providing a therapy allowing healthy resolutions of real-life problems. We present fourteen clinical case studies in chapters 5 through 11.

The objection may be raised in current circles that our proposed approach lacks an evidence-base. Our response is twofold. First of all, as we shall show, the approach is very much evidence-based and has been used successfully with a good number of patients. Secondly, the proactive observations of the clinical psychologist Jonathan Shedler (2010; 2015) are quite relevant here. In questioning the purported superiority of "evidence-based" therapies, Shedler offers several quite important arguments. First, he argues that the very term "evidence-based" is a loaded term, in fact equated with what he calls a "manualized treatment," most often equated with the brief, highly structured cognitive behavioral therapy (CBT). Such an approach may overemphasize symptom suppression instead of exploring and addressing the motivational factors that lead to psychopathology.

Shedler's reading of the literature suggests that despite claims to the contrary, psychodynamic therapies are more effective than other approaches. What is important for our purposes here is Shedler's listing of seven features essential to psychodynamic therapy: (1) focus on affect and expression of emotion; (2) exploration of attempts to avoid distressing thoughts and feelings; (3) identification of recurring themes and patterns; (4) discussion of past experience with a developmental focus; (5) focus on interpersonal relations; (6) focus on the therapy relationship; and (7) exploration of fantasy life.

Shedler's critique of CBT may be too strong, throwing out the baby with the bath water. It is undeniable that some practitioners apply CBT in a somewhat mechanical way. Yet much of Aaron Beck's approach as the founder of CBT can be seen as replacing a negative life view with a more positive one (Beck, 1963; 1967). However, a prominent critique of this approach argues that CBT over-emphasizes symptom suppression instead of exploring and addressing the motivational factors that lead to psychopathology. In our terms, this attempt runs parallel to replacing a tragic Greek vision of events with a hopeful biblical view.

It is quite possible for a psychodynamic therapy to be trapped in a negative Greek mind-set and a cognitive behavioral therapy to be pushing for a positive view of life, just not delving deeply enough in exploring the foundational motivational variables that underwrite human development. Much of the emphasis on behavioral change influencing inner attitudinal life rather than the reverse causality derives from the work of social psychologist Leon Festinger in his theory of cognitive dissonance (Festinger, 1957). Act first and inner emotions will follow, as the Hebrew people responded to God as they accepted the Law: "*naaseh v'nishma*" (Exodus 24:7) (act and you will come to understand).

In any case, the essential features Shedler lists are present in our conception of a biblical approach to mental health and how it fits into a depth positive hopeful view of life. First, as we just mentioned above, biblical narratives absolutely focus on affect and emotion, but not at the expense of action. Second, biblical figures experience all sorts of distressing thoughts and emotions, yet are provided the strength to work their way through them. They don't have to avoid or evade them. Third, biblical narratives emphasize recurring themes and patterns. Fourth, the entire biblical presentation is focused on how the past influences the future. We are not trapped by the past, but we are rooted in it and cannot avoid dealing with it. Fifth, the entire focus of biblical narratives is on interpersonal relations ("It is not good for man to be alone," Genesis 2:18). Sixth, biblical narratives focus on the relationship between a human being and God, and thus lend themselves quite well to a focus on the relationship between patient and therapist. Finally, seventh, biblical narratives have a life and logic of their own, resting on the journey a person must make in his own relationship with God. Yet when a biblical figure may stray too far from his life mission, God will refocus him. This model precludes over-structuring therapy sessions in advance and letting patients speak freely about whatever is on their mind. At the same time, the therapist must focus the patient when his free associations are being used to evade the central problem the patient is trying to deal with.

In a very real sense, the Greek mind created an antithesis between mythos and logos. In the *Republic*, Plato declares that "there is an old quarrel between philosophy and poetry" (607b). Henri Frankfort and his group at the Oriental Institute of the University of Chicago published a number of fascinating books on this topic at in the 1940s through the 1970s (Frankfort et al., 1946; 1972). The essence of this work is that philosophy and later Greek history was in many ways opposed to the earlier mythic structure.[4] Not so for the Hebrew Bible, where earlier legends blend into later history in a relatively non-antagonistic seamless way, making it difficult to exactly pin down where legend ends and history begins. Perhaps this was one of Freud's great insights, expressed so well in Euripides' great drama *The Bacchae* and Thomas Mann's novella, *Death in Venice* (1925) regarding the return of the repressed (again see the previously cited work of Yerushalmi, 1991, 95). This ever-repeating cycle represents Freud's tragic understanding of the psychological processes intrinsic to a deterministic universe.

This is in marked contrast to the Hebrew Scripture's ringing and hopeful proclamation of an unambivalent resolution of the Oedipus complex:

> And He shall turn the heart of the fathers to the children,
> And the heart of the children to their fathers. (Malachi 3:22–24)

The present book will describe how both secular and pastoral/rabbinic approaches to psychotherapy can be enhanced by de-situating biblical narratives and thinking from their formal theological context and employing them in a psychotherapeutic way to promote life rather than simply to prevent suicide. This represents a positive way to promote an individual's capacity to activate and mobilize innate, perhaps even divinely endowed, domains of resiliency to overcoming major life challenges. Although the aim of this book in some ways parallels that of a positive psychology (see Seligman and Csíkszentmihályi, 2000). We will argue in the next chapter that the aims go beyond those of positive psychology in addressing patients whose life views may not be altered by a simple sense of learned efficacy.

NOTES

1. The authors would like to thank Ms. Dashka Slater for permission to use the quote taken from her father's (Philip Slater's) publication "The Glory of Hera."

2. The irony of a rabbi using a term originally attributed to Pontius Pilate over the fate of Jesus (Matthew 27:24) was not lost on the senior author.

3. Alcibiades was a gifted and flamboyant Athenian statesman and general whose shifting of sides during the Peloponnesian War in the fifth century B.C.E. earned him a reputation for cunning and treachery. Good looking and rich, he was also notorious for his extravagant lifestyle and loose morals. Never short of enemies or admirers—amongst whom was Socrates—he was one of the most colorful leaders in the history of Classical Athens.

4. Hunter (1982) however observes that Thucydides, like Herodotus, treats mythical legends as if they had a basis in history, and the characters who appear in myths as if they were real people, she concludes that "one cannot discover in the works of Herodotus and Thucydides a distinction between historical and mythical time" (Hunter, 1982, 103). On the contrary, Thucydides' conviction that "the past is similar to the present" leads him to explicate even the mythical past in light of the present, in a reverse of the process which he recommends to his reader in dealing with the future (Hunter, 1971; 1982, 102–3).

Chapter Two

Biblical Psychology

Positive Psychology and Beyond

The field of positive psychology at the subjective level is about valued subjective experiences: well-being, contentment, and satisfaction (in the past); hope and optimism (for the future); and flow and happiness (in the present). At the individual level, it is about positive individual traits: the capacity for love and vocation, courage, interpersonal skill, aesthetic sensibility, perseverance, forgiveness, originality, future mindedness, spirituality, high talent, and wisdom. At the group level, it is about the civic virtues and the institutions that move individuals toward better citizenship: responsibility, nurturance, altruism, civility, moderation, tolerance, and work ethic. (Martin P. Seligman and Mihály Csíkszentmihályi, Positive Psychology: An Introduction: *American Psychologist*, 2000, 55, 5–14)[1]

The Creator of the world has Himself become subordinate to Necessity which He created and which, without at all seeking or desiring it has become the sovereign of the universe. . . . We must try to stand up against Necessity itself, try to free the living and feeling Parmenides from dead and altogether indifferent power. (Lev Shestov, *Athens and Jerusalem*, 1966, 85–86, 91–92)[2]

In France I had almost always seen the spirit of religion and the spirit of freedom pursuing courses diametrically opposed to each other; but in America I found that they were intimately united, and they reigned in common over the same country. (Alexis de Tocqueville, *Democracy in America*, 1863, 394)

The question we wish to raise in this chapter is how our conception of biblical psychology differs from the now very fashionable positive psychology. Examination of this question requires an explication of the origins of the positive psychology movement.

POSITIVE PSYCHOLOGY

The origins of positive psychology as a distinctive branch of psychology stems from the groundbreaking work of Martin Seligman and his associates (1975) on "learned helplessness," which later led to its antidote: "learned efficacy" or "learned optimism." The "learned helplessness" paradigm emerges from a series of empirical investigations beginning in 1967 regarding dogs being unable to avoid receiving electric shocks regardless of how they responded to any given situation. This produces in dogs a sort of behavioral paralysis and an unwillingness to act since their experience has taught them that there is no possibility of changing their circumstances in order to avoid or relieve pain, even when an option to escape their circumstances is presented.

Although there is always danger in too facilely generalizing human behavior from that of animals, Seligman extrapolates a general theory of depression from this model. People who have undergone experiences where they have been unable to avoid or stop negative reinforcements and/or experiences are likely to experience a sort of emotional paralysis, a "learned helplessness," and a depression. A person learns he cannot affect his circumstances and thus becomes emotionally depressed and develops a negative view of life, may we call it a "negative psychology," perhaps corresponding to some degree to the helpless tragic view of life emerging from a psychology based on a Greek tragic view of life discussed in the previous chapter.

However, in later work, Seligman (2011) begins to study the possibility of reversing "learned helplessness" in dogs by providing them some control over its outcomes. This control seems to reverse the sense of learned helplessness and produce a sense of "learned efficacy" or "learned optimism." This then can lift the dog out of its behavioral paralysis and motivate it to act. The trick here becomes to get the dog to act in this new environment where it is not helpless. Once it does, the dog will learn it has some control over its environment. So it is with people according to this paradigm. Give a helpless and depressed person some control over his life, and his depression will lift and he will begin to exert some control over his life.

In a 2000 paper Seligman and Csíkszentmihályi present an introduction to a special issue of the *American Psychologist* on positive psychology wherein they that,

> [T]he field of positive psychology at the subjective level is about valued subjective experiences: well-being, contentment, and satisfaction (in the past); hope and optimism (for the future); and flow and happiness (in the present). At the individual level, it is about positive individual traits: the capacity for love and vocation, courage, interpersonal skill, aesthetic sensibility, perseverance, forgiveness, originality, future mindedness, spirituality, high talent, and wisdom. At the group level, it is about the civic virtues and the institutions that

move individuals toward better citizenship, responsibility, nurturance, altruism, civility, moderation, tolerance, and work ethic. (5)

This is an insightful model as far as it goes and it has become very influential in the fields of psychology counseling and even coaching, but does it go far enough in dealing with the actual life problems people feel, and especially the capacity to cope for the more emotionally deep and sensitive human being. Can findings on dogs be aptly translated into more than the surface of the human condition? What if a person has suffered such early trauma as a child, and such a sense of helplessness, that no subsequent experience of having control over his environment is sufficient to overcome his sense of helplessness and victimhood?

Catastrophizing as a Search for Meaning

In an intriguing set of papers, Abramson, Seligman, and Teasdale (1978) and Peterson and Seligman (1984) studied the following three underlying factors of explanatory style for the causality of bad events: internality (it's me) versus externality, stability (it's going to last forever) versus instability, and globalism (it's going to undermine everything) versus specificity. They argued that individuals who entertained internal, stable, and global explanations for bad events showed emotional, motivational, and cognitive disturbances in their wake. A later empirical study by part of this same team (Peterson et al., 1998) reported findings that this "catastrophizing" style (attributing bad events to global causes) predicted mortality, especially among males, and predicted accidental or violent deaths especially well.

In an independent study, the senior author along with colleagues and students (Kaplan et al., 2007) studied the relationship between meaninglessness and suicidality. In the absence of an inherent meaning structure of life, undergraduate students tended to "catastrophize" and generalize singular negative hypothetical events with which they were presented. Further, this tendency tended to be linked with greater levels of depression and hence more positive attitudes towards suicide, and physician-assisted suicide for both men and women. The question for us becomes from where this catastrophizing cognitive style derives. Is it simply a product of direct personal experience, or does it emerge from an underlying cultural world view? Let us compare the biblical and Greek stories of creation.

TWO VIEWS OF CREATION

The ancient Greek poet Hesiod expresses the Greek view well. According to Hesiod, in the beginning there was Chaos, which has often been interpreted as a moving formless mass, from which the cosmos and the gods originated.

Yet the implication of the term "chaos," is complete disorder and confusion which must be controlled and subdued. Zeus can almost be seen as a punitive prison warden.

The Greek view of creation is deterministic, asserting that nature creates the gods and in fact governs them: "Earth and Sky foretold that Cronus would lose his rule to his own son" (Apollodorus 1:5). In the Olympian Theogony, nature exists before the gods. Sky (the male) marries Earth (the female) and produces, first the hundred-handed monsters, and then the Cyclopes. The family pathology then immediately commences, as the father takes the children away from the mother. "Sky tied them (the Cyclopes) up and threw them into Tartarus, a dark and gloomy place in Hades as far from earth as earth is from the sky and again had children by Earth, the so-called Titans." Such action of course breeds reaction and Earth repays Sky in spades.

> Grieved at the loss of the children who were thrown into Tartarus, Earth persuaded the Titans to attack their father and gave Cronus a steel sickle. . . . Cronus cut off his father's genitals and threw them into the sea. . . . Having thus eliminated their Father the Titans brought back their brother who had been hurled to Tartarus and gave the rule to Cronus. (Apollodorus, Library of 1.1.4)

Thus, the Oedipal conflict is born, and indeed, ingrained through the Furies into the fabric of the natural world. Indeed, it seems to be an unchanging law of nature, foretold by Earth and Sky. When Earth and Sky foretold that Cronus would lose the rule to his own son, he devoured his offspring as they were born. The infant Zeus is saved through a ruse. When Zeus reaches adulthood, he makes war on Cronus and the Titans, and defeats him, fulfilling the prophecy of Earth and Sky. The drama of infanticide continues. Zeus himself is informed that his own son would displace him. To forestall this, he devoured his wife with the embryo in her womb. Nevertheless, Zeus is not all powerful, subject himself to the natural force of *Necessity* which itself is controlled by the Fates and the Furies (ibid., 1.1.5, 1.2.1, 1.3.6, Aeschylus, *Prometheus Bound*, 514–517).

The biblical view of creation is dramatic and provides a counter-narrative. The biblical view of creation is the exact opposite. God exists prior to nature and in fact creates the heaven and the earth (Snell, 1953). "In the beginning, God created the heaven and the earth." God then proceeds, as a potter, to create form out of the unformed (*tohu vovohu*). *Tohu vovohu* is not *chaos* which needs to be controlled and subdued, but a formlessness which needs to be shaped and educated. The God of the Hebrew Bible is a sculptor and an artist, perhaps even a therapist, and not a prison warden or a jailor. Let us examine His method.

First, God divides lightness from darkness. Then He divides water from dry land. At this point, God begins to prepare this world for the entrance of man. First, He has the earth bring forth vegetation. He then places living creatures in the sea and fowls in the sky. Now God places living creatures on the earth, cattle, creeping things, and other beasts. The world is now ready for man in God's plan. God creates the human being, male and female, His ultimate handiwork, in His own image and gives them dominion over all in nature He has created (Genesis 1). It is important to emphasize that the biblical "unformed" is not equivalent to the Greek "chaos." Therefore, nature does not have to be subdued but shaped. God is neither seen as a tyrant nor a Procrustes,[3] but as a potter, differentiating as necessary, but not destroying.

Fate versus Freedom: Two Views of Prophecy

The previously mentioned Lev Shestov argues that Greek sense of pessimism carried down through much of Western philosophy. It has subordinated the biblical proclamation of human freedom to the enslaving concepts of fate (*moira*) and necessity (*ananke*).

> The Creator of the world has Himself become subordinate to Necessity which He created and which, without at all seeking or desiring it has become the sovereign of the universe. . . . We must try to stand up against Necessity itself, try to free the living and feeling Parmenides from dead and altogether indifferent power. (Lev Shestov, *Athens and Jerusalem*, 1966, 85–86, 91–92)

Freud correctly understood that a terrible determinism was implicitly bundled within the oedipal conflict. Yet he saw no ultimate way out. Let us repeat once again the profound observation of Yosef Yerushalmi cited in the previous chapter. "Like Sisyphus pushing his rock, Oedipus and Laius must contend forever. At one point in the cycle the father must be slain by the son; at another, that of the return of the repressed, the father returns; the return is only illusion, for the cycle will begin again" (Yerushalmi, 1991, 95). This ever-repeating cycle represents Freud's tragic understanding of the psychological processes intrinsic to a deterministic universe. Again, this is in marked contrast to the Hebrew Scripture's ringing proclamation of an unambivalently resolution of the Oedipus complex mentioned in chapter 1:

> And He shall turn the heart of the fathers to the children,
> And the heart of the children to their fathers. (Malachi 3:22–24)

But we still have not isolated the element that accounts for the biblical transformation of the seemingly *tragic* situations the Graeco-Roman characters face. Let us do so now. It is nothing less than the availability or unavailability of hope. The empirical and clinical work of Aaron Beck and his colleagues is critical in this regard in pinpointing the suicidal implications of hopelessness rather than simple depression per se. In other words, what seems to be most dangerous with regard to eventual suicide is not simply one's present circumstances, as dire as they may be but a lack of a hope that things will get any better (Beck et al., 1974; Bedrosian and Beck, 1979; Beck, Steer, and Carbin, 1988; Beck et al., 1990; Beck, 1996; Brown et al., 2000). In a recent study, Troister, D'Agata, and Holden (2015) found that a "psychache" scale (derived from the term coined by Shneidman) more accurately predicted suicide risk among undergraduate students than either the Beck Depression Inventory II or the Beck Hopelessness Scale.

Hope and Hopelessness in Greek and Biblical Narratives

Let us hone in on the sense of hope versus hopelessness in ancient Greek and biblical Hesiod's account of the beautiful but amoral Pandora is sadly an account of how hopeless life is. It is not a stretch to say that Zeus, the head god in the Greek pantheon, had no real interest or compassion for man, and indeed may have feared being displaced by man if he empowered him. Prometheus ("forethought" in ancient Greek) and his half brother Epimetheus ("afterthought"), both cousins of Zeus who joined him in his war against his father Cronus, are assigned the responsibility of creating man. Prometheus shapes man out of mud, and Athena, daughter of Zeus, breathes life into him. Prometheus had assigned Epimetheus the task of giving the creatures of the earth their various qualities, such as swiftness, cunning, strength, fur, wings. Unfortunately, by the time he reached man, Epimetheus had given out all the good qualities and there were none left for man.

The untrustworthy Zeus compounds the damage by deciding to make life difficult for men by withholding from them the knowledge of fire, presumably in retaliation for a slight on the part of Prometheus—Zeus has been offered a meat sacrifice without fat. Fire was critical to the generation of light and heat necessary to hold the environment at bay and to provide the basis for technological and medical advance. By withholding this knowledge, Zeus, the father god, is keeping man subservient to nature.

Prometheus rebels against Zeus (at least in part) in order to help man and does so, stealing fire from Mount Olympus, the home of the gods. Prometheus hides the fire in a hollow fennel stalk, and brings it to man, releasing him from his dependency. Zeus soon learns what had been done and, enraged, creates Pandora (meaning all-gifted), a beautiful but amoral and deceitful creature, as a punishment, and sends her to Epimetheus, the naïve half-brother of the wise Prometheus, along with a box as a "gift." One day, Pandora decided to open the box that Zeus had sent along with her. The box contained all the evils in the world, which flew out as soon as Pandora opened it. She closed the lid as quickly as she could, but too late; only hope remained locked in the box, and unavailable to people (Hesiod, *Theogony*, 533–615; *Works and Days,* 53–105; Plato, *Protagoras*, 320c–322a).

The following points stand out in this narrative:

1. Zeus is trying to keep man dependent by withholding the knowledge of fire from him.
2. Prometheus rebels and steals fire to bring man autonomy.
3. Zeus, enraged, punishes man by sending Epimetheus the seductive but amoral woman, Pandora along with an urn.
4. Pandora opens up the urn, unleashing all the evils of the world, making man more dependent again. Hope alone is locked up in the urn, and thus inaccessible to man.

This is bad enough, but Zeus is not finished playing with people. Zeus, for no specified reason, sends a great flood to destroy the Bronze race of men. He does not warn an innocent couple, Deucalion (the son of Prometheus) and Pyrrha (the daughter of Pandora and Epimetheus) of the approaching flood, nor does he provide them any means to save themselves.

However, Prometheus once again rebels against Zeus by warning Deucalion of the coming flood and provides instructions on the sly to Deucalion and Pyrrha on how to build a boat. Deucalion and Pyrrha are saved by this boat from the flood. When the flood is over, Deucalion and Pyrrha emerge from the boat. Deucalion sacrifices to Zeus and asks him for a renewal of the human race. Zeus agrees but has the last laugh. He arranges to repopulate the world in a very odd and malevolent way. Both Deucalion and Pyrrha throw stones over their shoulders. Men will spring from stones cast by Deucalion and women from stones cast by Pyrrha. His stones become men and hers become women.

Several points stand out in this narrative:

1. Zeus orders the flood out of a sense of personal affront rather than out of any moral sense.
2. Second, once again, Prometheus must rebel against Zeus to preserve mankind. This time he steals the blueprint for an ark and gives it to Deucalion and Pyrrha. Thus, the father-destroyer and the son-savior are distinct.
3. Third, men and women are perceived as emerging from separate sources, rather than from joint parentage. Zeus repopulates the world through cloning!
4. Finally, Zeus fails to promise not to send another flood if he so chooses.

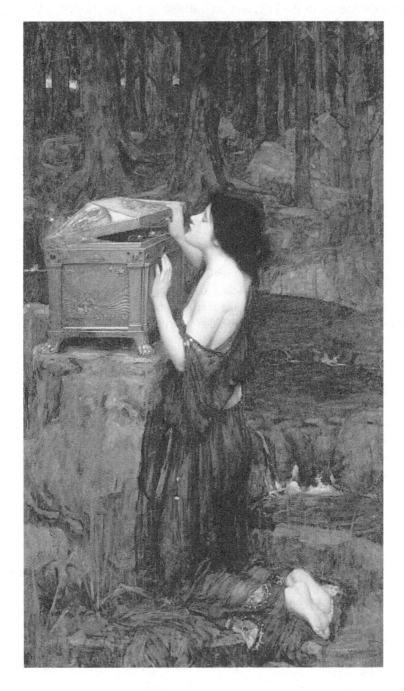

Figure 2.1. *Pandora*, John William Waterhouse (1896). Image courtesy of the Art Renewal Center® www.artrenewal.org.

Greek characters are caught in a deterministic tragic trap, much like B'rer Rabbit in Uncle Remus' tale of *The Tar Baby*. Br'er Fox constructs a lump of tar and puts clothing on it. When Br'er Rabbit comes along he addresses the "tar baby" amiably, but receives no response. Br'er Rabbit becomes offended by what he perceives as the tar baby's lack of manners, punches it, and becomes stuck. The more he punches, the more stuck he becomes, until he becomes a helpless prey to his arch-enemy Br'er Fox. In this view people cannot change their situations and attempts to do so are not only futile but may well backfire (Lester and Pinkney, 1987).

Hope is not only absent but a complete illusion. Indeed, the esteemed classicist, E. R. Dodds (1970), insists that the warning of the oracle to Oedipus is unconditional. "He will kill his father." In other words, *consequence Y will occur independent of which antecedent X you choose*. Greek characters are damned if they do and damned if they don't, and there is no way out. Furthermore, prayer will not help, as the chorus chants at the conclusion of Sophocles' Antigone. "Pray thou no more; for mortals have no escape from destined woe" (Sophocles, *Antigone*, 1345). This, of course is central to the state of "learned helplessness" postulated by Seligman (1992) and to the hopelessness discussed by Beck (1996). Here, the human being is unable to change his outcomes through changing his behaviors, and moreover, there is no hope he will be able to do so in the future! People carrying this set of stories around then may well be expected to be at higher risk for suicide than those with more positive narratives.

In contrast, the Hebrew Scriptures do provide these narratives, portraying hope and meaning in a very different way. To begin with, the biblical God does not want man to be subservient to nature but have dominion over it, which he must use wisely. Rather than withholding fire from man to keep him dependent, God is portrayed as providing the means for Adam to invent fire after his expulsion from Eden because He has compassion for the human beings He has created (Midrash Rabbah 11:2).

This Jewish concern for a moral human-kind is central to the story of Noah and the flood. As the story begins, the biblical God sends the flood to destroy the men whom he had created because of their wickedness, corruption, and lawlessness. Yet Noah is described as an exception, a just man and perfect in his generation and as "walking with God." God Himself warns Noah of the coming flood and provides him with an exact blueprint for an ark which will save him and his family. God is rewarding Noah for his obedience. Thus, Noah does not need to be a Promethean figure rebelling against God. God also instructs Noah to bring a male and female of each species on board the ark. After the flood ceases, all the living creatures, male and female, come out from the ark and repopulate the earth through their sexual union. Finally, God places a rainbow in the heavens as a sign of His covenant with man that He will not send another flood to destroy man. The bow becomes the very symbol of hope (Genesis 6–9).

A number of points stand out in this narrative:

1. The biblical God brings the flood out of outrage with regard to the immoral behavior of the human beings He has created.
2. God willingly gives Noah the blueprint for the ark because he is a just man who walks with God. In other words, Noah is rewarded for his obedience.
3. Thus the biblical God both brings the flood but also provides the ark to save mankind. Males and females from each species repopulate the world through their sexual union.
4. The biblical God places a rainbow in the heaven as a promise He will send no more floods.

Let us complete the Story of the Tar Baby. Br'er Rabbit is able to use his wits to escape Br'er Fox's trap. He tricks Br'er Fox into throwing him into a briar patch, which unknown to Br'er Fox, is a hospitable shelter for Br'er Rabbit. The warning of the biblical prophet is conditional. To return to the Oedipus

Figure 2.2. *Landscape with Noah's Peace Offering* (1803). Joseph Anton Koch.

example, "If you do so-and-so, you will kill your father. But if you not do it, you won't. The warning "if X, then Y" implies that "if *not* X, then *not* Y." There is a way out of difficult situations. People can, and even do, change. Further, in the biblical view, prayer will help "Even if a sword's edge lies on the neck of a man he should not hold himself back from prayer" (Babylonian Talmud, Berachot 10a).

The idea that people can change is of course central to Seligman's state of "learned optimism" and to the emergent field of positive psychology discussed previously. However, we would like to stress again how important a person's underlying narrative structure can be. The sad example today of youth born to affluence and seemingly all sorts of objective freedom engaged in a sad series of antisocial and even illegal acts is a case in point. There is even a name for this social disorder—"affluenza."

In other words, a person culturally conditioned in this negative way may simply discount any positive experience—an exception that proves the rule. Consider the Greek story of Zeno the Stoic. His success as the founder of the philosophical school of Stoicism is not sufficient to serve as protection to him against the mild life stressor of fracturing his toe on a rock on the way home from giving a lecture. The result—he interprets this mild mishap as a sign from the gods that he should depart, and he holds his breath until he dies. He becomes depressed and suicidal over a minor stressor (see chapter 6).

In contrast, may not a person experience behaviorally a lack of control over events in his life, yet still not give up a sense of hope? Are there not people who have a positive and hopeful world view that transcends and withstands personal negative experience? Is this not the message of Victor Frankl (1962) and Natan Sharansky (1998), the first a survivor of Nazi concentration camps, and the second a survivor of imprisonment in the Soviet Gulag? For such persons, negative experiences of helplessness do not seem to be internalized.

For some people, then, a sense of helplessness is not simply a product of empirical experience but of something quite deeper: a loss of a positive meaning structure, perhaps out of some earlier cultural trauma or even a world view where the only source of meaning is a tragic worldview such as that offered by ancient Greek society—man is obsessed with finding meaning. The radical idea emanating from the Hebrew Bible that God created nature and is thus able to change what seem to be immutable natural laws seems to lend itself to a sense of personal freedom and the ability to overcome misfortune, to survive and even thrive.

In a classic paper in clinical psychology, Zubin and Spring (1977) propose a stress-vulnerability model with regard to schizophrenia. The essence of this paper is that the effects of a stressor on a person are moderated by the degree of vulnerability that person experiences. In other words, a given stressor might overwhelm the defenses of a highly vulnerable person, but leave unaffected a less vulnerable person. Put another way, it may take a very serious stressor to overwhelm a relatively nonvulnerable person, but a less serious stressor to overwhelm a more vulnerable person.

The Greek Zeno obviously displays a high vulnerability to a relatively mild stressor—stubbing his toe. In contrast to Zeno, the biblical story of Job provides a stellar example of an individual who holds on to a positive meaning structure, and a belief in his Creator, despite knowing he is being unjustly punished and then criticized and abandoned by his wife and friends. He rightly complains and understandably shows despair, but he does not break (again see chapter 6).

What cultural conditioning accounts for this difference? We have argued that it is nothing less than the age-old conflict between Athens and Jerusalem. Consider the contrasting views of creation stated in these bedrock cultures. The Greek and biblical creation stories embody two radically different world views. Nature precedes the gods in the Greek version, but God precedes nature in the biblical account. The modern scholar Bruno Snell (1982) argues that differences in the respective orderings are not just chronological, but logical and psychological as well. The previously discussed Lev Shestov states it this way in his seminal work *Athens and Jerusalem*: "The Creator of the world has Himself become subordinate to Necessity which He created and which, without at all seeking or desiring it has become the sovereign of the universe" (Lev Shestov, *Athens and Jerusalem,* 1966, 85–86). This is "philosophical European man" for Shestov, who must learn to stand up against Necessity itself, try to free the living and feeling Parmenides from dead and altogether indifferent power (91–92).

Freud seems unable or at least unwilling to use biblical master stories as a foundation for developing a psychological theory of the human condition (Cantz, 2012; 2015; Kaplan, 1987; 1990a; 1998; 2002; 2012; 2013; Kaplan and Anderson, 2013; Kaplan and Schwartz, 2008). Freud is one of Shestov's "European men," and as such seems not even willing to consider Shestov's radical conception that God created nature and is thus able to change what seems to be immutable natural laws (for example, the immutable conflict between father and son foretold by earth and sky. Freud thus remains trapped within the cyclical Greek mind set and is left without the counter-narrative that biblical psychology provides. Freud tries his best to bring the unconscious father-son conflict to conscious awareness in order to make it amenable to control. Yet he has no real way of transforming it in the way that Erich Wellisch has called for.

As we argued in chapter 1, Freud's lack of a counter-narrative leaves him unable to offer his patients any real sense of hope in a happier life that a biblical psychology may provide, but just an amelioration of an unhappy one. That Freud seems be aware of the limitations of psychoanalysis in this regard is reflected in his often-quoted statement at the end of his essay on the psychotherapy of hysteria. Let us repeat Freud's response to the honest question of an unhappy patient: "you will see for yourself that much has been gained if we succeed in turning your hysterical misery into common unhappiness" (Freud and Breuer, *Studies on Hysteria*, 1895/2004, 306).

This is hardly a positive world view. However, our group of biblical psychologists are "American," not "European," and as such are less trapped by the negative Greek mind set so central to The Enlightenment described by Shestov. In his classic work, *Democracy in America*, Alexis de Tocqueville (1863) puts it this way:

> The philosophers of the eighteenth century explained the gradual decay of religious faith in a very simple manner. Religious zeal, said they, must necessarily fail, the more generally liberty is established and knowledge diffused. Unfortunately, facts are by no means in accordance with their theory. There are certain populations in Europe whose unbelief is only equaled by their ignorance and their debasement, whilst in America one of the freest and most enlightened nations in the world fulfils all the outward duties of religious fervor. (394)
>
> Upon my arrival in the United States, the religious aspect of the country was the first thing that struck my attention; and the longer I stayed there the more did I perceive the great political consequences resulting from this state of things, to which I was unaccustomed. In France I had almost always seen the spirit of religion and the spirit of freedom pursuing courses diametrically opposed to each other; but in America I found that they were intimately united, and that they reigned in common over the same country. (394)

The position of biblical psychology is unique in the sense that it goes beyond between traditional psychotherapy wherein the aim is to reduce or eliminate pathological symptoms by offering a means of achieving psychological maturity and living a meaningful, fulfilled life. Consider the biblical story of Job (also presented in chapter 6) in contrast to that of Zeno the Stoic. Zeno is overwhelmed by a relatively mild if not innocuous stressor (stubbing his toe) and holds his breath until he dies. Job, experiencing calamitous misfortunes and losses, one after another continues to hold on to a hopeful positive view of life. In other words, his inner life view protects him from the life stressors he is experiencing. He refuses to feel helpless despite experiencing severe misfortunes. To employ the language of Zubin and Spring, Zeno has high vulnerability to even mild life stressors, while Job is able to withstand even severe life stressors. We will treat this contrast in more depth in chapter 6.

Where Does Biblical Psychology Fit?

Table 2.1 presents the differences between the behavioral and psychodynamic views with regard to a negative versus positive view of life. While the behavioral level might be sufficient to understand and treat the reactions of some people, those with an underlying positive or negative world view may well require a deeper psychological intervention.

Unlike so many Greek heroes such as Agamemnon, Achilles, and even Odysseus who Erich Auerbach faults for their failure to psychologically advance during the course of their lives, biblical figures such as Abraham, Isaac, and Jacob are depicted as more holistic personas, for it is only in the course of an eventful life that men are differentiated into full individuality; and it is this history of a personality which the Hebrew Bible (Old Testament) presents to us as the formation undergone by those whom God has chosen as his examples (Auerbach, 1968, 18).

This returns us to the critical distinction between the understanding that Greeks and Hebrews endorse towards their respective deities. Unlike in Greek thought, the biblical world view is premised on a non-adversarial conception of God. The biblical God is not an impediment to man's autonomy nor an existential threat, such as Zeus is to Prometheus, but instead represents a realistic yet hopeful composite between "good" object and "bad" object; for example, "I have set before thee life and death, the blessing and the curse; therefore, choose life, that thou mayest live, thou and thy seed" (Deut. 30:19). Unlike Oedipus, who was doomed to tragedy as a result of following the cryptic and destructive prophesies of the Delphic Oracle (who was herself a proxy for the Zeus), Abraham exercised the Divinely instilled capacity for personal agency, choosing life for "thou and thy seed" (Deut. 30:19).

Regrettably, as it relates to the contemporary academic climate, the cultural uniqueness of the Bible has either been minimized or, in many cases, even conflated with the Greek tradition (cf. Brown, 1994; Cantz, 2012; Cantz and Kaplan, 2013; Glenn, 1977). Efforts at exonerating the Bible from Hellenized interpretations, such as that made by Phipps (1988), have done little to shift this exegetical discourse towards a de-Hellenized reading of the Hebrew

Table 2.1. Positive versus Traditional Psychology at the Behavioral and Psychodynamic Level

Depth of intervention/ Underlying view of life	Behavioral level intervention	Psychodynamic level intervention
Negative/helplessness/ Greek	Traditional psychology	Psychoanalysis
Positive/optimism/biblical	Positive psychology	Biblical psychology

Scriptures. It is therefore unfortunate as much as is it telling that mainstream Western attitude frames the God the Hebrew Bible through Hellenized lenses, portraying Him as a jealous, vengeful and punitive character when, in ideology the Hebraic attitude regarding God's essence epitomizes a more realistic balance between moral judgement and divine compassion: Roth puts it this way:

> The Creator is the Father, not in the physical sense of the old Greek Mythologies, but in the Moral sense He cares, that He approves and disapproves, that He punishes and forgives, loving those who live as He would wish, hating those who live as He would not wish. (Roth, 1970, 182–83)

This relationship with a personal, loving Deity led McFadyen (1904) to write that,

> It was this that made [the Hebrew] a worshipper, while the Greek remained an artist and a critic. It was this that lightened the mystery of suffering, lifted much of life's sadness, and helped the Hebrew to overcome the world. (47)

There is no question that positive psychology provides a framework for a positive approach to life. Yet biblical psychology can be seen as deepening positive psychology to offer a more historically based direction for the development of a leading-edge psychotherapeutic approach. This approach draws from the deep lessons embedded in biblical narratives—lessons that echo down through the generations into the present day and invite the discerning mental health practitioner, *regardless* of presence or absence of any formal religious affiliation, to explore the native wisdom of the Bible as it applies to the human condition.

NOTES

1. The authors would like to thank the American Psychological Association and the *American Psychologist* for permission to use the quote taken from your publications.

2. The authors would like to thank Ohio University Press for permission to use the quote taken from your publication.

3. In the Greek myth, Procrustes owned a bed, in which he invited every passer-by to spend the night, and where he set to work on them with his smith's hammer, to stretch them to fit. In later tellings, if the guest proved too tall, Procrustes would amputate the excess length; nobody ever fit the bed exactly.

Chapter Three

A Brief History of Views of Suicide

Biblical versus Greek Perspectives

To be or not to be, that is the question, whether 'tis nobler in the mind to suffer the slings and arrows of outrageous fortune, or to take arms against a sea of troubles, and by opposing end them. (William Shakespeare, *Hamlet,* 1881, Act III, Scene 1)

The philosopher may choose his own mode of death as he chooses a ship or house. He leaves life as he would a banquet-when it is time. (Seneca, *Epistle,* 1918, 70.11)

See I have put before you today life and death, blessing and curse, and you shall choose life so that you and your seed shall live. (Deuteronomy 30:19)

Hamlet's ponderings are found in the best-known soliloquy in Western letters.[1] This musing on suicide grows clearer in each succeeding line. First a hint: "Whether 'tis nobler in the mind to suffer the slings and arrows of outrageous fortune, or to take arms against a sea of troubles, and by opposing end them." He then addresses the question of death head on: "To die: to sleep; no more; and, by a sleep to say we end the heartache and the thousand natural shocks that flesh is heir to, 'tis a consummation devoutly to be wished." Finally, he poses the question of suicide directly: "For who would bear the whips and scorns of time . . . when he himself might his quietus make with a bare bodkin [dagger]?" (Shakespeare, *Hamlet,* Act 3, Sc. 1, lines 55–75). Seldom has the question of life and death been posed so earnestly. Hamlet places life and its attendant suffering in one hand and death and the supposed cessation of suffering in the other.[2]

The centrality of the question of suicide in the human agenda has also been stated very directly by the French existentialist Albert Camus: "Judging whether life is or is not worth living amounts to answering the fundamental question of philosophy" (Camus 1955, 3). There has been no agreement on this question in Western society and hence on the permissibility of suicide.

HISTORICAL VIEWS OF SUICIDE

Suicide in the Ancient Greek and Roman Worlds

The ancient Greek and biblical worlds had diametrically opposite views of life, death, and suicide. Let us turn to the Greeks (and Romans) first. Suicidologist Henry Romilly Fedden (1938, 70–85) has placed Greek attitudes toward suicide into three camps: Pythagoras, Aristotle, and the Epicureans were opposed to it; Plato and Socrates took a guarded middle position; and the Cynics and Stoics accepted it. Although this view is oversimplified, it provides an acceptable beginning for a discussion of these schools of thought.

The Pythagoreans

For the Pythagoreans, suicide is a rebellion against an almost mathematical discipline set by the gods. Death comes when it should, and at that time it can be welcomed. There is a set number of souls, according to Pythagoras, that is available in the world at any one time. Killing oneself creates a gap by upsetting this mathematical equilibrium, and thus we must reject it. Despite this philosophy, several accounts portrayed Pythagoras as letting himself be killed or actively committing suicide. According to one account, Pythagoras allowed pursuers to catch and kill him in preference to trampling on a field of beans (Diognes Laertius, 8.45).

Socrates

Three general themes in the teachings of Socrates eased the road to suicide in the classical period. First, he made several references to the nature of the afterworld. For Socrates, Hades (if it existed at all) was not so frightening a place as it was to the Homeric hero. In the closing section of Plato's *Apology* (41a–42a), Socrates asks rhetorically:

> If on arrival in the other world, beyond the reach of our so-called justice, one will find there the true judges who are said to preside in those courts, Minos and Rhadamanthes and Aeacus and Triptolemus . . . to meet Orpheus and Musaeus, Hesiod and Homer . . . would that be an unrewarding journey? . . .

> What would one not give . . . to be able to question the leader of that great host
> against Troy, or Odysseus, or Sisyphus?

Second, Socrates posited a conflictual and unfortunate relationship between body and soul. "The soul is a helpless prisoner chained hand and foot in the body compelled to view reality not directly but only through its prison bars, and wallowing in utter ignorance" (*Phaedo,* 83a). Only the soul can perceive "Ideal Truth," but it cannot do so while it must perceive reality through the use of the five bodily senses. Thus, the real attainment of truth can come only in the higher world when souls can perceive directly—without the interference of the body. This position does not necessarily lead to a direct call to suicide, but it does encourage the philosopher to believe that separation from earthly life is the only road to the "Ideal" human existence.

The third point that may have facilitated suicide was Socrates' general view, which he expressed in different forms on a number of occasions, that philosophy is "preparation for death." While awaiting execution after his trial, Socrates maintains in an argument to Simmias and Cebes:

> Other people are likely not to be aware that those who pursue philosophy aright study nothing but dying and being dead. Now if this is true, it would be absurd to be eager for nothing but this all their lives, and then to be troubled when that came for which they had all along been eagerly practicing. (*Phaedo,* 64a)

Later in this dialogue, Socrates argues that death frees the soul, allowing the attainment of pure knowledge.

> For, if pure knowledge is impossible while the body is with us, one of two things must follow. Either it cannot be acquired at all or only when we are dead: for then the soul will be by itself apart from the body, but not before. (*Phaedo,* 66e)

True philosophers practice dying and thus fear death less than other people do (*Phaedo,* 68a). The argument continues along the line that, unlike the ordinary person, the philosopher understands that death is not a great evil (*Phaedo,* 68d). Thus, it seems only a short step for Cebes to ask Socrates what the grounds are for saying that suicide is not legitimate (*Phaedo,* 62a). Socrates concedes Cebes' point (*Phaedo,* 62b) and gives the famous guard-post allegory as an argument against suicide. Life is a sorry business, but we must not leave our guard-post unless we are relieved (Phaedo, 62b–c).

Although Socrates seemed to be full of life energy, he epitomized Greek thinking in his view of death. All of his life is only to die; all of philosophy is but preparation for death. Xenophon offered his view of Socrates' trial in his usual direct, matter-of-fact style: he completely agreed with Socrates that at that point "to die was better for him than to live" (Xenophon, *Apology,* 31).

Plato

Plato's views on suicide seem a bit more complicated. On the one hand, he called for the denial of a regular burial for a suicide (*Laws,* 9.12). On the other hand, at least according to Olympiodorus, Plato seemed to admit that "suicide may be proper to the worthy man, to him of a middle character, and to the multitude and depraved." To the worthy person, as in the *Phaedo* (62b–c); to one of a middle character, as in *The Republic* (3.406d), if he "is afflicted with a long and incurable disease, as being useless to the city"; and to the vulgar character, as in *The Laws* (8.838), if he is "possessed with certain incurable passions, such as being enamored of his mother . . . and who is incapable of governing himself" (Plotinus, *On Suicide,* 1a).

Plato offers several additional comments on suicide in *The Laws.* In one entry, Plato condemns suicide on the grounds that it "imposes an unjust judgment of death on oneself in a spirit of slothful and abject cowardice." (9.837 c7). Plato also suggests that suicide may be permissible for people killing themselves as a result of intense moral disgrace (9.854 c4–5).

Plotinus

Plotinus, the third-century C.E. neo-Platonist, agreed with Plato's view that death is to be welcomed by the philosopher, but not sought before its proper time: "You should not expel the soul from the body. For in departing, it will retain something (of the more passive life), which is necessary in this case to its departure" (Plotinus, *On Suicide,* 1.9). Plotinus followed Plato in suggesting that there may indeed be times when suicide becomes necessary: "The soul is not to be separated from the body while a further proficiency is yet possible." Porphyry noted that when he himself was contemplating suicide, Plotinus convinced him that it was not a rational decision but was based on too much black bile.

Aristotle

Aristotle seemed less obsessed with the idea of suicide than Plato, his mentor, was; the subject occupies only a few lines in his many extant writings. He argues that, for certain reasons, suicide is the act of a coward: for example, suicide as an escape from "poverty or disappointed love or bodily or mental anguish is the deed of a coward. The suicide braves death not for some noble object but to escape ill" (*Ethics,* 3.7). Aristotle adds that suicide is an injustice against the state, which the state may punish. Unlike Socrates' allegory in the *Phaedo,* Aristotle does not mention that humans are the property of the gods, but only as obligated to the state.

> But the man who cuts his throat in a fit of temper is voluntarily doing an injury which the law does not allow. It follows that the suicide commits an injustice. But against whom? Is it not the State rather than him-self? For he suffers of his own volition, and nobody suffers injustice voluntarily. It is for this reason that the State attaches a penalty, which takes the form of a stigma put on one who has destroyed himself, on the ground that he is guilty of the offense against the State. (*Ethics,* 5.11)

Although there was no monolithic doctrine on suicide in the later Greco-Roman philosophical traditions, it is clear that suicide was widely accepted as within the limits of normal options.

The Cynics

Beginning with Diogenes of Sinope, the Cynic school of philosophy taught the importance of living simply and renouncing all attachments. They lived as wandering beggars with no possessions of their own, maintaining the sparest of dress and diet.

> Poor to begin with, or renouncing their property voluntarily they lived as beggars. Possessing no houses of their own, they passed the day in the streets, or in other public places; the nights they spent in porticos, or wherever else chance might find them. Furniture they had none. A bed seemed superfluous. The simple Greek dress was by them made still simpler. . . . In scantiness of diet, they even surpassed the very limited requirements of their countrymen. (Zeller 1885, 317–18)

Diogenes undertook self-mortification when his teacher was not sufficiently severe. Should life become unsupportable, they reserved for themselves the right of suicide. When the seriously ill Antisthenes cried out, "Who will release me from these pains?" Diogenes answered, "This," and showed him a dagger. "I said," replied Antisthenes, "from my pains, not from life." About this, Diogenes Laertius (the chronicler) commented: "It was thought that he showed some weakness in bearing his malady through love of life" (Diogenes Laertius, 6.18). Although there are contradictory accounts, Diogenes Laertius reported that the Cynic Diogenes committed suicide by holding his breath (6.76), as did two later Cynics, Metrocles (6.95) and Menippus (6.100).

The Epicureans

The Epicureans operated according to a moderate pleasure principle. Epicurus, the father of Epicureanism, put it simply: "Pleasure is the beginning and end of living happily" (Diogenes Laertius, 10.128). On the surface, Epicurus seems to have been indifferent to questions of death and suicide: "Death is nothing to us, since when we are, death has not come, and when death has come, we are not" (10.125). At times, he seems to have been opposed to suicide: "The wise man will not withdraw himself from life" (10.120). But close examination indicates a somewhat more complicated position. Epicurus defined happiness in terms of internal rather than external states. Whereas Plato justified suicide under intolerable external circumstances, Epicurus seemed to do so in terms of avoiding internal suffering. Unlike Epicurus, Hegesias of Cyrene concluded that life contains more pain than pleasure; therefore, the only logical outcome is suicide. The "preacher of death" argued his viewpoint so well, according to Cicero, that a wave of suicides took place in Alexandria, and Ptolemy II had to banish Hegesias from the land (Cicero, *Tusc. Disp.,* 1.34.83).

The Stoics

The Stoics seemed to regard neither life nor death as very important. At the same time, they seemed almost obsessed with the idea of suicide as a way of overcoming their fear of death. In a sense, the Stoics attempted to conquer death by choosing it on their own terms. At best, the philosopher should commit suicide not to escape suffering but to avoid restrictions in carrying out life, since he should be as unaffected by suffering as by any other emotions.

The Stoics did not accept the idea of a caring and loving deity, and they were also too deep as thinkers to place much permanent value on so limited a prospect as human success. They knew that they must fulfill their moral and social duty, but they could never desire reward, recognition, or love, and could never even feel secure that their good acts would produce a good result.

Zeno, the founder of the Stoic school, defined the goal of life as living in agreement with nature (Diogenes Laertius, 7.87). If such an agreement exists, life is good; if it does not exist, suicide becomes the wise choice (7.130). Therefore, Zeno was said to have killed himself (perhaps out of sheer irritation) when he wrenched his toe by stumbling on his way home from the stoa. He held his breath until he died (7.20). We will discuss his death in detail in chapter 6. His successor, Cleanthes, fasted to death. Initially, Cleanthes fasted to cure a boil on his gum; ultimately, however, "he had advanced so far on his journey toward death, he would not retreat," and he starved himself to death (7.176).

The Roman Stoics basically agreed with their earlier Greek counterparts—with one important shift. The question was no longer whether or when to kill oneself when life became intolerable, but how to do so in the right way. This attribute can be seen in a sampling of the writings of Cicero. Suicide, Cicero argues, is no great evil.

> When a man's circumstances contain a preponderance of things in accordance with nature, it is appropriate for him to remain alive: when he possesses or sees in prospect a majority of the contrary things, it is appropriate for the wise man to quit life, although he is happy, and also for the foolish man to remain in life although he is miserable. . . . And very often it is appropriate for the wise man to abandon life at a moment when he is enjoying supreme happiness, if an opportunity offers for making a timely exit. For the Stoic view is that happiness, which means life in harmony with nature, is a matter of seizing the right moment. (*De Finibus,* 3.60 and 61)

In the *Tusculan Disputations,* Cicero depicts death as freeing humans from chains. The gods in their benevolence have prepared for humans a haven and refuge after their departure from worldly life (1.18). Some philosophers disagreed with this, and some Stoics even felt that the soul is not immortal. Indeed, while earthly life is not wholly evil, the afterlife holds far more joy (1.84).

Cicero cites the deaths of Socrates and Cato as examples that suicide is permissible, but only when the gods themselves have given a valid reason. One must not break the prison bonds except in obedience to the magistrate. The human soul should be dissociated from the body during life by means of philosophy and virtue, for such a life will best prepare the soul for the afterlife. It is highly desirable for one to quit the sorrows of this world to gain the joys of the next (1.71–75).

Much the same view can be seen in a sampling of the declamations of the elder Seneca (ca. 40 C.E.). These declamations were a series of arguments on a variety of subjects and were widely used as training for law students. Whatever may have been the various opinions in individual cases, suicide was hardly shocking to either the speakers or the listeners.

A man whose wife and three children have died in a fire tries to hang himself, but he is cut down and saved by a passerby. Is the passerby guilty of an offense? The passerby argues that a person must have hope and that, in any case, if the man had truly wanted to hang himself, he should have done so immediately after the fire. The accuser argues: "It is a wrong done me if I have to die at your will when I should have died at mine." The one who attempted suicide is not accused; rather, the one who stopped him is accused (Seneca, *Controversiae,* 5.1).

Suicide is also a major subject in the letters of Lucius Anneaus Seneca, the brilliant Roman writer and statesman. The younger Seneca's writings show a deep concern and awareness of death. Man is always no more "than a moment ahead of the universal doom" (Seneca, *Ep.,* 71.15). Hope for the betterment of the human condition is false. "Truth doesn't grow and neither does virtue" (*Ep.*, 71.16). One must continue to try but not because there is any hope of success. Pacurius held his own wake every night, believing that anyone who can say "my life is lived" rises daily from his bed to a sense of something gained (*Ep.*, 12.8–10).

One may hope for good but must always be prepared for the worst. People discover too late that they "stand in the shadow of death, of exile and suffering" (*Ep.*, 24.12–15). The thinking man does well to feel terror before so dire a fate. Death provides a release from these horrors. Every day we stand nearer the end; every hour urges us toward the bank from which we must fall. One should not be afraid to leave the present field of action (120). Death is so far from being terrible that "by its grace all things lose their terrors." For Seneca, it seems, life is what is terrifying and death is what provides release (24).

According to the younger Seneca, the events of earthly existence are paltry and not worth any emotional involvement. The questions of who wins the Battle of Pharsalus or an election are insignificant (Seneca, *Ep.*, 71). A person may leave the world if he feels that he has overstayed his welcome (120). The human body is an unpleasantness to be endured only as long as one wishes, and when one thinks fit, one may dissolve the partnership with this puny clay (65.22).

The Stoic felt bound by necessity and sought a sense of freedom and release. In this area, among others, the philosophy of Stoicism seems to suffer from a sort of constipation. One should escape from this life whenever she chooses, and she should die when the means are at hand: "Choose any part of nature and tell it to let you out" (Seneca, *Ep.*, 117.23–24). One should pick the means by which to quit life, for the option of suicide leaves the road to freedom open. To grumble is pointless, since life holds no one fast. "Do you like life, then live on. Do you dislike it? Then you're free to return to the place you came from" (70.15). The philosopher may choose his own mode of death just as he chooses a ship or a house. He leaves life as he would a banquet—when it is time (*Ep.*, 70.11; Plotinus, *On Suicide*, 1.9).

Seneca would not destroy himself merely to avoid pain, for the philosopher must be above pain: "I shall make my exit, not because of actual pain but because the pain is likely to prove a burr to everything that makes life worthwhile" (58.36). The person who dies because of pain is weak; the person who lives to suffer is a fool. Ultimately, a person is not trapped:

> You see that yawning precipice? It leads to liberty. You see that flood, that river, that well? Liberty houses within them. You see that stunted, parched, and sorry tree? From each branch, liberty hangs. Your neck, your throat, your heart are so many ways of escape from slavery. . . . Do you inquire the road to freedom? You shall find it in every vein of your body. (Seneca, *De Ira*, 3.15.3–4)

Seneca and his wife, Paulina, put these thoughts into action, calmly cutting their wrists at the order of the Emperor Nero, Seneca's former student. This consistency between thought and action was exemplified in the advice Seneca gave to the incurably ill Marcellinus, who was contemplating—and ultimately did commit—suicide.

> Be not tormented, my Marcellinus, as if you were deliberating any great matter. Life is a thing of no dignity or importance. Your very slaves, your animals possess it in common with yourself, but it is a great thing to die honorably, prudently, bravely. Think how long you have been engaged in the same dull course: eating, sleeping, and indulging your appetites. This has been the circle. Not only a prudent, brave, or a wretched man may wish to die, but even a fastidious one. (Seneca, *Ep.*, 77.6)

This rash of philosophical suicides seems to have been associated with a generally pessimistic view of human existence. The human being is not an exalted creation; and the gods are limited in power and not loving to man. Fear of the seemingly unavoidable changes in the cycle of life pushes people to destruction and oblivion, no matter how great their accomplishments are. There is a fatalistic preoccupation with the end of life in a hostile universe.

The works of ancient biographers such as Plutarch and Diogenes Laertius recount many historical suicide tales: Pythagoras, Socrates, Zeno, Demosthenes, the statesman Marc Antony, the stoic philosopher Seneca, and his wife Paulina. In addition, Graeco-Roman literature provides a number of examples of collective suicide in the ancient world, in which men slaughtered their families and then themselves (Cohen, 1982).

The famous English poet John Donne (1608) lists three pages of such historical suicides in his iconic work *Biathanatos*. Thus it is not surprising that some 16 suicides are described it the 26 surviving plays of Sophocles and Euripides alone. They are reflective of the suicidal tendencies of the Graeco-Roman society. At the end of this chapter, we will turn to an examination of suicide and self-destructive behavior in the plays of Sophocles and Euripides, and to a lesser extent Aeschylus.

Suicide in the Biblical World

Judaism

Some contemporary suicidologists (e.g., Fedden, 1938, 30; Alvarez, 1970, 51; Shneidman, 1985, 30) have argued that there is no specific anti-suicide teaching in the Hebrew Bible. In the rabbinic view, however, Hebrew thought opposes not only suicide but also self-wounding. Judaism places the issue of suicide in terms of the larger context of views of life versus death. The Talmudic tradition condemns suicide as a most heinous sin. But the

Figure 3.1.   *The Death of Seneca* (1612–1613). Peter Paul Rubens.

subject evokes little discussion. The minutiae in the laws of Sabbath obser-
vance or animal sacrifices in the Temple occupy far more space in the literature. In the eight volumes of the *Aruch Hashulchan*, only one page covers the
subject of suicide (Yorah Deah, 345).

The biblical basis for the Jewish injunction against suicide has been derived from the Noahide laws: "For your lifeblood too, I will require a reckoning" (Genesis 9:5). This statement has been seen as a prohibition not only
against suicide but also against any form of self-mutilation (*Baba Kamma,*

91b, BT). The Hebrew Bible contains several additional prohibitions regarding self-mutilation, for example: "Ye are the children of the Lord your God: Ye shall not cut yourselves, nor make any baldness between your eyes for the dead" (Deuteronomy 14:1). Much the same prohibition is given specifically to the priests in Leviticus: "They shall not make baldness upon their head, neither shall they shave off the corners of their beard, nor make any cuttings in their flesh" (Leviticus 21:5).

The prohibition against suicide is clear in rabbinic law. For example, a suicide is not given full burial honors. Rending one's garments and delivering memorial addresses and certain other rites to honor the dead are not performed for a suicide. The definition of a suicide, however, requires intent, full wits, non-deficiency in behavior, and non-inebriation (*Yorah Deah,* 345). There are also exceptions to the prohibition against suicide. According to the Talmud (*Sanhedrin,* 74a), one is obliged to accept death when the alternative is to be forced to commit adultery, murder, or idolatry. We should emphasize that this means allowing oneself to be killed under certain prescribed circumstances, not actively killing oneself.

But the Jewish law on suicide is only one narrow aspect of a far wider and more important idea: that God loves humankind without qualification and indeed created humans in his own image. God has thus given the Torah to humans as a guide for living rather than merely as a preparation for death: "Ye shall therefore keep my statutes, and mine ordinances, which if a man do, he shall live by them: I am the Lord" (Leviticus 18:5). The same idea is constant throughout the Bible and the rabbinic writings.

Christianity

Christianity is called the daughter religion of Judaism and is based partially on the same Hebrew Bible. One would thus expect it to demonstrate the same life-centeredness, belief in a loving God, and general repugnance toward suicide. And in a sense, it does, especially in its more modern forms. At the same time, Christianity grew up within the Greco-Roman world in world in which Judaism lived, and its leaders were influenced by pagan cults in addition to Jewish apocalyptic movements, as well as a Platonic ambivalence toward life and death and even by the Stoic elevation of suicide disguised as a kind of martyrdom. Consequently, a part of Christianity blended intense eschatological excitement with the chronic depression of Greek philosophy. The Circumcelliones and the Donatists of the fourth century C.E. tended to engage in martyr suicides often seeking to provoke and even invite Romans to kill them

Despite his insistence on the voluntary aspects of the death of Jesus, St. Augustine (354–438) strongly condemned suicide in the *City of God* as "a detestable crime and a damnable sin" (1.27). He based this prohibition on his interpretation of Deuteronomy 5:17: "Thou shalt not kill" (1:20). He considered even the suicides of Judas Iscariot and of the Roman matron Lucretia to be evil, and he portrayed Jesus as urging flight from persecution rather than self-murder (1.17, 19, 22). One must not commit suicide out of magnanimity, because of physical violation of chastity, or to avoid future sin. Augustine declared his preference for the saintly Job over the suicidal Cato (1.24). He condemned dominant Donatist passion for quasi-martyrdom by suicide (cf. Willis, 1950).

Christian thinking on suicide after Augustine reflected the political and legal changes from the Roman Empire to medieval Christendom. With the post-Constantinian success of Christianity, martyrdom, or dying for the faith, was no longer an issue within the old Roman Empire (though it remained so for Christian missionaries who sought to convert pagan tribesmen outside the boundaries of Christian civilization). The second Council of Orleans (533) produced the church's first official disapproval of suicide by denying funeral rites to suicides who were accused of crimes. The Council of Braga (563) extended this ban to all suicides. In 590, the Council of Antisidor forbade the church to accept offerings for the souls of suicides.

Aquinas comes out strongly against suicide in his *Summa Theologica* (1485). Despite his argument that Jesus was the voluntary indirect cause of his own death (*Summa,* 3.47.1), Aquinas attempts to demolish pagan arguments for suicide. He reiterates Augustine's argument from *City of God* (1.20) that associates suicide with murder (2.2.64.5). Aquinas then adds three arguments of his own. First, suicide is unnatural: everyone bears an instinctive charity toward himself and should thus desire to do himself no harm. Suicide, being both unnatural and uncharitable, is a mortal sin. Second, an individual is a member of a social unit. Thus, Aquinas echoes the Aristotelian argument that suicide is antisocial. Third, life is the gift of God: though it is given, it remains God's property; therefore, only God can pronounce the sentence of life and death: "I will kill and I will make to live" (Deuteronomy 32:39). In summary, then, the Christian church slowly but surely formalized its opposition to suicide.

Suicide in Later History

Dante's *Divine Comedy* (1308–1321) reflects this formalized anti-suicide view of the church in its placement of the "violent against themselves" in the wood of the suicides in the second round of the seventh circle of Hell. The souls of the suicides are encased in thorny trees where the leaves are eaten by harpies, causing their wounds to bleed. Only as long as the blood flows are the souls of the trees able to speak. They are permitted to speak only through that which injures and destroys them (Dante Alighieri, *The Inferno*, canto 13).

The English poet and churchman John Donne (1608) expresses a very different point of view in his classic work on suicide, *Biathanatos* (1648, 29). He argues that, under certain limited conditions, suicide might not be a sin: "[F]or we say . . . that this may be done only, when the Honor of God may be promoted by that way and no other" (136). However, Donne did present a general plea for charity toward suicides, and he offered a proof that no set of rules can govern all instances (145). Of all later Christian thinkers, John Donne (1572–1631) was unique in seeing the implications in the voluntary death of Christ for a Christian tolerance of suicide.

For Donne, Christ's death was brave and voluntary: "[I]t is a heroic act of fortitude, if a man when an urgent occasion is presented, expose himself to a certain and assured death as he did" (*Biathanatos,* 3.4.5). Donne thus views the passion of Christ as a Greek altruistic suicide: He was a martyr who gave his life to redeem mankind. Many of the early Christian martyrs also seemed suicidal in nature: "And that Apollonia and others, who prevented the fury of the executioners, and cast themselves into the fire, did therein imitate this act of our Savior, of giving up his soul, before he was constrained to do it." This behavior certainly stands in marked contrast to that of the Jewish martyrs of faith, who tried to avoid death if at all possible and to live in a way that did not compromise their faith.

A very different point of view was taken by an English clergyman named Adams at the beginning of the eighteenth century. In a publication entitled *An Essay Concerning Self-Murder* (1700), Adams declares that human life is God's own property that He entrusts to humans only for a certain end. Therefore, human beings have no liberty to destroy it. Adams extends this viewpoint into the political realm. A person may hazard her life for her country, but she may not destroy herself for it. Another English clergyman, the Reverend Tuke, attempted to bridge this gap by differentiating between two kinds of suicide, one permissible and the other not.

> There be two sorts of voluntarie deaths, the one lawful and honest such as the death of Martyrs, the other dishonest and unlawful, when men have neyther lawfull calling, nor honest endes, as of Peregrinus, who burnt himself in a pile of wood, thinking thereby to live forever in men's remembrance. (1613, 21)

In Germany some centuries later, Immanuel Kant (1785) argued strongly against suicide because he felt that it was incompatible with the affirmation of a universal law of self-love. At about the same time, however, Johann Wolfgang von Goethe (1774) romanticized suicide in his novel *The Sorrows of Young Werther.* Indeed, the publication of Goethe's book was followed by a veritable epidemic of romantic suicides throughout Europe.

Many of the most prominent names in French philosophy were sympathetic to suicide. Voltaire, for example, argued in his selected letters (1733) and later in his philosophical dictionary (1764) that at times suicide must be defensible, even though his own temperament was opposed to it. While regarding it as abnormal, he admitted the possibility of its social and moral validity.

Paul d'Holbach (1770) strongly favored the permissibility of suicide on two grounds: first, suicide is not contrary to the laws of nature; second, suicide is not antisocial. The individual's contract with society is based on mutual benefit. Therefore, if society can give him nothing, the suicide has every right to consider the contract void.

Jean-Jacques Rousseau, too, was sympathetic. The twenty-first letter in his *Nouvelle Héloise* (1761) contains an extensive apologia for suicide from a young man disillusioned with life. Like d'Holbach, he says that, first, suicide is not against the laws of nature: that is, it is up to us to leave life when it no longer seems good. Second, suicide is not akin to deserting one's post (see Plato's argument in chapter 2) but is like moving to a more hospitable town. Third, suicide does not remove one from the providence of God; it destroys one's body but not one's soul, which actually comes closer to God through death. Fourth, suffering sometimes becomes unendurable. Fifth, the scriptures have no word to say against suicide.

At the same time, France produced a great voice against suicide. Madame Anne Louise de Stael, in her 1814 essay *Reflections on Suicide,* reverses the support for suicide she had shown in an earlier essay she wrote, entitled *On the Influence of Passions* (1796), by offering a threefold argument: first, pain serves to regenerate the soul, and thus to escape from pain through suicide is a refusal to recognize the possibilities of one's own nature; second, God never abandons the true believer, so there is no reason or right to commit suicide; finally, suicide is not consonant with the moral dignity of humankind.

In England, David Hume demurs, agreeing basically with Voltaire, d'Holbach, and Rousseau, and going even further in *An Essay on Suicide* published in 1894. For suicide to be criminal, he argues, it must be a transgression of duty against God, one's self, or one's neighbors. That it cannot be the first stems from Hume's assertion that all our powers are received from our creator. Therefore, suicide can be no more ungodly than any other form of death. That suicide cannot involve a transgression against one's self seemed obvious to Hume, as no one has ever thrown away his life while it was worth keeping. That suicide does not involve transgression against one's neighbors was also obvious to him. All one's obligations to do good to society, according to Hume, imply something reciprocal. Therefore, as long as one receives benefit from society, one is obligated to promote its interests; but when one withdraws altogether from society, one is no longer so bound.

Views in contemporary Western society are similarly mixed. The American psychiatrist Thomas Szasz (1962; 1971) has attacked the view that suicide is necessarily a manifestation of mental illness and of mental illness generally. Suicide, he has argued, is a product of choice by an agent in response to problems in living, not a symptom of disease. Such a choice, he maintained, must be respected by psychiatrists, police, and others who might attempt to intervene. To do otherwise involves the infantilizing and dehumanizing of the suicidal person, robbing the individual of their freedom to make autonomous decisions that affect their welfare.

On the other side, an equally compelling anti-suicide position has been taken by Austrian psychiatrist Erwin Ringel, the founder of the International Association for Suicide Prevention. Ringel (1981) has argued that suicide cannot be freely chosen, and thus he opposes libertarian attitudes toward suicide, including those that would allow planned deaths for the terminally ill. Arguing that every human life is important, he presents the purpose of suicide prevention as the reinvigoration of human life—through the help of psychiatry and crisis intervention—for all human beings.

R. B. Brandt (1975) and Lebacqz and Englehardt (1977) have taken middle-ground positions. Brandt, a past president of the American Philosophical Association, has followed Hume in his attempt to distinguish between rational and irrational suicide. His opinion is that a person may, on utilitarian grounds, reach a rational decision to take his life but that the rational decision process is often distorted by emotional disturbances. He has argued that intervention to prevent suicide may be justified if the decision to take one's life is an irrational one. However, if the decision is rational, such an intervention is not justified; furthermore, Brandt has even argued for an obligation to assist a person attempting a rational suicide.

Lebacqz, a professor of Christian ethics, and Englehardt, a professor of the philosophy of medicine, have taken a slightly different approach. While acknowledging on libertarian grounds that people may have a *prima facie* right to commit suicide, they have maintained that this right is nonetheless usually overridden by contravening duties that grow out of our covenantal relationships with others. Still, there may be a right to suicide in at least three kinds of cases: voluntary euthanasia, covenantal suicide, and symbolic protest, for in these cases suicide would affirm the covenants we have with others.

Christopher Cowley (2006), however, strongly disagrees with Brandt's position, arguing that the concept of rationality is not appropriately ascribed—or withheld—to the victim or the act or the desire to commit the act. Since the suicide victim has no future, it makes no sense to call his act rational or irrational. The more appropriate reaction to a declared desire for suicide, or to the news of a successful suicide, is horror and pity, and these are absent, in Cowley's view, from Brandt's account, as is a humble acknowledgement of the profound mystery at the heart of any suicide.[3]

These views, of course, represent only a sample of those existing in past and present Western society. However, they do reflect the confusion and vacillation with regard to many issues involving suicide. Is suicide to be viewed as mental illness, when judgment is, by definition, distorted and irrational, or can the choice be viewed as a rational decision? What implications would this definition have for mental-health professionals, religious leaders, and concerned laypeople? Should they respect an individual's "right to die" and even assist that person? Or are they morally bound to attempt to preserve life even against the expressed will of the potential suicide? To whom does an individual's life belong—to herself, to the state, or to God? And, finally, how is suicide related to the basic idea of freedom? Suicide must be understood in the context of the larger issues of life and death and the historical antecedents to this problem.

Studies of the attitudes of African and Asian societies toward suicide also indicate variation (Bohannan, 1960; Elwin, 1943; Hankoff, 1979; Thakur, 1963; Yap, 1958; Ohara, 1961). India practiced *suttee,* the custom in which widows were placed on the funeral pyres of their husbands (Thakur, 1963). Japanese history is filled with incidents of suicide, ranging from the traditional story of the forty-seven *ronin,* in which servants killed themselves *en masse* on their master's death, via the practice of *hara-kiri* or *seppuku* (conducted by the Samurai warriors), to the modern Kamikaze pilots, who dive-bombed to their deaths in World War II (Ohara, 1961; Tatai and Kato, 1974). Suicide in China has never been ritualized to the same extent as in Japan and has thus attracted less attention. Yet suicide has played an important role throughout Chinese history, and an astounding number of eminent men and women are reported to have taken their own lives. These suicides were often committed as expiation for violations of loyalties, even if they were committed inadvertently (Yap, 1958; Lindell, 1973; Rin, 1975).

DEFINITIONS OF SUICIDE

In his book, *Definition of Suicide,* Edwin Shneidman (1985), the father of the suicidology movement in America, has offered what many regard as a state-of-the-art definition of suicide: "Currently in the Western world, suicide is a conscious act of self-induced annihilation, best understood as a multidimensional malaise in a needful individual who defines an issue for which suicide is perceived as the best solution" (Shneidman, 1985, 203). Shneidman's emphasis on "currently" reflects his awareness that the meaning of suicide may vary from one historical period to another; his emphasis on "Western world" implicitly recognizes that the meaning of suicide may be a function of the cultural matrix in which it occurs; the word "conscious" limits suicide to *human* acts, while the word "act" calls for a narrowing of our use of the term "suicide" to a particular behavior that leads to death. As such, this passage seems to suggest that the word "suicide" not be so readily used to refer to attempts and/or threats. The word "self-induced" indicates a death by one's own hand, and "annihilation" is meant to imply the end of experiential aspects of life and of the actual cessation of life itself. Suicide thus represents the permanent cessation of individual consciousness.

Shneidman's attempt to fix stringent criteria for the suicidal act finds an echo in Jewish law. Here, someone mentally ill cannot be classified as a suicide. The Talmud (*Semahot* 2:2) defines an intentional suicide as follows. It is not one who climbed to the top of a tree and fell down and died, nor one who ascended to the top of a roof and fell down and died, as these may have been accidents. Rather a willful suicide is one who calls out "Look, I am going to the top of the roof or the top of the tree, and I will throw myself down that I may die." A person found strangled or hanging from a tree or lying dead on a sword is presumed not to have committed suicide intentionally (Rosner, 1970; 1998).

Nevertheless, Shneidman's definition fails to capture many nuances apparent in the suicides that we explore in this book (Kaplan, 1998b). First, Jewish law, for example, addresses the question of when a person is compelled to accept death rather than to actively commit suicide. Second, many Greek suicidal themes, especially in the plays of Euripides, take the form of ritual murder, in which the victim does not literally take his or her own life. Iphigenia, for example, allows herself, without protest, to be sacrificed by others (Euripides, *Iphigenia in Aulis*). Another example is Macaria, who refuses the chance to escape her sacrifice by means of a lottery (Euripides, *Heracleidae*). Third, Shneidman's definition leaves open the relationship between martyrdom and suicide: where does one end and the other begin? Our examination of Greco-Roman, Jewish, and especially Christian materials shows how complicated this question can be. Fourth, many of the suicides in ancient narratives may not be fully "conscious." Sophocles' Ajax is a good example of this: he kills himself while in a state of severe depression and agitation (Sophocles, *Ajax*). Finally, the question arises as to whether the individual equates suicide with total "self-annihilation." What if he believes in an afterlife?

Still, Shneidman and Farberow (1957) have argued that "suicidal logic" presupposes a belief in one's immortality after death. Thus, a potential suicide thinks that she will be able to experience others' reactions to her death. She may think, "You'll be sorry after I kill myself." Equally destructive is the belief that the world ends with one's own death. Such a breakdown is evident in Eugene Ionesco's play *Exit the King* (1967). Here the dying King Berenger shows no investment in the future: when told by his wife that "the younger generation's expanding the universe," the king replies, "I'm dying." When he is told that they are "conquering new constellations," he again

replies, "I'm dying." Finally, when he is informed that the younger generation is "boldly battering at the gates of Heaven," he responds, "They can
knock them flat for all I care" (67). Berenger has lost any investment in the
world beyond him.

Many of the assumptions underlying Shneidman's definition of suicide
are thus tenuous. More useful for present purposes is Durkheim's definition
in his classic study *Le Suicide* (1897/1951): "all cases of death resulting
directly or indirectly from a positive or negative act of the victim himself,
which he knows will produce this result" (44). Durkheim's inclusion of the
word "indirectly" in his definition of suicide suggests that martyrs may
sometimes be classified as suicides. Durkheim's taxonomy of suicide types is
also extremely valuable. In *Le Suicide,* he suggests three common types of
suicide: *egoistic, altruistic,* and *anomic.* Egoistic suicides are people insuffi-
ciently bonded to the society around them. Altruistic suicides lack the autonomy to differentiate themselves from the surrounding milieu. Anomic suicides occur when there is confusion or disruption in an individual's relationship to the society around him. In addition, this work suggests a non-suicidal
category (which Durkheim labels "religious") that unites the individual personality with society (336). Durkheim's thinking seems overly influenced by
outmoded utopian idealism, and his reference to religion is vague. Nevertheless, he seems to be groping toward the possibility of a category where there
is unity or congruence between *individuation* and *attachment.*

An understanding of the processes of individuation and attachment is
essential to the problem of healthy versus pathological human development
and specifically to the problems of suicide and suicide prevention (Kaplan,
1987; 1988; 1990b; 1998a; 1998b). The individuation-deindividuation refers
to the degree to which an individual can stand on her own two feet—that is,
can show autonomous or independent thought, feeling, and action. An individuated person is *separated* or *differentiated* from those around her but is
not necessarily *detached* from them. The attachment-detachment dimension
describes the degree to which an individual can extend her hand to another—
that is, can show a capacity for bonding or cooperating with others in
thought, feeling, and action. An attached individual is *integrated* or *involved*
with those around her but is not necessarily *enmeshed.* An excellent study by
M. D. Faber (1970) has noted sixteen suicides and self-mutilations in the
twenty-six extant plays of Sophocles and Euripides. There is a seventeenth:
Jocasta in Euripides' *Phoenissae.* However, many of these suicides, especially those in Euripides, fall into a pattern of ritual murder, in which the person
does not actually raise a hand against himself.

In these dramas, character after character is led to a suicidal end. Faber
has used Durkheim's three categories of suicide discussed above to argue
that the suicides in Sophocles tend to be primarily egoistic (initially outward
destructive tendencies that are turned inward), while those in Euripides tend

to be primarily altruistic (basically inward destructive tendencies that are sometimes disguised as outwardly heroic or martyr-like acts). Some cases in the plays of both playwrights may fall into Durkheim's anomic type.

Suicides in Greek Tragedy

Given the prevalence of the theme of suicide in ancient Greek (and Roman) culture, it is not surprising that some 16 suicides occur in the 26 surviving plays of Sophocles and Euripides alone. Only one suicide occurs in the 7 surviving plays of the third great Greek tragedian, Aeschylus.[4] There are approximately 223 characters (exclusive of unspecified figures such as the Greek chorus) who appear in the 26 plays of Sophocles and Euripides, some in more than one play.[5] Sixteen suicides (including one self-mutilation) can be found in the 26 surviving plays of Sophocles and Euripides, including 12 by female characters. Eight instances of suicidal behavior (including one self-mutilation) can be found among the approximately 62 characters in the seven plays of Sophocles, yielding a suicide rate of 12.9%. Of these, four of the suicides occur among the 44 male characters depicted in Sophocles (9.1%) and the remaining four among the 18 female characters in Sophocles' plays (22.2%). This gender difference in suicide is even more pronounced in the 19 surviving plays of Euripides. Here, approximately 161 characters are depicted with no suicides occurring among the 113 male figures (0%) and eight among the 48 female characters (16.7%). Only one suicide, a male character Eteocles, occurs in the seven surviving plays of the third great Greek tragedian, Aeschylus. Granted, these characters are fictional, but their depiction provides a unique portal into the way the Greek tragedians viewed Greek society.

Emil Durkheim (1897/1951) distinguished three distinctive types of suicides: (1) egoistic suicides resulting from an isolation of self from society; (2) altruistic suicides resulting from a lack of differentiation between self and society and; (3) anomic suicides, referring to a confusion in boundaries between self and society. Most of Sophocles' depicted suicides are egoistic, while most of the suicides depicted by Euripides' are altruistic. Several of each are anomic. Table 3.1 applies Durkheim's typology to suicides in Greek tragedy. We briefly examine these suicides below. We will cite the translations collected in *The Complete Greek Drama* by Oates and O'Neill (1938).

Sophocles' Suicides

Let us begins with the eight Sophocles suicides/self-destructive behaviors. A prime example of Sophoclean egoistic suicide is the Greek warrior Ajax in the play bearing his name. Ajax has gone mad with jealousy because Achilles' armor has been given to Odysseus; so, in a frenzied state, he tries to murder Odysseus. The goddess Athena prevents him from doing so by de-

Table 3.1.   Suicides in Greek Tragedy

Character	Gender	Source	Method	Type
Ajax	M	Ajax (Sophocles)	Sword	Egoistic
Deianeira	F	The Trachinae (Sophocles)	Sword	Egoistic
Eurydice	F	Antigone (Sophocles)	Knife	Egoistic
Haemon	M	Antigone (Sophocles)	Sword	Egoistic
Jocasta	F	Oedipus Rex (Sophocles)	Hanging	Egoistic
Oedipus	M	Oedipus Rex (Sophocles)	Self-Blinding	Egoistic
Antigone	F	Antigone (Sophocles)	Hanging	Anomic
Heracles	M	The Trachinae (Sophocles)	Burning	Anomic
Hermione	F	Andromache (Euripides)	Suicidal Threats	Anomic
Phaedra	F	Hippolytus (Euripides)	Hanging	Anomic
Alcestis	F	Alcestis (Euripides)	Poisoned	Altruistic
Evadne	F	The Suppliants (Euripides)	Burning	Altruistic
Iphigenia	F	Iphigenia in Aulis (Euripides)	Ax	Altruistic
Macaria	F	The Heracleiadae (Euripides)	Knife	Altruistic
Menoeceus	F	The Phoenissae (Euripides)	Jumped	Altruistic
Polyxena	F	Hecuba (Euripides)	Sword	Altruistic

M = Male; F = Female

flecting his anger so that he slaughters a herd of sheep instead. The text makes clear that Athena not only wants to restrain Ajax but to humiliate him deeply as well, and to mock him in his madness in front of Odysseus. As Ajax's rage passes, it is replaced by a potentially self-destructive depression, which is not uncommon among egoistic suicides. Ajax first contemplates murdering Odysseus, and then himself.

Ajax's suicidal aims are even more clearly articulated in his ruminations about his lost honor in the eyes of his father. An honorable suicide may be his only solution: the egoistic nature of Ajax's suicide is already hinted at in his initial inclination toward homicide (also shown by Oedipus and Haemon), in his rejection of tears as cowardly, and in his excessive concern with honor in his relationship with his father. In his final talk with his young son, Ajax reveals his own sadly erroneous views of human development. The childhood years are sweet in their innocence, before a man must prove his manliness in facing life's tragic tribulations. The pattern that Ajax prescribes for his son appears to describe his own childhood. Ajax himself was broken to his father's "stern rugged code" and plucked early from his mother's embraces. Ajax falls on his sword and dies, the very epitome of an egoistic suicide. We will discuss this suicide in more detail in chapter 5 in comparison to the non-suicide of Elijah.

Oedipus Rex contains one egoistic suicide (Jocasta) and one egoistic self-mutilation (Oedipus himself). *Oedipus Rex* begins with the priest of Zeus telling King Oedipus of the ravages of the plague on the city of Thebes. Creon announces that the plague is due to the unavenged murder of Laius and describes the circumstances surrounding that unresolved crime. Oedipus volunteers to reopen the search for the murderer of Laius, cursing the killer to a life of misery and solitude. Oedipus seems obsessed with past family connections that, at least on a conscious level, are not his. There is no one to lighten the burden of excessive responsibility that Oedipus takes on. The unfolding of the terrible secret continues in earnest. Oedipus summons Tiresias, the blind oracle, who, like the seer in the legend of Narcissus, speaks in unfathomable riddles and points to the dangers of self-knowledge: "Alas, how dreadful to have wisdom where it profits not the wise!" (316–17). He tries to leave, but Oedipus will not permit it. Tiresias speaks again, but the riddles are so maddening that even when he finally and bluntly accuses Oedipus of being the killer, Oedipus does not understand him. Oedipus becomes furious, accusing both Tiresias and Creon of lying and plotting against him; but at the same time, he wants to know more. Tiresias again resorts to riddles, reminding Oedipus of his prowess in deciphering the riddle of the Sphinx.

This same pattern continues through the play. Oedipus becomes more and more obsessed with the need to get at what the audience knows will be a most unwelcome truth. Oedipus calls in one reluctant party after another, and he gives them all the same Hobson's choice of revealing to him the awful truth about his past or incurring his wrath by withholding information. Still, Oedipus insists on charging full speed ahead to attain the knowledge that will prove to be his undoing, first with Jocasta, then with a messenger, and finally with the herdsman whom Oedipus forces the herdsman to reveal the last piece in the horrible puzzle, and he finally sees his position clearly: He has murdered his father, Laius, himself, and he has married Jocasta, his mother. He is now determined to kill Jocasta, believing that it was through her that he was cursed from his birth on: Oedipus rushes into the palace, where he finds that Jocasta has hanged herself. Oedipus then puts out his own eyes. We will return to Oedipus's self-blinding in chapter 9 contrasting it with the biblical story of Moses who also uttered suicidal thoughts.

Sophocles' *Antigone* portrays three suicides, those of Antigone, Haemon, and Eurydice. Antigone, the daughter of Oedipus and Jocasta, has long been viewed in Western thought as a sterling example of a highly individuated and idealistic woman who ably senses the conflict between the higher moral law and the wickedness of an earthly ruler. When faced with Creon's decree that her brother Polyneices should remain unburied, she invokes the authority of the law of the gods and buries him. However, closer scrutiny reveals a far more complex character. She has over-identified with her family of origin and with the opinion of the community at large; she is also obsessed with death. Antigone's idealism masks the driving force of her life: the fulfillment of the curse of the house of Labdacus with which the play begins. Her hopelessness is so profound that it can only lead to self-destruction.

This theme echoes throughout the play. After she has been condemned by Creon, her uncle and King of Thebes to be buried alive, Antigone repeats her depressive obsession with thoughts of a noble death, and this theme develops as the play proceeds. Antigone now sees death as preferable to life, as freedom from life's miseries. Antigone also seems thoroughly indifferent to Haemon, her fiancé: She remains strangely silent in the face of his father Creon's attacks on him. Furthermore, Antigone is exceptionally insolent in her confrontation with Creon. Yet she later laments that she will die alone, forlorn, and friendless. She expresses her embeddedness with her family of origin further in her method of suicide, which mimics that of her mother.

Haemon, son of Creon and the fiancé of Antigone, enters midway through the play (628–30), "grieving for the doom of his promised bride Antigone." What develops is an accelerating step-by-step struggle between father and son. The leader of the chorus warns Creon of Haemon's suicidal state, but Creon chooses to ignore it for too long. When he at last relents, it is too late. Haemon's emotions reach a peak when Creon interrupts his son's mourning for the dead Antigone. Creon's attempts at intervention are useless at this point and, in all likelihood, seem to Haemon to be another effort by his father to reestablish control. Haemon reacts violently: he tries to stab his father. When he fails at this, he turns his murderous wrath inward and falls on his own sword. Haemon's suicide is egoistic. He feels controlled by his father, and his resultant rage, like that of Oedipus, is first projected outward against his father and then inverted inward against himself.

The final suicide in Sophocles' *Antigone* is that of Eurydice, the wife of Creon and the mother of Haemon. She enters late in the play and has only one speech. She has heard of the family disaster and asks the messenger to repeat the story. Upon hearing of Haemon's suicide, Eurydice silently returns to her house. Her silence justifiably arouses concern from both the leader of the chorus and the messenger. Then the messenger reports that Eurydice, too, has killed herself: the messenger's further description reveals Eurydice's rage toward her husband, blaming him not only for the death of Haemon but also for the death of her other son, Megareus. This hostility is characteristic of egoistic suicides. In chapter 11, we will return to a consideration of the suicide of Antigone in comparison to the life affirmation and motherhood exhibited by the biblical Ruth.

Two final Sophoclean suicides occur in *The Trachiniae*: the anomic self-stabbing of Deianeira, the unhappy wife of Heracles, and Heracles' own egoistic self-burning. In her first speech, Deianeira expresses great conflict between her gratitude toward Heracles for fighting for her hand and delivering her from dangers and her anger at his prolonged absence from her after their marriage. She feels abandoned and resentful toward him but seems able to express these feelings only through excessive concern. Deianeira goes on to chide her son, Hyllus, for not having looked for his father. Her uncertainty toward Heracles surfaces in her hesitance to accept what should be the good news of Heracles' safety—and indeed, his triumph.

Even after she comes to believe this news, her joy is short-lived, rapidly followed by a desire to know why he was away so long and by her great misgivings about the future. Deianeira's misgivings are borne out as she learns the truth about the love affair of Heracles and Iole, whom Deianeira has already befriended and welcomed into her house. It is the pursuit of this love that has kept Heracles away so long. Deianeira's unrealistic and idealized self-expectations seem to prevent her from openly expressing a well-justified anger and hurt (Faber, 1970, 56). Rather, she seems bewildered and hapless, and she goes so far as to excuse Heracles and Iole, at least on the conscious level: she will not say a harsh word about either of them. At the same time, however, Deianeira struggles with an inner fury that threatens to break out of control, though she cannot accept her own anger. Finally, she decides to send Heracles a robe that she had dipped in the blood of the centaur Nessus many years earlier, after he was mortally wounded by Heracles' poisoned arrow. As he lay dying, Nessus had instructed Deianeira to take some of the blood from around the wound and to use it as a charm on her husband—so that he would never look at another woman.

Nessus's response contains a riddle typical in Greek theatre. Might he not have meant that Heracles will die before he looks at another woman? Deianeira seems to ignore the hints of danger in the gift: she treats it only as a love potion, though she has hinted at a far more sinister intent slightly earlier. On the one hand, Deianeira cannot accept responsibility for having done any wrong, even when she is accused of this by her son, Hyllus; on the other, she walks away rather than defending herself because she knows or fears that at some level she has done something wrong. It is this smallness, timidity, and excessive concern with others' opinion of her that distinguishes her from a more actively aggressive personality such as Medea. These characteristics were no doubt accentuated by the total failure of her father to protect her from the sexual advances of the river god Achelous. Indeed, her treasured Heracles saved her from that ravishment as well. This embedded, altruistic quality surfaces along with egoistic anger turned inward, Deianeira's vacillation and confusion about the boundaries between self and other are typical of an anomic suicide. At this point Deianeira resolves to take her own life: "How be it, I am resolved that, if he is to fall, at the same time I also shall be swept from life; for no woman, could bear to live with an evil name, if she rejoices that her nature is not evil" (718–20). She cannot go on living with a feeling of being seen as less altruistic than she has always seemed to herself. She offers no expression of sympathy or remorse toward her husband. Both the anger and embeddedness in Deianeira's suicide are evident in the fact that she stabs herself in her own marriage bed, presumably the same bed Heracles intends to share with Iole.

Euripides' Suicides

Suicides in the plays of Euripides are very different from those of Sophocles' characters. Many seem like ritual deaths or martyrdoms in which the victims submit passively to group demands. These are mostly altruistic people with insufficient boundaries in relationship to the outside world. Some are anomic, with confused boundaries. Suicides occur in seven of Euripides' 19 extant plays: *Hippolytus, The Phoenissae, The Suppliants, Iphigenia in Aulis, The Heracleidae, Alcestis,* and *Hecuba.* An eighth play, *Andromache,* portrays an attempted suicide.

In *Hippolytus,* Phaedra, the wife of King Theseus of Athens, is caught in a miserable family situation, and at the same time she has unrealistic expectations of herself. By Aphrodite's design, she falls madly in love with her stepson Hippolytus. Though she resists her passion, with great misery to herself, her servant betrays her secret to Hippolytus. Phaedra then hangs herself, leaving behind a note that falsely accuses Hippolytus of raping her. Theseus believes the note and pronounces a curse of death on his son. The curse is soon fulfilled, and the truth of Hippolytus's innocence is revealed too late. According to this play, the gods are selfish and cruel, utterly without compassion toward humans. Aphrodite plots to destroy Hippolytus for living in chastity: she has filled his stepmother, Phaedra, with passion for him, and has turned the heart of his father against him. Phaedra mixes an exaggerated sense of honor and guilt with a tendency toward self-punishment.

Phaedra's punitive conscience is accompanied by low self-esteem engendered by her fears of misogyny and her unhappiness and helplessness at being a woman. This view is echoed by the chorus and by Hippolytus, who delivers a particularly sharp attack on women. Women are vile and filthy: "I can never satisfy my hate for women, no! Not even though some say this is ever my theme, for of a truth they always are evil. So, either let someone prove them chaste, or let me still trample on them forever" (665–67). Phaedra suffers under the burden of a family background that rivals that of Oedipus. Her mother had slept with a white bull, her sister had been raped by Dionysus, and she herself is the "third to suffer" (337–40).

Caught in a conflict between Aphrodite and Artemis, Phaedra sees no way out but suicide. Phaedra destroys herself because, much like Sophocles' Antigone, she is embedded in a miserable situation. At the same time, she has an unrealistic expectation of herself. Vacillating between the altruistic and egoistic positions leads Phaedra to an anomic suicide. We will return to Phaedra's suicide in chapter 10 in comparison to the overcoming of suicidal thoughts on the part of the biblical Rebecca.

In *The Phoenissae*, Euripides treats the story of Oedipus's family quite differently from the way Sophocles does in his trilogy. Euripides portrays Antigone as a naïve young woman who is eager to sneak a look at the attacking army. Jocasta is still living, and Oedipus sits shut up in a house in Thebes, feeling miserable about himself and his misfortunes and cursing his sons, who have put him there. There are two altruistic suicides in *The Phoenissae*—Menoeceus, Creon's son, and Jocasta. The seer Tiresias taunts the Thebans that the city can be saved from the invaders only by the death of a young unmarried man to repay the earth for the slaying of Ares' dragon. This is the very essence of a Hobson's choice: an apparent pressure to destroy either one's own life or that of one's city. Menoeceus pretends to let Creon persuade him to flee the city, but he secretly goes to the appropriate site and stabs himself. Menoeceus genuinely believes that he must give precedence to the city over his own private needs and indeed his own life, so he offers his life as a gift, and his suicide must thus be classified as altruistic.

The second suicide, Jocasta, has failed to reconcile her two sons, Eteocles and Polyneices, with each other. They are greedy and ambitious, and Oedipus himself is predictably pessimistic. Jocasta is certain that one will kill the other in a duel, and she warns Antigone: "Daughter, thy brothers are in danger of their life" (1268). Jocasta then links her sons' imminent deaths with her own: "If I can forestall the onset of my sons, I may yet live; but if they be dead, I will lay me down and die with them" (1281–82). She kills herself after discovering that her sons have indeed killed each other at the Seventh Gate of Thebes. Jocasta's suicide has already been counted in Sophocles' *Oedipus Rex*.

Euripides' *The Suppliants* treats the story of Oedipus's children from a different angle. Here the families of the seven champions who fought against Thebes come to seek help from Athens and Theseus, its king. *The Suppliants* depicts the different mentalities of Theseus and Evadne: Theseus is open, flexible, confident, and at the same time serious; Evadne is uncommunicative, flighty, and lacking confidence both in herself and in the world around her. She is without a stopper, and ultimately, she becomes an anomic suicide. While many Euripidean characters are heavily embedded in their life patterns, Theseus is a clear-thinking, balanced man who sizes up situations well, can recognize flaws in his own character, and can treat others empathetically and considerately. His optimism is unusual among Euripidean characters.

Euripides portrays the gods, especially Athena, as friendly and encouraging to Theseus. Are the gods good to Theseus because he has a positive approach to living, or is his approach to living positive because the gods are

good to him? In any case, Theseus stands in marked contrast to Evadne, the
wife of Capaneus, the first man to scale the walls in the attack on Thebes
where he was struck dead by a thunderbolt thrown by Zeus. Evadne is not
caught up in an inescapable destructive environment. Rather, her largely
personal problems impel her to jump into the funeral pyre of her husband.
Morbid and depressed, she is "resolved not to save her life, or to prove untrue
to her husband." She seeks some recognition or notice, especially from her
father, and will "leap from this rack in honor's cause." She tries to hide her
purpose from her father, but she clearly also wants attention. She resorts to
riddles: "It would but anger thee to hear what I intend, and so I fain would
keep thee ignorant, my father" (1050). She adds: "Thou wouldst not wisely
judge my purpose" (1053). Yet, at the very same time, Evadne, like Sophocles' Antigone, wants her deed to be a model for all Argos. Evadne's final
challenge to Iphis, her father, before she leaps onto her husband's funeral
pyre, is worth examining: "'Tis all one; thou shalt never catch me in thy
grasp, lo! I cast me down, no joy to thee, but to myself and to my husband
blazing on the pyre with me" (1070–71). Indeed, it seems less important for
her to burn with her husband than that he burn with her. The father then
commences a long soliloquy on his own troubles in old age (1080–1113),
showing little concern for Evadne herself. Perhaps her father's indifference is
the root of Evadne's anomic behavior and her suicide as she vacillates errati-
cally between a desire for enmeshment and fear of any human contact.

Consider now *Iphignia in Aulis*. Euripides' Iphigenia, daughter of Agamemnon, is an altruistic suicide in Durkheim's terms. She accepts willingly,
almost gladly, a seer's order that she must be sacrificed before her father's
army will be able to sail for Troy. This is ritual murder, not suicide in the
contemporary use of the word; however, in this play there is no real distinction. The play's characters are encumbered with the same problem as so
many other characters of Greek drama—the general cheapness of human life
in the heroic view of man. There is the usual foreboding of calamity. Agamemnon declares this very clearly at the beginning of the play. Hubris will
be followed by nemesis, and every human is born to grief. Agamemnon
laments: "Woe's me for mortal men! None have been happy yet" (162–63).
All must go as the fates will. Again, in Agamemnon's words: "Woe, woe is
me, unhappy, caught by fate, outwitted by the cunning of the gods"
(442–45). Nevertheless, Agamemnon still feels compelled to kill Iphigenia,
even when Menelaus relents in his demands for her sacrifice. Indeed, Iphigenia herself seems to avoid any active attempt to evade her death. She grasps
for a freedom that she does not have by trying to make her death seem
voluntary instead of obligatory: "I have chosen death: it is my own free
choice. I have put cowardice away from me. Honor is mine now. O mother,
say I am right" (1375–77). Iphigenia is a dependent young girl who attempts
to ingratiate herself with her father by offending her mother: "O mother,

blame me not! Let me go first, and put my arms about my father's neck" (633–34). Yet the theme of abandonment is constant: "Mother, my father has gone, left me, betrayed and alone" (1317–20).

Iphigenia is at first horrified at the suggestion of her sacrifice. However, she finally accepts her situation bravely, as suits a woman from a heroic family. In addition, she wishes to defend her father against what she perceives as the anger of her mother toward him: "Oh, hate him not—my father, and your husband" (1453). Agamemnon, weak and indecisive, seems unable to commit himself to any course of action that will preserve his daughter's life. The success of the expedition to Troy, his own prestige, and his fear of an attack on his own city seem more important to him. These problems seem serious enough, but the biggest difficulty again is that classical Greek society offers no stopper, no way out. What is Iphigenia to do? Who is to explain to her that this situation is another Sphinx riddle that offers only a road to obliteration? It seems normal to Iphigenia that she should die in a heroic attempt to help the army and thereby salve her father's feelings, win his approval, and fulfill her family's tradition. This negation of self demonstrates Iphigenia's suicide to be altruistic. She is unable to free herself from the group pressure around her.

The Heracleidae begins after the death of Heracles. Afterwards, his family seeks refuge in Athens from his old enemy, King Eurystheus of Argos, who wishes to kill them. Demophon of Athens is willing to help the fugitives, but an oracle pronounces that a girl of noble descent must be sacrificed to the goddess Persephone in order for him to defeat the Argives. Once again, the characters are faced with a Hobson's choice: the safety of the family versus an individual life. Heracles' daughter Macaria learns of the trouble from Iolaus, her father's old friend, and she seems to take total responsibility for her brothers while neglecting herself. Iolaus takes advantage of this self-sacrificing streak in Macaria to pressure her, not very subtly, to resolve the state's perplexity by offering herself as the victim. Macaria takes the bait, revealing a willingness to let herself be sacrificed for others.

Death is welcome to her as long as it is glorious and she has freely chosen it. Iolaus is greatly moved by Macaria's altruistic gesture, praising her as the true daughter of Heracles. He suggests a fairer method, a lottery involving Macaria and her sisters, but Macaria will have none of this. Her sacrifice for others has no meaning if it is imposed through a lottery, nor does she seem to want to avoid the sacrifice through winning the lottery: "My death shall no chance lot decide, there is no graciousness in that peace, old Friend. But if ye accept and will avail you of my readiness, freely do I offer my life for those, and without constraint" (541–43). She wishes to protect her sisters, but it is also possible that an altruistic suicidal urge underlies this dramatic gesture in the name of others She echoes Seneca saying that one fulfills one's purpose in life most fully by the way one leaves it: "For I, by loving not my life too well have found a treasure very fair, a glorious means to leave it" (532–33). This wins the approval of those around her: "Who can speak more noble words or do more noble deeds henceforth forever?" (534–35). Again: "Daughter, thou art his own true child, no other man's but Heracles; that godlike soul" (539).

She travels the high road of heroism as her fathers did before her. Through her self-sacrifice, Macaria likewise fulfills the way of her father, Heracles. Perhaps more important, she seeks his approval, but she must do it freely: "Stand by and veil my body with my robe, for I will go even to the dreadful doom of sacrifice, seeing whose daughter I avow myself" (563–65). This seems to be the epitome of altruistic suicide: she must die to fulfill her father's glory, but she must have the heroic sense that she has chosen it freely.

Consider now Euripides' *Hecuba*. Polyxena, prisoner of the Greek conquerors after the fall of Troy and the last surviving daughter of Queen Hecuba, is another altruistic suicide. Her sense of *noblesse oblige* makes it impossible for her to escape the ritual death demanded of her. The play commences with the Greek fleet ready to return home after sacking Troy. The ghost of Achilles appears and demands that a virgin be sacrificed on his tomb before the fleet can sail. Primal terrors horrify the protagonists: "O'er the summit of his tomb appeared Achilles' phantom, and for his guerdon he would have one of the luckless maids of Troy" (97). The ghost demands: "Whither away so fast, ye Danai, leaving my tomb without its prize" (114). At the very moment of Polygene's sacrifice, Achilles' son raises the knife and invites his dead sire to come drink the black blood of a pure virgin. Euripides' characters seem laden with a sort of primal guilt simply because they exist. For them, the pristine simple world of nature is not to be reworked or improved by man's labors or even by his mere existence. Its virginity is not to be disturbed.

Man can expiate the innate foulness of his existence only by returning something in its virgin state to the monstrous and hellish earth that demands its due. What better sacrifice than a young virgin who will now be devoted only to earth and to no one else? This overwhelming sense of primal guilt adds to the daily pressures of life in captivity to push Polyxena to her death. First, there is her sense of ruin and outrage: "For my own life, its ruin and its outrage, never a tear I shed; nay death is become to me a happier lot than life" (210–11). The duty of the hero is to act heroically; indeed, she prefers death to unheroic behavior. Rather than rebuke her executioners for murdering her, she forgives them, Like Iphigenia and Macaria, she seeks to create the illusion of control over her own death: "Of my free will I die; let none lay hand on me; for bravely will I yield my neck" (559–62). The Greeks are impressed with the bravery of their Trojan captive, and they unbind her. Polyxena then voluntarily tears open her robe, sinks to her knee, and bares her breast. Her heroic sense of *noblesse oblige* leads her on to altruistic suicide: "Young prince, if 'tis my breast thou'dst strike, lo! Here it is, strike home! Or if at my neck thy sword thou'lt aim, behold! That neck is bared" (563–65).

From Polyxena's point of view, this becomes an altruistic suicide, or martyrdom. She needs to feel that she is dying freely because she cannot confront her captors with their injustice.[6] From the point of view of the Greeks, her ritual sacrifice is a necessary evil, part of the Hobson's choice with which they confronted themselves. Achilles' son is emotionally torn about the necessity of killing a girl so heroic and brave, "half glad, half sorry in his pity for the maid, cleft with the steel the channels of her breath" (560). He almost seems to wish that he would not have to kill Polyxena, but there is no stopper, no way out.

In *Alcestis*, one of Euripides' most puzzling plays, King Admetus of Thessaly is told that the fates demand his death unless he can find someone who is willing to die in his place. His aged parents sharply refuse his request, but Alcestis, his young and beautiful wife, offers herself. Both general and personal motives seem to be prompting Alcestis in her decision. The demands of the gods of the underworld are inexorable and horrifying; not even the Olympian gods can overrule them. In the opening scene, the god (Death) meets Apollo in a deadly serious debate for the life of Alcestis. Humans do not really have a right to enjoy their life on the earth: who they are or what they have accomplished mean nothing. In the end, the netherworld makes demands, and all of this means that one of the characters must die. Alcestis is the one who will satisfy Death's claims. Man's situation is, in its deepest sense, cheerless and hopeless. He may be met at any moment by the cruel demands of mysterious forces that show him neither mercy nor understanding. Alcestis accepts this view: "But these things are a god's doing and are thus" (297–98). It is perhaps more natural for an intelligent, concerned woman like Alcestis to accept these demands than for a selfish and hypocritical coward such as Admetus.

On the personal level, Alcestis's motives for substituting her life for Admetus's are quite complex: she is not a heroic or epic figure, nor does she speak of her debt to heroic ancestors. Rather, she is a lady of the noblest kind. When the day of her death arrives, she bathes, dresses in her best finery, and prays to the goddess of the earth to watch over her children. She seeks to comfort each servant in the house individually as they weep sorrowfully over her. Like so many Greek heroines, she bewails the loss of intimacy in her marriage bed. She puts Admetus first, even before her own life, and seems unable to fulfill herself unless she gives her unworthy husband her entire existence. On the other hand, Admetus's only concern about his wife's sacrificial death is the fact that he will be abandoned. Alcestis's puzzling response to Admetus seems to reveal another aspect of her psyche: "But, torn from you, I would not live with fatherless children, nor have I hoarded up those gifts of youth in which I found delight" (283–85). This statement makes no sense on the surface. Why are the children better off losing Alcestis than losing Admetus? Alcestis appears to be one of those women who must always cover up for a miserably inferior husband. She feels totally responsible for him and can never consider looking at her situation in any other way, whether it kills her with one blow, as here, or makes her life miserable for many years, day by day. Perhaps she fears showing her own weakness or dealing decisively with an unrewarding marriage. Perhaps she is simply disillusioned, and she is leaving the field and abandoning a totally dependent husband.

The choice here is not the classic Hobson's dilemma of Greek drama. Other protagonists who are offered a chance to die in Admetus's place have refused. This is not the heroism that proves so destructive to Ajax or the house of Atreus. Instead, it is a false sense of responsibility rooted in Alcestis's over-idealized conception of herself and an insufficient differentiation from her environment.

The complex plot of Euripides' *Andromache* includes one surrender to be murdered (Andromache) and one attempted anomic suicide (Hermione), both unsuccessful. Andromache, the widow of the Trojan hero Hector, is now a slave concubine of Neoptolemus, son of Achilles. While Neoptolemus is away at Delphi, his jealous wife, Hermione, and her father, Menelaus, threaten to kill Andromache's son unless Andromache surrenders herself to them to be put to death in his stead. When she does so, Menelaus announces that both will be killed. They are saved only by the timely arrival of old Peleus, father of Achilles. As much a coward as a bully, Menelaus withdraws, leaving his prisoners to Peleus. At her father's departure, Hermione goes into a panic. She is deeply afraid of what her husband (Neoptolemus) will say when he hears about her plotting; he might send her away in scandal. This leads her to thoughts of suicide, for now her deeds will make her abominable in the eyes of all men. Only the quick action of her servants restrains her from hanging herself and later stabbing herself. The suicide attempt by Hermione is anomic: it is initiated by Menelaus's cowardly abandonment of her, in conjunction with her overdependence on him. In that family, clearly, troubled relationships have been passed down from one generation to the next. Yet Hermione's suicide seems to be prevented by her returning home to her father's house, with its seeming protection. Orestes enters her life to rescue her from her immediate difficulty. The arrival of a father figure twice saves characters in this play: first, Peleus arrives to save Andromache and her son from Menelaus and Hermione; second, as despicable as Menelaus himself may be, his home proves to be a suicide-preventive haven for Hermione.

A Comparison of Sophocles and Euripides

In Faber's view, Sophocles and Euripides differ in their dramatization of the suicidal act and the underlying motivation. Suicide in Sophocles is ordinarily an active, aggressive self-murderous act (Ajax, Oedipus, Jocasta, Haemon, Eurydice, Deianeira), an act which expresses anger toward significant others and guilt over the breakdown of the idealized self. The self-destructive behavior of Heracles and Antigone are the only exceptions and tend to be more like the suicides depicted by Euripides. For Euripides, suicide (Alcestis, Polyxena, Evadne, Macaria, Iphigenia, and Menoeceus, all women except the last) is a more passive, acquiescing, self-sacrificial act, an act in which anticipation for and anxiety regarding the future is more conspicuous than anger over loss or guilt for past deeds (Faber, 93, 94).

In contrast to Sophocles, where suicide is a savagely aggressive act provoked by the need to expiate failure, to attack the significant other, to resurrect the good self by punishing the bad self,—in short, an act that announces the terrible toll human beings are prone to exact for themselves for what they have *done*, or for what they believe others have *done*, Euripides is preoccupied with suicide as a phenomenon intimately bound up with the problem of *choice*, with the problem of allowing oneself to become a person who is unlike the person one imagines oneself to be by *doing* something "bad" or unacceptable, something that forces one to "face up to" the truth of one's character. As far as suicide is concerned, Sophocles is a playwright of guilt, Euripides of anxiety.

Biblical Suicides

There are only six suicides in the entire Hebrew Bible. This is not surprising given the biblical and post-biblical attitudes toward suicide. The biblical basis for the injunction against suicide has been derived from the Noahide laws: "For your lifeblood too, I will require a reckoning" (Genesis 9:5). This statement has been seen in Talmudic law as a prohibition not only against suicide but also against any form of self-mutilation (*Baba Kamma*, 91b). The Hebrew Bible contains several additional prohibitions regarding self-mutilation, (Deuteronomy 14:1 and Leviticus 21:5). It is noteworthy that a number of suicide prevention stories occur, notably absent in Greek accounts. We will cite the translation provided in the fourteenth printing of *The Holy Scriptures According to the Masoretic Text* provided by The Jewish Publication Society of America (1985).

Table 3.2 applies Durkheim's terminology to the much smaller number in biblical narratives. Only six suicides can be found in the entire Hebrew Scriptures (Old Testament), all by men, and none in the Pentateuch. Chronologically, they are as follows: the self-stabbing of Abimelech (Judges 9:54);

the crushing of Samson (Judges 16:30); the self-stabbing of Saul (1 Samuel 31:14; 2 Samuel 1:6; 1 Chronicles 10:4) and his armor-bearer (1 Samuel 31:15; 1 Chronicles 10:5); the hanging of Ahitophel (2 Samuel 17:23); and the burning of Zimri (1 Kings 16:18). They can be classified as egoistic, altruistic and covenantal (in the service of a relationship with God).[7]

Let us examine the three egoistic suicides first. Ahitophel, a counselor of King David, has joined Absalom's rebellion. But when he perceives that Absalom has been tricked into following a foolhardy plan that is certain to lead to David's victory, Ahitophel sets his house in order and strangles himself: "And when Ahitophel saw that his counsel was not followed, he saddled his ass and arose, and got himself home unto the city; and set his house in order, and strangled himself; and he died and was buried in the sepulcher of his father" (2 Samuel 17:23).

Several reasons, all egoistic, have probably prompted Ahitophel's suicide. First, he now fears that Absalom's attempt to overthrow David is doomed and that he will die a traitor's death. Second, and less likely, is Ahitophel's disgust at Absalom's conduct in setting aside his counsel, which has wounded Ahitophel's pride and disappointed his ambition. Third, David's curse may have prompted Ahitophel to hang himself (*Makkot,* 4a).

Finally, rabbinic writers have also argued that, since Ahitophel is a suicide, his family inherits his estate. If he were to be executed as a rebel, his possessions would be forfeited to the king. Ahitophel thus seems to be an egoistic suicide (and is listed in the Mishna (*Sanhedrin,* 10:2) as among those who have forfeited their share in the world to come.

Zimri is also an egoistic suicide, with seemingly no redeeming qualities. King Elah of Israel passes his days drinking in his palace while his warriors

Table 3.2.   Suicides in the Hebrew Bible

Character	Gender	Source	Method	Type
Saul	M	1 Samuel 31:4	Sword	Covenantal
		2 Samuel 1:6		
		1 Chronicles 10:4		
Saul's Armor-Bearer	M	1 Samuel 31:5	Sword	Altruistic
		1 Chronicles 10:5		
Ahitophel	M	2 Samuel 17:23	Strangling	Egoistic
Zimri	M	1 Kings 16:18	Burning	Egoistic
Abimelech	M	Judges 9:54	Sword	Egoistic
Samson	M	Judges 16:30	Crushing	Covenantal

M = Male; F = Female

battle the Philistines. Zimri, a high-ranking officer, takes advantage of this situation, assassinates Elah, and mounts the throne. His reign, however, lasts only seven days. As soon as the news of King Elah's murder reaches the army on the battlefield, they pronounce General Omri to be king and lay siege to the palace. When Zimri sees that he is unable to hold out against the siege, he sets fire to the palace and perishes in the flames: "And it came to pass, when Zimri saw that the city was taken that he went into the castle of the king's house, and burnt the king's house over him with fire, and he died" (1 Kings 16:18).

Abimelech's suicide is also egoistic. After carving out a principality for himself in Israel by means of various brutalities, he is mortally wounded by a millstone that a woman throws from a fortress he is besieging. Realizing that he is dying, Abimelech asks his armor-bearer to finish him off so that it will not be said that a woman has killed him. This act of hubris qualifies him as an egoistic suicide.

And a certain woman cast an upper millstone upon Abimelech's head, and broke his skull. Then he called quickly to the young man, his armor-bearer, and said to him: "Draw your sword and kill me, lest men say of me, 'A woman killed him.'" So his young man thrust him through, and he died (Judges 9:53–57).

Samson, the great defender and leader of the Israelites, represents an example of a covenantal suicide. We must remember that he had been blinded and publicly mocked by the Philistines. Faced with torture and death, Samson asked God for the strength to take as many Philistines with him as possible; when granted his request, he pulled down the central pillars of the temple of Dagon, killing thousands in one last blow: And Samson called to the Lord, saying, "O Lord God, remember me, I pray! Strengthen me, I pray, just this once." And Samson took hold of the two middle pillars which supported the temple, and braced himself against them, one on his right and the other on his left. Then Samson said, "Let me die with the Philistines!" And he pushed with all his might, and the temple fell on the lords and on all the people who were in it (Judges 16:28–30).

It is tempting to see Samson as the biblical equivalent of Sophocles' Ajax. Samson, like Ajax, has fallen from his previous state of leadership. Is he, too, using suicide to restore his lost image in the eyes of others? Closer examination indicates that Samson's suicide is not egoistic like that of Ajax: he is not alienated from his society but is very much a part of the people of Israel. His uncut hair is part of his Nazarite consecration to God, not a symbol of macho heroism. He loses his strength when he abandons his consecration by falling to the wiles of Delilah and having his hair cut. His death is not an attempt to restore his own lost honor at the expense of his people, but it comes about in his effort to strike a telling blow against the enemies of Israel. Is Samson's suicide, therefore, altruistic and self-sacrificing?

Arguing against this classification is that Samson does not suffer from a failing sense of his own personality; rather, he calls on God to strengthen him in his final attempt to destroy the Philistines. His purpose is not self-annihilation but the carrying out of his divinely ordained mission to free Israel from the Philistines. Samson's suicide thus seems to be neither egoistic nor altruistic; rather, it may be labeled covenantal in the sense that it is in the service of the biblical God, with neither over-isolation nor over-integration in his boundaries with his society. Significantly, his final action in life leads to a long period of peace (Judges 13).

A second covenantal suicide is that of King Saul. Rabbinic literature has regarded King Saul as a man of great stature, the anointed of the Lord. Yet his reign was marked by series of mistakes, ending with his own suicide during a losing battle against the Philistines on Mount Gilboa. Saul has seen three of his sons and many of his fighters slain, and he himself is severely wounded. Surrounded by enemies and not wishing to be taken prisoner and exposed to the mockery and brutality of the Philistines, King Saul entreats his armor-bearer to kill him. The latter refuses, and Saul falls on his own sword: "Then Saul said to his armor-bearer: 'Draw your sword, and thrust me through with it, lest these uncircumcised men come and thrust me through and abuse me.' But his armor-bearer would not, for he was greatly afraid. Therefore, Saul took a sword, and fell on it" (1 Samuel 31:4).

The suicide of Saul has been taken by commentators in different ways. The Midrash Rabbah (on Gen. 9:5) has pointed to Saul as an example of a permissible suicide (see also *Midrash Rabbah,* 34.13 and *Shulchan Aruch, Yoreh Deah,* 345.3). One commentator has considered Saul as a special case because, before the final battle with the Philistines, he has received a message from the witch of Endor that he will die. Thus, by taking his own life, he is not defying Providence. Other commentators have viewed Saul as an example of a suicide who takes his own life in order to avoid greater profanation of the divine name. In this view, Saul fears that if he is captured alive by the Philistines, they will desecrate his body, either by torture or by forcing him to commit idolatrous acts. This interpretation implies that suicide may be permissible if it is committed in order to prevent dishonor to God's name rather than for personal reasons. As such, Saul's suicide can be classified as altruistic—perhaps better, covenantal, rather than as either egoistic or altruistic.

The suicide of Saul's armor-bearer can be classified as altruistic because of his seeming lack of differentiation from Saul: "And when his armor-bearer saw that Saul was dead, he also fell on his sword, and died with him" (1 Samuel 31:5). The biblical passage tells us that the armor-bearer first refuses to kill Saul and then falls on his own sword in response to Saul's suicide. In a related narrative, an Amalekite comes to David and reports that he has assisted in Saul's suicide; for this, David orders him killed (2 Samuel

1:9–10,13–16). Commentaries have seen David as behaving correctly in condemning the Amalekite to death, even though the Amalekite was simply following Saul's orders in assisting the latter to die (Ralbag on 2 Samuel 1:14).

There is no example of Durkheim's anomic suicide in the Hebrew Bible; the six suicides seem to be either egoistic, altruistic, or covenantal. The most sympathetic rabbinic treatment is given to the covenantal suicides (Samson and Saul). The harshest judgments are applied to suicides that seem clearly egoistic (Ahitophel, Zimri, and Abimelech).

The important point here is the far fewer number of suicides in the Hebrew Scriptures. Whatever their motivation, it is important to emphasize the 16 suicides in the 26 surviving plays of Sophocles and Euripides (or 17 if we include the 7 surviving plays of Aeschylus) in comparison to the much smaller number of 6 occurring in biblical narratives.[8]

Comparative Statistics of Greek versus Biblical Suicides

Let us now offer some comparative statistics based on the total number of characters in these two source documents. As we mentioned previously, there are approximately 223 personalities appearing in the 26 plays of Sophocles and Euripides, some appearing in more than one play. This yields a suicide rate of 16/223 or 7.2%. If we include the 41 characters depicted in the plays of Aeschylus as well, we tally 17 suicides out of a total of 264 characters or a slightly lower suicidal behavior rate of 6.4%.

In contrast, some 2,855 different people (2,730 men and 1125 women) are mentioned in the 39 books of the Hebrew Scriptures spanning a period of 3,330 years (see Zfiffer, 2006). Only six are identified as completed suicides (see Table 3.2), yielding an overall suicide rate of 6/2855 or .02%, including none by women. If we limit our estimate of the total number of biblical characters to the 1,778 identified by one title or another such as King, Queen, Prophet, Judge, Military Commander, etc. (again see Zfiffer, 2006), the suicide rate increases slightly to 6/1778 or .03% Both of these rates are extraordinary lower than the suicide rates emerging in Greek tragedy, whether we compare these biblical rates to the 7.2 % suicide rates in the 26 plays of Sophocles and Euripides (respective Chi-Squares = 141.39 and 85.19, p<.001 in both cases) or to the 6.4% suicide rate for the 264 characters when we include the 7 plays of Aeschylus (respective Chi-Squares= 128.05 and 76.85. p<.001 in both cases).

Biblical Suicide Preventions

Perhaps even more to the point are the six suicide-preventing, indeed life-promoting, narratives described in Scriptures. Job, for example, expresses a clear wish for suicide out of the depths of his affliction (Job 7:15). Yet Job does not commit suicide and indeed seems to recover his faith. "Though he slay me, yet I will trust in Him" (Job 13:15). The prophet Elijah represents another example of suicide prevention. He clearly expresses a wish to die, but recovers his strength after being given food and drink and is allowed to rest (1 Kings 19:8). Moses expresses suicidal wishes to God when he is in the desert. Moses feels overwhelmed by his burdens which he feels he must shoulder alone (Numbers 11:14–15). Once again, God successfully intervenes by offering Moses a chance to have his burden shared (Numbers 11:16–17). David (Psalm 22) also expresses weariness of life, Rebecca (Genesis 27–28) becomes dismayed at the thought of her son Isaac marrying a Hittite woman, and Jonah several times expresses the wish to die. God is portrayed as intervening in these cases as well. In other words, the Hebrew Scriptures seem to provide a psychological stopper for people in despair which seems unavailable to figures in the Greaco-Roman literature.

The plan for the remainder of this book is as follows: chapter 4 will present evidence-based research with regard to the following seven risk factors for suicide: (1) Feeling isolated and ignored; (2) Feeling one's life is without meaning; (3) Feeling exiled from one's homeland as a refugee; (4) Feeling one is unable to express one's own needs with others; (5) Feeling as an adopted child that one is unable to trust enough to seek or accept help; (6) Feeling abandoned by one's child leaving the family nest and building his/ her own life; and (7) Feeling doomed by a dysfunctional (incestuous) family of origin.

We compare Greek and biblical narratives regarding each of these evidence-based suicide risk factors, demonstrating how Greek narratives lead to self-destructive behaviors while biblical narratives provide a safe way out of these dilemmas. We will discuss each of the biblical suicide prevention-life

Table 3.3.   Suicide Preventions in the Hebrew Bible

Character	Gender	Source	Method
Rebecca	F	Genesis 27–28	Appropriate Matchmaking
Moses	M	Numbers 11	Support and practical advice
Elijah	M	1 Kings 18–19	Protected withdrawal and nurturance
Jonah	M	Jonah	Protected withdrawal and guidance
David	M	Psalms 22	Renewal of faith in God
Job	M	Job	Renewal of relationship

M = Male; F = Female

promotion stories presented in table 3.3, and add to this mix the story of Ruth. We will contrast them with four of the Greek suicide stories discussed in table 3.2 along with the stories of Zeno the Stoic, Narcissus, and the Roman general, Coriolanus, around the seven evidence-based risk factors for suicide outlined above and to be discussed in chapter 4.

Chapter 5 will contrast Elijah with Ajax around the effects of isolation; chapter 6, Job with Zeno around the effects the lack of an intrinsic meaning structure; chapter 7, David with Coriolanus around the effects of being a refugee; chapter 8 Jonah with Narcissus around the effects of conflict of one's one needs with those of others; chapter 9, Moses with Oedipus around the effects of being expelled from one's nuclear family; chapter 10, Rebecca against Phaedra around the empty nest syndrome; and finally, chapter 11, Ruth with Antigone around the issue of a dysfunctional, even incestuous, family of origin.

NOTES

1. Some of the material in this chapter has been abridged, with permission by William B. Eerdmans Publisher from a book by the senior author: Kalman J. Kaplan and Matthew B. Schwartz *A Psychology of Hope: A Biblical Response to Tragedy and Suicide* (2008).

2. Significantly, Hamlet has rejected suicide earlier in the play on the religious grounds that the "Everlasting hath fix'd his canon 'gainst self-slaughter" (ibid., Act I, Scene II, lines 335–336). Hamlet's famous soliloquy cited earlier in this chapter has Hamlet reject suicide on more prosaic grounds: if there is consciousness after death, then the mental torment that drove one to suicide will persist (ibid., Act III, Scene 1, lines 63–67). Finally, at the end of the play, Horatio tells the dying Hamlet that he (Horatio) is "more an antique Roman than a Dane" meaning that he wishes to take his own life (as many Romans have done) and follow Hamlet unto death. Hamlet begs him to "absent thee from felicity awhile and . . . live to draw thy breath in pain to tell my story" (ibid., Act V, Scene II, lines 377–386).

3. Philosopher Margaret Battin (1996) discusses aspects of the arguments regarding suicide in her book: *The Death Debate: Ethical Issues in Suicide*.

4. Only one semi-overt act of self-destruction occurs in the seven surviving plays of Aeschylus, the third great Greek tragedian; specifically, in *The Seven Against Thebes*, where Eteocles, son of Oedipus and Jocasta, rushes to the battlefield, insisting the gods are eager for his death (ll. 692–719).

5. Generally, we do not count Greek choruses as characters as they are not candidates for suicidal behavior.

6. Contrast the altruistic Greek heroine with Rabbi Akiba, who at the moment of his brutal torture and murder at the hands of the Romans recited the Shema: ("Hear O Israel, the Lord is our God, the Lord is one"). Akiba reconfirms his faith in God and in life and does not need to seek illusory control by pretending to die willingly. He psychologically and spiritually is able to reject the idea of Romans control over his death, without resorting to a suicidal explanations.

7. A covenantal suicide is, of course, not part of the Durkheimian typology, but is our contribution, employing the previous discussed term introduced by Lebacqz and Englehardt (1977).

8. Only one suicide, Judas Iscariot, appears in the Christian New Testament either by hanging (Matthew 27:5) or falling and bursting open (Acts 1:18). Other suicides have been reported in the non-rabbinic writings of the Second Temple period as well. In the apocryphal book of 1 Maccabees, for example, Eleazar sacrifices himself by darting beneath the elephant of an enemy general and running his sword into it (1 Maccabees 6:46). In the book of 2

Maccabees, two acts of suicide are recorded: first, that of Ptolemy, and second, that of Ragesh (Razis). Ptolemy, an advocate of the Judeans at the Syrian Court of King Antiochus Eupator, poisons himself after being accused of treason (2 Maccabees 10:12). Ragesh first attempts unsuccessfully to die on his sword rather than fall into the hands of the Syrians (2 Maccabees 14:41–42). He subsequently succeeds in disemboweling himself after throwing himself from a wall (2 Maccabees 14:43–46). The historian Flavius Josephus also mentions a number of suicides in his work *Wars of the Jews,* including the mass suicides at Jotapata in 69 C.E. and Masada in 73 C.E. (see the surveys of Koch, 2005 and Shemesh, 2009). In Josephus's account (*Wars of the Jews,* 7:598–603), the 900 Jewish defenders of Masada (Sicarii Nationalists) kill themselves *en masse* rather than surrender to the Romans The first parts of the speech Josephus attributes to their leader Eliezer Ben Yair are decidedly non-Jewish. For example, Ben Yair argues that God had given the Sicarii freedom to choose their own kind of death (*Wars of the Jews,* 7:600–601), then he says that the revolt against the Roman Empire has failed because God had sentenced the Jewish race to extinction; therefore, let the defenders of Masada take their own lives. Josephus then gives Ben-Yair an even more explicitly Greek argument: "Death gives freedom to the soul which then returns to a wonderful abode where it dwells with God. Death is much like sleep" (7:601–2). He then portrays Ben Yair as citing as a good example the Indian Brahmins, who bring on their own deaths with great pleasure and courage in their desire for death and immortality (7:602).

Finally, Ben Yair is portrayed as stressing the great suffering of the Jews during the war, the immense trauma of the destruction of Jerusalem, and he reaches a peak of intensity when he depicts a man watching his wife and children being carried off by heartless enemies (7:602–3). The listeners respond with deep emotion to his plea, and according to Josephus, go forward with a mass suicide.

Although Masada has become a symbol of bravery in much of the modern world, its lesson for Israel is that Masada must not fall again, rather than the aggrandizement of suicide. Significantly, it is never once mentioned in rabbinic literature, and references to it are conspicuously absent in *Yosippon,* a later Hebrew account of the Jewish revolt, which portrays the defenders fighting against the Romans to the death (Ben Gurion, *Sefer Yosippon,* chap. 87).

No Talmudic passage can be taken as praising suicide or glorifying heroism in the Greek sense, nor is there an obsession with death as the solution to life's problems or with the issue of control. Nevertheless, according to the Talmud, suicide can be permissible and even preferred in select instances in which a person is faced with forced apostasy or tortures that might be more horrifying than death. The great scholar Rabbi Hanina ben Teradion, who was burned to death by his Roman persecutors with a Torah scroll wrapped around him, would not even open his mouth so as to breathe in the flames and die more quickly: "Let him who gave me my soul take it away but no one should injure himself." In other words, he refused to advance his own death actively. The Roman executioner, impressed by the personal greatness of Rabbi Hanina and the terrible awe of the moment, wanted to be joined to him (*Tosefot Avodah Zarah,* 18a; *Maharsha*). He offered to end Hanina's torture by removing the wet sponges from around his heart, which had artificially prolonged his life. Rabbi Hanina approved this, and he assured the executioner of a portion in the world to come. The executioner then removed the sponges, and, knowing that he himself would now be severely punished by the Romans, he leaped into the fire. Both were assigned a place in the world to come (*Avodah Zarah,* 18a; *Sifre* and *Yalkut Shimoni* on Deut. 32:4). The story of the 400 boys and girls who leaped into the sea rather than be sent to lives of prostitution in Rome is comparable (*Gittin,* 57b). There is a similar story in *Lamentations Rabbah,* 1.45, where the basic principle is that if "they feared lest idol worshippers force them to sin by means of unbearable tortures, then it is commanded to destroy oneself" (*Tosafot, Avodah Zarah,* 18a; *Gittin,* 57b; see also Rabbi Jacob Emden, *Hagahot*). At such a point it may be more desirable to sanctify God's holy name by suicide than to sin. Again, this is not an approbation of suicide per se, nor an obsession with issues of control, as in many of the Greek suicides. Human life remains an object of great importance. We should note that the young people in *Gittin* 57 and the elders in the parallel story in *Lamentations Rabbah* asked for a rabbinic opinion before leaping into the sea, so that they would not lose their share in the world to come. Gittin also describes the suicide of Hannah after the martyrdom of her seven sons, and *Avodah Zarah* 18b recounts the suicide of Beruria, the wife of Rabbi Meier.

Other Talmudic suicides include the Hasmonean princess who was loved by her former slave, Herod (*Baba Batra,* 3b), a Roman officer who saved the life of Rabben Gamlieh (*Taanit,* 29a) and the suicides of a mother and father after the father threw their son from the roof for receiving food from a guest without permission (*Hullin,* 94a). Another suicide involved a student whose name was falsely besmirched by a prostitute (*Berachot,* 23a). The Talmud (*Semachot,* chaps. 2 and 5) also relates two incidents of childhood suicide, the first involving the son of Gornos of Lydda, who ran away from school, and the second, that of a child in Bnei B'rak, who broke a bottle on the Sabbath. Each child killed himself after his father threatened to punish him; neither was ruled an intentional suicide. Two more suicides are mentioned in the *Midrash Rabbah.* The first (*Ecclesiastes Rabbah* 10:7) describes a pagan eunuch of the emperor of Rome who attempted to embarrass Rabbi Akiba. When the eunuch was shamed in return, he killed himself. The second (*Genesis Rabbah* 65:22) describes the suicide of Jakum of Tzeroth who, after taunting Rabbi Joseph Meshitha, inflicted as self-punishment the four modes of execution typically sentenced by the courts: he stoned, burned, strangled, and decapitated himself. There are a number of significant suicides in later Jewish history as well, including five hundred Jews at York in the twelfth century, hundreds in Verdun, France, in 1326, and many more in response to the Spanish Inquisition. While it is not our intention to create a laundry list here, there have been periods of external persecutions throughout Jewish history that have put Jews in the position of choosing apostasy or suicide (Haberman, 1946). Durkheim's aforementioned observation on the comparatively higher rate of suicide among Jews in late nineteenth-century Bavaria and the suicides among Jews in Central and Eastern Europe in the 1930s and during World War II are also clearly connected to external forces. The importance of the theme of suicide in modern Yiddish literature has been explored in a work by Janet Hadda (1988), who has focused largely on suicidogenic family themes. Famous Jewish suicides in modern times include that of Otto Weininger, the self-hating Jewish intellectual who in 1903 shot himself in Ludwig van Beethoven's apartment; Ernst Toller, a playwright and revolutionary who killed himself in New York in 1939 in despair after the fall of Madrid to Francisco Franco; and Samuel Zygelbojm, who in 1943 committed suicide in London to protest the indifference of Polish, British, and other authorities to reports of the Holocaust and the savage destruction of the Warsaw Ghetto. According to some accounts, Sigmund Freud, who was suffering from a painful and incurable illness, also took his own life.

It is obviously incorrect, then, to claim that there are no suicides in biblical and later Jewish history. Individual suicides have occurred despite the injunctions against them. Nevertheless, suicide is strongly prohibited in biblical and later Jewish thought, and when it has appeared within the culture, it may represent individual idiosyncrasies, impossible external situations, or profound Greco-Roman influences. The basic Jewish preference for life over death as expressed in the Hebrew Bible has never changed, nor has suicide ever been idealized as an end in itself.

Chapter Four

Seven Evidence-Based
Risk Factors for Suicide

A number of psychosocial risk factors have also been reported to be significantly associated with the risk of suicide. They include marital disruption, unemployment, lower socio-economic status, living alone, a recent migration, early parental deprivation, family history of suicidal behavior and psychopathology, poor physical health and stressful life events. (Cheng, Chen, Chen and Jenkins, 2000, *The British Journal of Psychiatry, 177 [4],* 360)[1]

Exogeneous and/or endogenous challengers elicit a crisis in all humans, but depending on the intensity of the elicited stress and the threshold for tolerating it, that is, one's vulnerability, the crisis will either be contained homeostatically, or lead to an episode of disorder. Vulnerability and episode stand in a trait-state relation, and markers for each must be provided to distinguish between them. (Zubin and Spring, 1977, *Journal of Abnormal Psychology, 86 [2],* 103)[2]

This chapter will review the evidence regarding seven risk factors for suicide: (1) Feeling isolated and ignored; (2) Feeling one's life is without meaning; (3) Feeling exiled from one's home or homeland as a refugee; (4) Feeling unable to be oneself with others; (5) Feeling as an adopted child that one is unable to trust enough to seek or accept help; (6) Feeling abandoned by one's child leaving the family nest and building his/her own life; and (7) Feeling doomed by an enmeshed and dysfunctional (even incestuous) family of origin.

Each of these factors can be seen as a stressor with regard to suicide. However, people may differ in their vulnerabilities to these stressors (c.f. Zubin and Spring, 1977). Exogeneous and/or endogenous challengers elicit a crisis in all humans, but depending on the intensity of the elicited stress and the threshold for tolerating it, that is, one's vulnerability, the crisis will either be contained homeostatically, or lead to an episode of disorder. In other words, a given stressor may overwhelm the defenses of a highly vulnerable person but be successfully navigated by someone who is not so vulnerable. This we will discuss at length in chapters 5 through 11. For now, let us concentrate on the stressors or risk factors themselves.

FEELING ISOLATED AND IGNORED

Feeling isolated and ignored can leave one feeling helpless and hopeless which can in turn lead to suicidal behavior. Durkheim (1897/1951), Dublin and Bunzel (1933), and Pretzel (1972) have summarized the sociological literature highlighting the importance of social isolation as a risk factor for suicide. Moustakas (1961) stressed the importance of existential loneliness in 1961 and was an influential writer throughout the turbulent 1960s.

Choron (1972) emphasized loneliness as a principal cause of suicide, and suggested that it is often the psychological make-up of the suicidal individual which prevents the establishment of healthy individuals. Dublin (1963) emphasized the experience of social isolation and lack of interpersonal connectedness as representing one of the more important indices when assessing the suicidality in an individual. Margolin and Teicher (1968) and Schneer, Kay, and Brozovsky (1968) found effects of early parental loss or separation on subsequent adolescent suicide. Barter, Swaback and Todd (1968) found that repeated attempters had suffered a higher percentage of parental loss than non-attempters. Dorpat (1973) and Dorpat and Ripley (1967) reported that early loss was associated with completed suicides and later loss with attempted suicides. Social isolation also has an important role as a risk factor in the review articles of Douglas (1967), Giddens (1971), Lester and Lester (1971), Maris (1969; 1981), and Martin (1968).

Feeling isolated seems to be a risk factor for suicide across the life span. Let us examine several studies of suicide conducted in the 1970s. Finch and Proznanski (1971) found that in younger patients a suicide or suicide attempt may reflect a sense of trying to establish a reunion with a lost person (see the review article of Lee, 1978). Isolation is a risk factor among older adults as well. Bock and Weber (1972) studied suicide among older adults in Pinellas County, Florida, between 1955 and 1963. They reported the following results: (1) the widowed exhibited higher suicide rates than the married, (2) this differential is partially explained by the greater social isolation of the widowed, especially the widowers, (3) the widowed can find in other types of relationships, alternatives to marriage which help prevent suicidal behavior, (4) widowers have greater difficulty than widows in making effective substitutions for the loss of their spouse, and (5) there appear to be limits to the effective mitigation of these alternatives for the widowed, especially the widowers.

In an excellent review of the effects of social isolation on suicide, Trout (1980) emphasized that the empirical literature indicates that social isolation had a primary and direct role in suicide. She draws several implications from this conclusion. First, that suicide attempters are appealing for help through suicidal behaviors, and that the character of the response is crucial in determining whether or not suicide will take place (Kobler and Stotland, 1964, 252).

However, Trout emphasizes that caring on the part of the helping contact might not be enough contact in itself. What is required, for Trout, is the right kind of interaction which allows an individual to function adequately in significant interpersonal relations with others. The suicidal individual must be able to express himself in a positive way in interpersonal situations. A destructive social contact may well be deleterious to the suicidal individual, making him more desperate. For Trout, a broad range implication of the literature on social isolation and suicide is the striking need for supportive and educational programs to deal with social isolation in a positive manner. Trout warned us back in 1980 that there was direct evidence that America and much of the West has become an interpersonally cold society, one with a lack of genuine warmth and empathy, and a lack of succorant persons and institutions. We can see this has occurred with a vengeance.

When there is a continued lack of helpful response from others, a person's suicidogenic feeling of being socially isolated is confirmed. As Stengel stated back in 1964,

> The importance of the fight against social isolation cannot be overrated because it involves not only the incidence of suicidal acts, but also of delinquency and much psychological illness. It is a problem which concerns society as a whole and which cannot be left to kindly volunteers and charitable organization. (Stengel, 1964, 38)

If anything, the situation has worsened considerably since then. Our society is fragmented and the traditional bonds of family have become frayed. People are more mobile, the institution of marriage is under attack, and economic pressures have pushed women away from their traditional roles as social emotional anchors of the family unit.

Connections with family members, friends, organizations, neighborhoods, religious organizations, and other communal outlet serve as potent protective factors against the risk of developing patterns of suicidal thoughts and behaviors (e.g., Borowsky et al., 2001; Knox et al., 2003; Oyama et al., 2004). More recently Daniel and Goldston (2012) have emphasized that a lack of connectedness to others along with a pervasive sense of hopelessness are two of the most significant risk factors associated with increased rate of suicidal thoughts and behaviors across the life span.

An ecological study of isolation and suicide by Martiello and Giacchi (2012) in Tuscany (Italy) found a positive correlation between suicide and measures of economic deprivation and social fragmentation for both men and women. The correlation analyses showed that suicide was significantly associated with many variables in men, but only with old age in women. The multiple regression analyses showed that the best predictors in men were education, single person households, and isolated houses. For women, the best predictors were the proportion of elderly people and income (this was also true for the weighted model, but in the opposite order). Among the best predictors, isolated houses may act as a marker for remoteness and isolation on a small scale.

Providing important elaboration around protective factors that lead suicidal individuals to seek out help when feeling socially isolated, Calear, Batterham, and Chistensen (2014) found that among those individuals who demonstrate high suicide literacy and low suicide stigma, suicidal ideation resulting from isolation was associated with an increase in positive attitudes toward seeking help from others, while individuals experiencing suicidal ideation had more negative attitudes toward help-seeking and lower intentions to seek help. This research further underscores the criticality of addressing suicidality as not only a clinical issue to be dealt with individually, but as a public safety initiative focused on education and de-stigmatization. The role that faith-based communities can play in furthering these aims can be deeply impactful by promoting faith, hope, and—perhaps most importantly—involvement in communal activities.

FEELING ONE'S LIFE IS WITHOUT MEANING

Feeling that one's life is without meaning or purpose is a terrible problem in modern society, leading the eminent psychiatrist and thinker Victor Frankl (1962) to comment that, "There is nothing in the world . . . that would so effectively help one to survive even the worst conditions, as the knowledge that there is a meaning in one's life" (126). The existential despair in individual experiences when they are unable to identify reasons that will allow them to continue living can be devastating. This emotional pain leads many to consider suicide as their only viable escape from life's miseries.

In Western society, personal meaning is often confused with success, where success is measured by a certain level of attainment of status and wealth. Economic pressures such as unemployment, under-employment, recessions, as well as other financial down-turns have increasingly negatively impacted the ways that individuals derive meaning from their lives since the loss of status and affluence contributes to feelings of failing at being "successful."

Within the current cultural climate in America and in much of the West, a reduction in these materialistic benchmarks for what is considered "successful" can lead to a personal loss of meaning and trigger an existential spiral that can lead to suicidal ideations and behaviors. Although we cannot know for certain the exact motives for those who have completed suicides, we can rely on the truism that they decided that life was no longer worth living at that moment—their choice inherently relies upon the assumption that they gave up searching for meaning in their lives.

To prevent a lack of meaning from developing, individuals must attach themselves to social supports who will help shift their paradigm of what it means to be successful, in effect recalibrating their entire meaning structure to emphasize the centrality of the dignity of human life, independent of success as it has been contemporaneously understood. A redefinition of meaning will help shift an individual's perspective, and lead to more what some have called "existential intelligence"—the ability to appreciate the "big" picture in life. This is essentially the biblical world view, which extends beyond one's immediate personal, social, and cultural context, permitting people the psychological latitude to appreciate that what problems exist today may not persist forever.

In a 1993 study, the senior author developed a new approach to measuring one's belief in a Creator. Rather than employ traditional measures of religiosity, Kaplan along with a colleague developed a more direct way of measuring belief in a Creator (Ross and Kaplan, 1993–1994; Kaplan and Ross, 1995). Life-ownership orientation was assessed by a 21 item Life-Ownership Orientation Questionnaire (LOOQ) which consisted of items reflecting different attitudes towards seven distinct areas of life. Respondents could indicate their beliefs as to whether these events and attitudes were God-oriented (reflecting a belief that different areas of life belonged to God), individual-oriented (reflecting a belief that these same areas of life belonged to the individual) or state-oriented (reflecting a belief that these areas of life belonged to the state/government). On the basis of their responses, college student subjects were classified as God-oriented, individual-oriented or state-oriented.

These scores were assessed against attitudes towards four life-death topics of concern: abortion, suicide, physician-assisted suicide and capital punishment. No students were classified as state-oriented so this type was dropped from the study. However, very interesting differences emerged in the response patterns of individual-oriented and God-oriented students. Results were as follows: individual-oriented respondents were more accepting of abortion, suicide and physician-assisted suicide than were God-oriented respondents. These two orientation types did not show significant differences in attitudes toward capital punishment. These results suggest that belief in a Creator serves as a prophylactic against the interference with the natural process of life at both ends of the life-span: birth and death.

Let us again cite the work of Abramson, Seligman, and Teasdale (1978), Peterson and Seligman (1984), and Peterson et al. (1998) regarding a "catastrophizing" explanatory style for the causality of bad events: internality (it's me) versus externality, stability (it's going to last forever) versus instability, and globosity (it's going to undermine everything) versus specificity. And how this catastrophizing style (attributing bad events to global causes) predicted mortality, especially among males, and predicted accidental or violent deaths especially well.

We have also discussed our independently conducted 2007 study, in which the senior author (Kaplan et al., 2007) along with colleagues and students studied the relationship between meaninglessness and suicidality. In the absence of an inherent meaning structure of life, undergraduate students tended to catastrophize and generalize singular negative hypothetical events with which they were presented. Further, this tendency tended to be linked with greater levels of depression and hence more positive attitudes towards suicide, and physician-assisted suicide for both men and women. However, the two genders differ as to the main dynamic of this effect. The effect for men is exclusively located on the front end of this causal chain (between catastrophizing and demoralization) while the relationship for women was located on the back end of this chain of causality (between demoralization and suicidality). Interestingly, traditional measures of religiosity (such as synagogue or church attendance) do not seem to play an important moderating influence in this sequential chain.

Kleiman and Beaver (2013) have recently found that presence of meaning in life accurately predicted decreased suicidal ideation as well as lower lifetime chances of attempted suicides. Further, this research concludes that even the *search*—not necessarily the presence—for meaning in life also predicted decreased suicidal ideation over time. These findings suggest that interventions that target increasing meaning-seeking and meaning-making in life may likely be an important factor to diminish suicide risk in individuals. This line of research has been supported by findings by Heisel and Flett (2015), who likewise concluded that there is a growing body of knowledge suggesting that establishing a personal meaning in life (MIL), contributes not only to general mental wellness and, but also potentially decreases future incidents of suicidal contemplations later in life. Kleiman and Bearver (2013) have recently found that presence of meaning in life accurately predicted decreased suicidal ideation as well as lower lifetime chances of attempted suicides. Further, this research concludes that even the *search*—not necessarily the presence—for meaning in life also predicted decreased suicidal ideation. This line of research has been supported by findings by Heisel, Neufeld, and

Flett (2015), who likewise concluded that there is a growing body of knowledge suggesting that establishing a personal meaning in life, contributes not only to general mental wellness but also decreases future incidents of suicidal contemplations later in life. In an intriguing study, Peterson et al. (1998) report that catastrophizing (attributing bad causes to global causes) predicted mortality, especially accidents and violent deaths, for males.

FEELING EXILED FROM ONE'S HOMELAND (AS A REFUGEE)

Experiencing oneself as a refugee or an outcast can deprive a person to creatively deal with adverse and even life-threatening situations. Although the prevalence of suicidal and other self-harming behaviors amongst refugee populations are difficult to reliably ascertain since official statistics are often not readily available (Centre for Suicide Prevention, 2010), it is impossible to ignore the preponderance of unofficial reports found in newspapers, magazines, and personal accounts. What the research community does know for certain, however, is that refugees and other asylum seekers tend to experience a significantly higher rate of mental health issues, often surviving or being witness to a variety of physical and psychological trauma (Silove, Austin, and Steel, 2007).

As a group, empirical research has consistently shown that homeless and runaway minors, more frequently suffer from abuse and neglect at the hands of their family members or caretakers, which also leads to an array of additional mental health issues, including depression, anxiety, and PTSD, to list some of the more prominent conditions. Finally, and perhaps most relevant to our discussion, these youths often find themselves feeling trapped in circumstances that may prompt them to act violently towards themselves (Martin, Rozanes, Pearce, and Allison, 1995). They have lost their home, family, and the social supports that many children and adolescents take for granted.

Many of these trends seem exaggerated among people forced to become refugees for social-political reason. Let us present some sociological evidence. As World War II ended (1946), the population of Hong Kong was just over 1,000,000; by 1955 it had almost doubled and it was estimated that a third of the residents were recent political refugees. Using hospital and police records, Yap (1958) showed that the annual suicide rate rose from a low figure of 3 per 100,000 in 1946 to 12 per 100,000 (Yap, 1958).

Alley (1982) reported a study of suicidal tendencies among Indochinese refugees. The Indochinese refugees have experienced more devastation than most Americans will know in a lifetime. The tremendous turmoil of war, the risking of one's life, the forced separation of families and relocation into the American culture have drastically changed the lives of every Indochinese individual. Nor do the emotional scars imprinted into the minds of these people disappear upon arrival into a neutral country. Rather, these psychological problems can show themselves as suicidal preoccupation, or attempts. This paper stresses related variables observed in those Indochinese people contemplating suicide. Of 4,192 Indochinese refugees sampled, 10 suicidally inclined refugees were identified. Clinical findings revealed that multiple determinants were operating conjointly in creating the high risk of any particular refugee in relation to suicide.

In a somewhat later study, Ponizovsky, Ritsner, and Modai (1999) reported a significantly higher 6-month prevalence rate of suicide ideation among Russian Jewish immigrant adolescents to Israel (10.9%) than among a comparable sample of Jews remaining in Russia (3.5%). However, the suicide ideation rate of indigenous Israeli Jews was not significantly lower (8.7%) than that of the Jewish immigrants from Russia.

In a summary of a conference panel on migration, refugees, and health risks, Carballo and Nerukar (2001) acknowledge the aims of settlement policies of European Union countries but point out that they have been largely ineffective. Despite the psychosocial risk factors experienced by migrants, relatively little is known about the dynamics involved or about what should and can be done to prevent or manage mental health problems related to migration. Language plays an important role in mental health, and barriers to good communication compound feelings of isolation and being "unwanted." Among rural Turkish workers in Amsterdam, only a few can speak Dutch, and the capacity to function and integrate into mainstream society has often been limited. Mental health problems such as neuroses are common, and over half of these immigrants say they worry and often regret their decision to move away from home.

In Germany, Nierukar reports that an estimated 13% of immigrants seen for depressive disorders develop problems during their initial 12 months away from home. Another 25% tend to have problems within the following 2 to 5 years. The relatively high incidence of depression among immigrants and their children in many EU countries has been associated with high rates of suicide, possibly linked to unemployment. In the Netherlands, where the unemployment rate among migrants in 1994 was 31% compared to 13% for Dutch nationals, the suicide rate among children of immigrants was five times as likely as Dutch children to commit suicide and Moroccan children three times as likely. Children, particularly girls, of Surinamese immigrants had a suicide rate 27.6 times higher than that of Dutch children. In the United Kingdom, suicide rates for women from the Indian subcontinent are also markedly higher than for men and are highest among girls ages 15 to 24. On the whole suicide among this immigrant group is two times the national average and 60% higher in the 25 to 34 age group. This pattern is also true with regard to attempted suicides.

In a cross-cultural, nation-wide study of all immigrant groups in Sweden, Ferrada-Noli (1997) analyzed over 10,000 suicides and possible suicides occurring during the period 1987–1991. The results indicated an over-representation of immigrants in the Swedish suicide statistics nation-wide. This overrepresentation was statistically significant among immigrants in Sweden from Russia, Finland, Germany, Denmark, and Norway. Other nationalities with an increased suicide incidence were from Poland, Hungary, Czechoslovakia, Austria, Korea, The Netherlands, France, Spain, and Uruguay. The risk of an immigrant dying of a cause related to suicide was found to be 1.5 times higher than that for a native Swede. Furthermore, the increased suicide rates observed among the immigrant groups in Sweden were found to be higher than in the respective countries of origin for 90% of the nationalities involved. In a follow-up paper, Ferrada-Noli (2014) reports suicide among immigrants had increased 10.3 % in 2012.

Rahman and Hafeez (2003, 393) found that 91% of Afghan women who had been residing in a refugee camp in Pakistan who were screened positive as meeting criteria for common mental disorders (e.g., major depression, PTSD, etc.), experienced a notable frequency of suicidal thoughts in the previous month, with 8% rating suicidal feelings as representing their most prominent psychological stressor. Other research has suggested that the lack of help-seeking behaviors amongst refugees due to an understandable reticence to trust official agencies and health care systems as well as cultural stigma around psychological disorders has posed challenges to providing preventive interventions, which is often compounded by social isolation and lack of social support, prior histories of mental health concerns, and simply not being directly assessed about potential suicidal or mental health issues (Cohen, 2008).

In 2011, Lester, Saito, and Ben Park reported evidence indicating that the suicide rate of Koreans living in Japan is twice as high as that of Koreans in South Korea. The authors speculate that higher suicide rate for the Koreans in Japan may have been influenced by the Japanese economic crisis, which may have been more devastating for the Koreans in Japan because of the discrimination they faced (Lester, Saito, and Ben Park, 2011).

A number of recently published studies have focused on Bhutanese refugees to the United States (Ao et al., 2012; Ellis et al., 2015; Hagaman et al., 2016) report an increase of suicides among Bhutanese refugees to the United States between 2009 and 2012. Suicide-risk factors emerging from these studies included poor health. Results identify overall factors such as disappointment with current unemployment, lack of resettlement services and social support, frustrations with separation from family as potential trigger factors for suicide, poor health, perceived burdensomeness and thwarted belongingness. Some important gender differences emerge. For male immigrants, stressors related to employment and providing for their families were related to feeling burdensome, and/or alienated from family and friends, whereas for women, stressors such an illiteracy, family conflict, and being separated from family members were more associated.

In non-refugee populations, these aforementioned dynamics likewise exist, but become manifest in different ways. Fortunately, empirically validated prevention strategies have been identified that significantly minimize suicidality amongst refugees and those who feel dispossessed. The importance of a robust social support system in close proximity to the suicidal individual perhaps represents the most potent protective factor (daCosta, 1993), as does increasing the quality of clinical and communications training among frontline health care workers (Wahoush, 2009). The need for meaningful culturally sensitive training attached to assessment for suicidality has increasingly garnered support in both clinical and research circles. Cultural variations in expressing suicidal intent and behaviors along with the associative thoughts and feelings has made culturally informed evaluations of paramount importance.

FEELING ONE IS UNABLE TO EXPRESS ONE'S OWN NEEDS WITH OTHERS

The profound disillusionment that accompanies feeling unable to be oneself with others can lead to an endless cycling between plunging into a relationship because of loneliness and leaving that same relationship because of boredom, and a feeling that one cannot be oneself. We will review and discuss the effects of this endless cycling of depression in relationships and loneliness without them with regard to self-destructive behavior. Of what should come as little surprise, amongst completed suicides, depression is the most common psychiatric disorder present, occurring in half to two thirds of cases (Rich et al., 1986; Henriksson et al., 1993; Conwell et al., 1996; Harwood et al., 2001).

A recent study and review article by Skodlar, Tomori, and Parnas (2008) points to two main risk factors for suicidal ideation in their sample of schizophrenia patients and in several other studies (Inskip et al., 1998; Palmer et al., 2005; Rossau et al., 1997; Nyman et al., 1986; Wiersma et al., 1998). The first precipitant is solitude with the inability to participate in human interactions, and the second is feelings of inferiority. These experiences seem to resemble ordinary depressive reactions, yet they may be reflective of a more basic self-alienation and incapacity for immersion in the shared world. Ignoring this experiential level of patients' disturbances may lead to trivialization (and misjudgment) of the experiences at the root of suicidality in schizophrenia. In a follow-up study, Skolar and Parnas (2010) reported that these two factors were associated with disturbances measured by the Examination of

Anomalous Self-Experience scale, that is, disorder of self-awareness and self-presence.

In a series of studies of prospective suicidal behavior over 20 years in the Chicago Follow-up Study of psychiatric patients, the senior author in conjunction with Martin Harrow has suggested different risk factors are predictive for different psychiatric disorders. Psychotic symptoms (i.e., hallucinations, delusions) at 2-years post-hospitalization predict later suicidal activity at 7.5 years post-hospitalization only for schizophrenia patients. Cognitive symptoms (poor processing speed, concreteness) at the 2-year follow-up predicted later suicidal activity only for the depressive group. Adequacy of overall functioning predicted later suicidal activity for both diagnostic groups (Kaplan and Harrow, 1996; 1999).

A more recent study highlights important gender differences in this regard (Kaplan, Harrow, and Faull, 2012). Poor early hospital global functioning is significantly associated with later suicidal activity only among male patients in both the schizophrenia and depressive patients, with no such effect emerging for women diagnosed with schizophrenia or nonpsychotic depression. Early display of psychotic symptoms is associated with later suicidality only for male schizophrenia patient.

In a recently published study across the entire 20-year study of these same patients, Kaplan, Harrow, and Clews (2016) report the following findings. Maximum suicidal activity (suicidal ideation, suicidal attempts, and suicide completions) generally declines over the three time periods (early, middle, and late follow-ups) following discharge from the acute psychiatric hospitalization for both males and females across diagnostic categories. There are two exceptions however: female schizophrenia patients and female bipolar patients. A weighted mean suicidal activity score tended to decrease across follow-ups for male patients in the schizophrenia, schizoaffective, and depressive diagnostic groups with an uneven trend in this direction for the male bipolar patients. No such pattern emerges for our female patients except for female depressives. Males' suicidal activity seems more triggered by psychotic symptoms and potential chronic disability while females' suicidal activity seems more triggered by affective symptoms.

In a somewhat older review of the literature, the senior author (Kaplan and Worth, 1992–1993) proposed a model wherein a leading cause of suicidal impulses was an inability to successfully integrate self and other, and this this may persist across the life span. The maturation process relies on successful integration of attachment and individuation (c.f. Ainsworth, 1982; 1989; Bowlby, 1969; 1973; 1977) at each life stage as a precondition to proceed to the next more developed stage (Kaplan and O'Connor, 1994). Kaplan's theory focuses on the process of moving from each of Erikson's life-stages of development (Erikson, 1950; 1968) to the next, more developed stage (see an excellent discussion by Ledgerwoord, 1999, in this regard).

In agreement with Erikson and the very important work of both Ainsworth and Bowlby, Kaplan and his colleagues argue that in order for the individual to mature through a stage, he or she must work through a natural ego crisis which accompanies that stage. For a suicidal person, one either loses his/her own identity or attachment to others. Such a choice is very disintegrative and can be seen as beginning at early school age.

According to Barker and Wright's classic work (1955), about 50% of the school age child (approximately ages 6 to 12) interactions are with other children as opposed to only 10% in this regard for 2-year-olds. Calhoun and Morse (1977), for example, have shown that failure in school and the experience of public ridicule can interact with an initially negative self-concept to cause long-lasting damage to a child's self-esteem.

The same problem occurs in adolescence (approximately ages 12 to 22). The work of Gould et al. (1974) and Shaffer (1974) highlights the prevalence of depressive symptoms among adolescent suicide attempters and adolescent suicide completers. Topol and Resnikoff (1982) have emphasized the importance of social isolation in youth suicide. They point out that adolescents who commit suicides have a personal history of difficulty in relating to peers. They rarely have close friends and are "non-joiners" who are often invisible to peers and teachers.

Now consider early adulthood (approximately ages 22 to 34). Katz (1968) discovered that healthy young adults learned to make decisions without seeking permission from their parents and moved toward closer relationships and assumption of the marital role (Katz, 1968). Vaillant (1977) found that the "best outcome" younger adulthood tended to be well-integrated and practical in late adolescence and early adulthood and the "worst outcome" young adults asocial in adolescence and early adulthood. Goldney (1981) found that the absence of a significant personal relationship was associated with depression and suicide attempts by 110 women aged 18 to 30. Maris (1971) described the prototypic young female suicide as married, having children, suffering from depression, and enmeshed in a marriage that has a history of conflict. Illifeld (1977) reports that job-related problems may represent a more important stressor for men than do family problems. Rygenstad (1982) found an increased incidence of separation, divorce, and unemployment in both men and women suicide attempters between the ages of 13 and 88.

Consider now middle-adulthood (ages 34 to 60), where a person in distress may present in therapy as a person who has lost his or her path and has been swallowed up in the life goals of others. In the words of Dante Alighieri in his epic poem, *The Divine Comedy*, and later of Charles of Orleans, "In the middle of my life, I found myself in a dark wood wandering" (Haasse, 1975). Neugarten (1973) has focused on the middle adult's increased preoccupation with his/her inner life, his or her "interiority" which enables one to look backward for the first time rather than forward. The dynamic of withdrawal to one's inner space is necessitated by the overwhelming demands of marriage and family life and may be associated with a sense of "burnout," just going through the motions. Slater and Depue (1981) found that exit events (e.g., separation, divorce, and death) differentiate suicidal depressed individuals from non-suicidal depressed individuals more than any other kind of loss. The suicidal middle-aged adult is likely to have been recently divorced or separated, to have lost a parent, or to have had a child leave home (Adams, Bouckoms and Streiner, 1982; Richman, 1981; Warren and Tomlinson-Keasey, 1987).

Suicide is a large problem for older adults (ages 60 to 75). An older adult of this age may report that many previous achievements have proved meaningless and many of his or her dreams are now out of grasp. Darbonne (1969) found that suicide notes of elderly individuals included more references to loneliness and isolation than those of any other age group. Miller (1979) found that older men who committed suicide were three times less likely to have a confidante than those who died of natural causes. Widowhood has been shown to increase the risk of suicide, especially among elderly males during the first six months of bereavement (Benson and Brodie, 1975; Berardo, 1968; Bock and Webber, 1972; MacMahon and Pugh, 1965). Bock and Webber found that suicidal and widowed elderly people were more socially isolated than those who were non-suicidal.

Among the oldest-old (76 plus), suicide may be triggered by physical decline and awareness of one's own mortality and life-finiteness. One expression is that Cumming and Henry (1961) have labeled disengagement which is indicated by increased preoccupation with the self and decreasing emotional investments in persons and objects in the environment. While Lawton (1980) has reported that residents of institutions of the aged seek out areas of high activity, Lemon et al. (1972) find that activity per se was not found to be significantly related to life satisfaction among new residents of a retirement community. In extreme form, an obsession with "keeping busy" may block the private time necessary to achieve a state of trans-generational continuity.

FEELING AS AN ADOPTED CHILD THAT ONE IS UNABLE TO TRUST ENOUGH TO SEEK OR ACCEPT HELP

Depression, impulsivity, and aggression during adolescence have been associated with both adoption and suicidal behavior. In a landmark secondary analysis on data from the National Longitudinal Study of Adolescent Health, Slap, Goodman and Huang (2001) report that attempted suicide is more common among adolescents who live with adoptive parents than among adolescents who live with biological parents. This association persists after adjusting for depression and aggression and is not explained by impulsivity as measured by a reported tendency to quickly make decisions. Yet another report finds no significant differences between the adopted and the non-adopted in attempting suicide (Feigleman, 2001).

Both the Slap et al. (2001) and Feigleman (2001) studies provide concise reviews on the conflicting conclusions about adoptee mental health (see Feigleman, 2005). Slap et al. (2001) argue that although a few studies find adoptees showing better adjustment than the non-adopted on some criteria, a somewhat larger number find no differences between the adopted and the non-adopted, and the greatest number of past studies show adoptees less well-adjusted than the non-adopted. One of the few factors most analysts agree on is that adoptees are over-represented among counseling patients (Miller, Fan, Christensen et al., 2000; Miller, Fan, Grievant et al., 2000).

In a more recent study, Anderson (2011) reports that child youth who enter the child welfare system and are put in an out-of-home placement can aggravate the existing health problems and may be at an increased risk for developing depressive symptoms, which has been shown to increase the risk for suicidal ideation. Being put in an out of home placement can aggravate and even compound existing psychological maladies (Harden, 2004; Newton, Litrownik, and Landsverk, 2000). Elevated risk of mental health outcomes such as depression continues due to the unusual stresses inherent in their situation, namely frequent relocations and temporary to prolonged separation from family of origin (Rubin et al., 2004; 2007; Taussig, Clyman, and Landsverk, 2001).

A penetrating demographic study by Berlin (1987) points to the deleterious effects of deculturation on native American adolescents. The study was occasioned by alarm emerging from the increasing number of suicides among adolescent and young adult male Indian suicides in the previous decade. Berlin cites research identifying a number of factors characterizing tribes with high suicide rates. These all involve lack of support for traditional cultural supports, including failure to adhere to traditional ways of living, to traditional religion, to clans and societies and the resulting chaotic family structure and adult alcoholism.

An excellent review article by Heikkinen, Aro, and Lonnqvist (1993) highlight the role of social support in modifying the effects of adverse life events with regard to suicidal behavior. They conclude from the studies they reviewed that social support was weaker among suicides, as measured by living alone, number of close friends, residence changes, and interaction between family members. Losses that significantly affect the social support system appear to function as a long-term risk factor for suicide, probably by causing social isolation and depression among the bereaved.

Eisenberg et al. (2007) proposed that an individual's emotions are related to negative feelings and emotional intensity, and that emotional regulation is the way an individual manages emotions. The researchers found that high emotional intensity in the subjects was associated with aggression and avoidance coping mechanisms and increased tendency towards anger. Children who were viewed as highly socially competent by their peers and school personnel were found to cope with anger in more constructive, nonaggressive ways.

Jones and Peacock (1992) studied anger in adolescents, emphasizing the importance of negative social interactions with parents, siblings, and friends. Siblings seemed to be rated as the major source of their anger. Although they reported that 76% of adolescents linked communicated anger with feelings of depression, there were no suicidal thoughts related to uncommunicated anger. Paul (1995), however, does list adolescent suicidal tendencies as one of the destructive outcomes of mishandled anger, along with depression, suicidal tendencies, eating disorders, bed-wetting, substance abuse, addictions, and overdependence.

In a major study of motives behind physician-assisted suicide, Kaplan et al. (1999–2000) report that many of Kevorkian's "suicides" in Michigan were described by relatives in a psychological autopsy study[3] as wanting to avoid "being a burden on others." Similar feelings were reported in a comparison of studies of physician-assisted suicide and euthanasia (Kaplan, Harrow, and Schneiderhan, 2002) in locations in several places around the world where physician-assisted suicide or euthanasia were being practiced legally, including The Netherlands (Hendin, 1994, 1995, 1998) Western Australia (Kissane, Street, and Nitchske, 1998) and even Oregon (Ganzini et al., 1998; Hendin, Foley, and White, 1998). This disparagement of "needing help" and "dependency" has become pathological in counter-dependent and increasingly isolated America today, and seems to becoming worse each year.

According to Joiner, Van Orden, Witte, and Rudd (2009) interpersonal theory of suicide, stresses related to feeling rejected from others—what Joiner refers to as "thwarted belongingness," which amounts to a visceral sense that one is utterly unable to form meaningful connections with others, often increases an individual's desire and risk for suicide. Feeling one is alone and unappreciated in one's life mission can deprive a person of the energy and drive to go on and lead to unchecked bad choices propelling a person to self-destruction. Feeling disconnected from others, particularly those who most people typically rely upon for emotional support, such as close friends and family, clergy, etc., can result in loneliness and isolation and a deep sense of personal lack of meaning in one's life.

Joiner (2005) also emphasizes the role that the self-perception of being a burden plays in factoring into the suicidal thoughts and actions of some individuals. Perceived burdensomeness is premised on the idea that one's very existence represents a significant burden on family, friends, and/or society. This attitude is exceptionally dangerous since it is based on the fundamental perception of a suicidal individual that his family and friends would be better off if only he were dead. And the frightening possibility exists that the suicidal individual's perceptions might be exactly accurate as to the attitudes of his family and friends in this increasingly selfish and counter-dependent world. They may wish him dead rather than as a burden.

Indeed, a strong association between elevated levels of perceived burdensomeness and suicidal ideation has been borne out in the research. DeCatanzaro (1995), for example, concluded that perceived burdensomeness directed toward family correlated with suicidal ideation among community participants and high-suicide-risk groups, such as military veterans and those with chronic mental health issues. Although identified for many years, only recently has the subject of perceived burdensomeness—the belief that one's existence represents a burden for family, friends, and/or society—along with a sense of low belongingness or social alienation become a main focus in suicide prevention research.

In an important review of the literature, Modrcin–McCarthy et al. (1998) report studies of childhood anger which they argue convincingly has been greatly misunderstood. They argue that anger may represent a healthy or unhealthy response in children experiencing small frustrations or great injustices. Paul (1995) views anger as a "natural, healthy appropriate life-enhancing emotion." It can occur when one feels unsupported and rejected. Anger can rise from small frustrations or great injustices, and it can be very appropriate, if channeled properly.

A child or teen, or even an adult may act out and become angry from both being denied a toy/reward and physical/verbal/emotional abuse by loved ones or by feeling unsupported in one's life and in one's own sense of mission and purpose. Anger itself is not dysfunctional, but the behaviors it may lead to, including suicidal behavior, can be and often are. For example, Fabes and Eisenberg (1992) studied white middle-class children, ranging in age from 3 to 5. They postulated that situations that elicited anger would be accompanied by an overt expression of anger. Children were found to be angry because of disagreement over possessions and in response to physical assault by a classmate.

In a series of novel studies aimed at providing direct support for this theory, Joiner, Pettit, Walker, and Voelz (2002) showed that trained raters reliably detected a substantial number of expressions of burdensomeness in suicide notes. More specifically, these studies confirmed that the notes of people who had died by suicide compared to those that survived suicide attempts as well as those who died by violent means compared to the notes of those who died by less violent means consistently indicated a notable pattern of perceived burdensomeness as a prominent motivating factor. Even when controlling for dominant suicide-related covariates like hopelessness, Van Orden, Lynam, Hollar, and Joiner (2006) found that a degree of perceived burdensomeness acted as a robust predictor of suicide attempt status and of current suicidal ideations amongst those engaged in outpatient treatment.

The link between belonging (or lack thereof) and suicidality has been authoritatively established for a number of diverse non-psychiatric populations, including college students, young adolescents, and elderly individuals. Viewed from another angle, suicide rates decrease during times of communal happiness and celebration (Joiner, Hollar, and Van Orden, 2006) and, perhaps counterintuitively, during periods of communal hardship or tragedy. To this end, two prominent examples can be found in the fact that there was a low rate of death by suicide in the U.S. on September 11, 2001, as there was the week after President Kennedy's assassination (Biller, 1977).

FEELING ABANDONED BY ONE'S CHILD LEAVING THE FAMILY NEST AND BUILDING HIS/HER OWN LIFE

The parental experience of children leaving home has been labeled the "empty nest" syndrome and can have important implications for one's mental health. The shift from daily parenting and a "full nest" to an "empty nest" can be a startling one. Many don't know what to do with themselves when the job of full-time parenting becomes a part-time one, or one managed from a distance. The transitions from full house to empty house, to half-full house to empty house again can create a cycle of ups and downs that can be difficult to manage. A recent book by Aronsson (2014) presents real stories showing how parents manage that period when children are preparing to leave the family home, either temporarily or permanently, and how to move forward in a healthy, even rewarding way.

Clinicians have observed a "temporal though not necessarily causal, relationship between the termination of child rearing and clinical depression" (Deykin et al., 1966). Bart (1971) reported that middle-age women in psychiatric hospitals stated that they had become depressed with their child leaving home, particularly those who had been over-involved in the mother role and who were not employed outside the house. Both Deykin and Bart suggest that depression is a function both of the loss of the parental role and the lack of other compensatory roles (such as employment or career).

In contrast to these clinical studies, household surveys using self-report mental health measures have found evidence inconsistent with the "empty nest syndrome." The presence of children in the home has frequently been associated with more symptoms of distress (Bernard, 1974) and lower life satisfaction (Campbell, Converse, and Rodgers, 1976; Converse and Rodgers, 1976). Pearlin and Lieberman (1977) found that married people who reported their last child had left home within the previous four years were not significantly different with regard to anxiety and depression than parents who did not report these events. Radloff (1980), in fact, conducted a large mental health interview of some 3,000 adults in representative samples in two communities (Washington County, Maryland, and Kansas City, Missouri). She reported that her analyses indicated that parents (both mothers and fathers) whose children were not living with them were significantly less depressed than matched parents whose children were still living with them.

A later study by Adelmann et al. (1989) suggested a more complicated pattern. Whether the empty-nest experience has positive or negative consequences for women's well-being at midlife may depend on their historical cohort membership and employment status. They argue that the evidence is mixed. Although the empty-nest syndrome is occasionally revealed in clinical samples (Bart, 1971; Curlee, 1969), other studies suggest that women in the empty-nest stage were found to have unchanging or even elevated well-being compared to women in previous stages (Axelson, 1960; Campbell, 1975; Deutscher, 1964; Lowenthal and Chiriboga, 1972; Rollins and Feldman, 1970).

A factor that may moderate the experience of the empty-nest period is whether the parent engages in paid employment and indeed has a career. One of the most interesting ideas in this regard is the "midlife crossover hypothesis" offered by Gutmann (1975), Neugarten (1968), and Rossi (1980) which contends that women who focus on their nurturant needs early in adulthood, though active involvement in motherhood, by midlife may be motivated to satisfy their as yet unmet achievement needs.

Adelmann et al. (1989) specifically compare two cohorts of women, one who reached adulthood during a period of strong social emphasis on women's maternal role, and an earlier cohort who were encouraged to enter the labor force during World War II. Their results indicated that both cohort and employment had important independent associations with women's well-being at midlife, but that the experience of the empty nest depends on both of these two factors.

A more recent study by Hobdy et al. (2007) examined the relationship between a person's attachment style and both adjustment and coping processes in adults during two specific life events involving both the loss of and a renegotiation of an attachment relationship: the launching of children from the family of origin and job loss, which represent both normative and nonnormative transitions, respectively. Their results failed to yield a significant multivariate life event by style interaction. However, a statistically significant multivariate main effect for life event and for attachment style was obtained. The data support the notion that securely attached individuals may be more equipped to meet developmental life challenges in adulthood, and extend previous work that was limited to women and the empty nest.

What can we conclude from all this? The parent, especially the mother, can indeed under some circumstances, experience depression and even possible suicidal impulses in reaction to her now grown up child leaving the family nest. Yet parents, especially mothers, are not all the same. Those with insecure attachment styles are more prone to pathological responses to their offspring going out on their own to build their own lives than are those with secure attachment styles.

Jane Bidder (2005) poignantly describes her experience of taking her oldest son to the university for the first time.

We drove 400 miles in silence through nerves on my son's part and concentration on my husband's as the luggage virtually obscured the car's back window. On arrival, my son's hall of residence, which had once won an architectural award, resembled a dirty cruise ship and his bedroom was slightly bigger than our downstairs lavatory. "I can't believe that I have worked so hard to end up in a place like this," said my son.

I went home in tears but I need not have. The next day, his enthusiasm shone down the phone. He had already had ten new friends in his room and gone on a pub crawl instead of attending the chancellor's welcome speech. And could I send the trainers that I had said he would need and he had insisted he would not.

Sending a child to university can be tough on the family left behind but few people confess to this because it makes them sound wet and clingy. We found that, after three rowdy children, the quiet was awkward when our son had gone, even though there had been times in the run-up to the A-level results when I couldn't wait to see the back of him.

Now I found myself waking in the night, wondering if he had made it back to hall.

I also found it hard to tidy his empty room and more than once laid the table for five instead of four.

"You will get used to it," said a colleague whose daughter went up the year before. Slowly I did, though I have learnt a lot on the way. The first is that one child's absence often affects siblings left behind. My remaining son and daughter, who often squabbled, grew closer because they were the only ones left.

Secondly, I learnt not to ring my student son every day because that unsettled him, though my daughter, who is now at university, happily chatters to me on a daily basis. Texting is better because student offspring can reply when they please. However, I was surprised when my son complained that he had not had parcels of goodies from home unlike some of his friends.

Now, twice a term, I send Jiffy bags of ginger cake, a silly postcard and a lottery ticket for fun. Another friend has set up a family chat group online so people can dip in and out.

Another tip is to help them to budget. One friend encourages her son to put most of his loan on an internet account for the interest and the rest in a current account for easy access. I have tried to get mine to withdraw a set sum each week but with little success.

Another mistake that we made was to pay for the contract on his mobile phones but, after the last bill, that is to end. Do trial runs, too, at the local launderette and send them with a bag of small change. Another parent advised me to write down basic recipes and get them to practice before they go. I also packed a first-aid kit and ran over meningitis warning signs.

Be aware that visiting for the first time can be odd because you are imposing on their new territory. Do not do anything to embarrass them. Instead of asking what they are eating and why their breath smells, take home-made soup and a new tube of toothpaste. A couple of goodbye tenners always goes down well.

Many students settle well without problems but what if you are not so lucky? One friend, whose son loathed his course, encouraged him to see his tutor fast and he was able to change. Leave it more than two or three weeks and it can be too late for that year.

Michele Elliott, director of Kidscape, warns parents to be vigilant for signs of depression and suicide. "If your child sounds different or is acting strangely, contact the tutor. It might be interfering but it is better than being too late."

Tell them about bad things that happen when they are away or they will resent you for shielding them. Before exams, suggest early nights. Finally, be prepared for the Christmas holidays. They will return with their own routines and will get up when you go to bed and vice versa. The key is give and take.

FEELING DOOMED BY A DYSFUNCTIONAL (ENMESHED) FAMILY OF ORIGIN

Experiencing seductive advances from one's parent can adversely affect an individual for the rest of his life. The occurrence of child abuse and neglect as a predisposing factor to suicidality in adolescents is commonly found (Brockington, 2001; Lange et al., 1999; Oates, 2004), especially amongst runaway and homeless youth (Kidd, 2007; Rew et al., 2001). This holds especially true for homeless adolescence, with Plunkett, O'Toole, Swantson, Oates, Shrimpton, and Parkinson (2001) finding that sexual abuse and suicidality were highly correlated. Not surprisingly however, many researchers have found a gendered correlation between sexual abuse and suicidal behaviors, being more commonly present in females (Brockington, 2001; Lange et al., 1999; Lester, 2003; Oates, 2004).

Family dysfunction generally can be seen as a risk factor for adolescent suicide. In a classic 1985 report of a study of youth suicides in Chicago, Maris offers the following observations deriving from his sample. Younger suicides as compared to older suicides were more likely to (1) be females, (2) have made multiple suicide attempts, (3) have been more interpersonally motivated, (4) have been more revenge-directed and more based in anger and an irritability, (5) have come from more multi-problem families of origin, (6) have been less health-compromised and have better long-term prognosis, (7) have been less likely to have worked and have had fewer financial resources, (8) have used more drugs and alcohol, when they drink at all, (9) have has more feelings of prolonged uselessness, (10) have had more intense, deep feelings, and more aggressive and erotic energies, (11) have tended to be more romantic and idealistic, (12) tended to be less emotionally independent and financially self-sufficient, (13) have had a less clearly developed and defined sense of personal identity and lower self-esteem, (14) have been more affected by the decline of common social goals and the increase of cultural relativism, and (15) have been more likely to be risk-takers, with greater impulsivity, and higher levels of dissatisfaction with their life accomplishments.

A follow-up studied by Haight and Hendrix (1998) examined some of the Maris results described above. Using a life history approach, they report different themes in the lives of two groups of older women recently relocated to a nursing home-those who are satisfied with their lives and those who are not. Twelve women were selected from a sample of 256 by their scores on a life satisfaction index of suicidal intent scale. Seventy-two hours of transcribed life histories were content-analyzed for dominant themes that contributed to either life satisfaction or suicidal intent. Strong overall themes emerged for both groups under the headings of childhood, families, role models, connectedness, confidantes, life involvement, death experience, and memories. However, the most important correlates to contribute to a lifetime pattern of suicidality were dysfunctional families of origin, poor role models, a feeling of isolation and a pessimistic outlook.

The senior author of this book in conjunction with Marshall Maldaver (Kaplan and Maldaver, 1993) examined the issue of family dysfunction in more detail. Concentrating primarily on parental marital pattern, Kaplan and Maldaver reported some 85 studies linking dysfunctional family structure variables to adolescent suicidal behavior. In these studies, judgments of enmeshment and disengagement were inferred from self-report measures, behavioral descriptions, and/or individual psychiatric diagnoses obtained from the parents of completed adolescent suicides. Our literature review indicated that among dysfunctional parental psychological structures on the part of the parents, disengaged marital patterns were the most lethal pattern for psychiatric adolescents, enmeshed marital patterns, the next most lethal, and rejection-intrusion patterns (one parent enmeshed and the other disengaged) the least. The least lethal structure was experiencing parents where neither member was enmeshed nor disengaged.

A similar pattern emerges with regard to attempted adolescent suicide, the greatest number of attempted suicides occurring for adolescents experiencing a disengaged parental type, and an approximately equal number of outcomes occurring with adolescents experiencing an enmeshed family pattern and with those experiencing a rejection–inclusion parental type.

Consider first the case of disengaged parents. Corder, Page, and Corder (1974) found that parents of adolescent attempters were perceived by their children as stringent disciplinarians, disengaged and unable to communicate.

McIntire and Angle (1973) reported that 56% of children who poisoned themselves reported a loss of communication with their parents (see also the studies of Chia, 1979; Garfinkel, Froese, and Hood, 1982; Parnitzke and Regel, 1973; Sathyavathi, 1975).

Consider now the enmeshed parental type. Hill (1970) compared the mother of suicidal and non-suicidal adolescent girls on a measure of empathy, finding that the mothers of the suicidal subjects were the least empathic and most symbiotic of all groups. Richman (1978) found a polarity between symbiosis and disengagement in families with suicidal children in the work of Litman and Tabachnik (1968), Wold (1968; 1970), Sarwer-Foner (1969), and Boszormenyi-Nagy and Spark (1973). The rejection-intrusion parental type can also be lethal. Wenz (1978) reports greater anomie and conflict among families of 55 completed suicides than among those of 55 matched controls. Similar results were obtained by McKenry, Tishler, and Kelly (1982), who found family conflict to be greater among adolescent suicides than among controls. The reader is also referred to the work of Kosky (1983), Pfeffer (1981), and Wenz (1979).

Kaplan and Maldaver (1993) also participated in an ongoing "psychological autopsy" study to address more directly the question of parental engagement styles of the families of 25 completed adolescent suicides as opposed to those of 25 controls (with adolescents who had no suicidal behavior) matched in terms of age, gender, and race and geographical area in three counties in and around Chicago. The families of 18 of the 25 completed suicides responded to the questionnaire, after their child's suicide. This sample consisted of the parents of 16 male completed suicides and 2 females. The control sample consisted of the parents of 23 male and 2 female adolescents.

They assessed marital style of the parents through an instrument developed by the senior author called the Individuation-Attachment Questionnaire (the IAQ) (see Kaplan, 1988; 1990b; 1998c). The IAQ consisted of 44 times designed to measure four separated tendencies: needs and fears of both individuation and attachment. Rather than view individuation and attachment as reciprocally antagonistic tendencies on a unidimensional distance line as did many family theorists and therapists (e.g., Minuchin, 1974), Kaplan has proposed a bidimensional view of distance where boundary formation (capacity to individuate) is seen as conceptually orthogonal from wall protection (need to detach). This allows the differentiation of marital types into enmeshed, disengaged, and rejection-intrusion pathological marital styles as opposed to integrated health parental marital styles.

Kaplan and Maldaver found that parental pathology as diagnosed by this IAQ self-report systematically differed between the suicide and control groups. The post-mortem responses of 3 of the families (16.7%) of the 18 completed suicides indicated a healthy parental marital classification, while 7 of the parental pairs (38.9%) were either enmeshed or disengaged or a rejection-intrusion type (one parent enmeshed and the other disengaged). The remaining 8 parental couples (44.4%) showed a mixed parental structure (one parent being either disengaged or enmeshed and the other healthy). The 25 control parents showed a diametrically opposite pattern. Ten (40%) had two healthy parents, 3 (12%) showed a pathological pattern (enmeshed, disengaged, or rejection-intrusion type), and 12 (48%) showed a mixed parental structure.

The role of dysfunctional patterns in one's family of origin on suicide has continued to remain an important topic in research and thinking. The physical and sexual abuse of children along with neglect have commonly been considered valid ways of measuring family dysfunction (Lester, 2003; Smyth and McLachlan, 2004; Wagner et al., 2003). While investigating poor family relationships, particularly in childhood and early adolescence, several research teams (Shagle and Barber, 1993; Wagner et al., 2003) have determined that poor parenting may cause serious issues in one's emotional and psychological developmental, including an increased rate of suicidal thoughts (Waldvogel, Rueter, and Oberg, 2008).

Several studies specifically point to the role of parental seductiveness on subsequent child and adolescent suicidality (Dwivedi, 1993; Dutton and Yamini, 1995; Kagan, 2009). The physical and sexual abuse of children along with neglect have commonly been considered valid ways of measuring family dysfunction (Smyth and MacLachlan, 2004).

A PRECIS FOR CHAPTERS 5 THROUGH 11

In each of chapters 5 through 11, we will compare a classical Greek or Roman narrative to a biblical one illustrating the seven risk factors discussed above. We will examine these narratives with the aim of illustrating contrasting vulnerabilities for the Graeco-Roman and biblical figures. Chapter 5 will discuss in detail the story of the suicide of the great Greek warrior Ajax. We will treat it as a clinical case, and describe how Ajax is allowed to leave his tent alone while isolated, depressed, and suicidal. We will present real-life clinical examples of two patients (one man and one woman) we have encountered who have demonstrated this *Ajax Syndrome*. We will counter this *Ajax Syndrome* with a treatment plan based on the biblical story of the prophet Elijah who clearly expresses the desire to die after a brutalizing set of encounters with the ruthless Queen Jezebel. Yet with responsive care Elijah overcomes his suicidal despair and goes on productively with his life. We will develop a clinical treatment plan deriving from this *Elijah Intervention*.

Chapter 6 will analyze the suicide of Zeno the Stoic as presented by Diogenes Laertius, the ancient Greek chronicler of people's lives. While Ajax was a mythic figure, Zeno was a historical figure, the founder of the philosophical school of Stoicism. Yet Zeno too kills himself after he stubs his toe on the way home from giving a speech at the *Stoa* (porch). And he does this by "holding his breath." Any perceptive reader must be startled by this strange story. Why does Zeno kill himself after such a minor mishap? What has motivated him to take his life? And why has Zeno been described as having done so in such an improbable if not impossible way? We will treat Zeno as a clinical case who kills himself in a vain attempt to give, through his strange death, meaning in his life. We will present two real-life clinical examples of two patients (one man and one woman) we have encountered who have demonstrated this *Zeno Syndrome*. We will describe our attempt to counter this *Zeno Syndrome* with a therapeutic intervention based on the famous biblical narrative of Job who rejects the thought of suicide even after being assailed with one catastrophe after another: the loss of his wealth, his children, and his health. We will outline a clinical treatment plan deriving from this *Job Intervention*.

In chapter 7 we will discuss the death of the famous Roman general Marcius whose military valor at Corioli against the Volsci won him the honorary name Coriolanus. Despite his heroism and brilliance in defeating the Volsci, Coriolanus's rigidity of character leads him to become embroiled in angry class arguments in Rome, and his outspoken insults to the plebeians leads to his banishment from his homeland. Infuriated and obsessed with wreaking revenge on Rome, he goes over to the Volsci and persuades them to attack Rome. Ultimately, Coriolanus is seen as disloyal to both Rome and the Volsci and he provokes the Volsci to kill him. His almost inhuman rigidity leads to his death. We will present real-life clinical examples of two patients we have encountered (one man and one woman) who have demonstrated this *Coriolanus Syndrome* We will counter this *Coriolanus Syndrome* with the narrative of the Israelite figure David who similarly must flee his homeland. David has gained great favor at Saul's court and popularity among the people. However, Saul grows jealous of David and seeks to kill him on numerous occasions (1 Samuel 18–26). David flees from the court for his life and runs as a fugitive with 600 loyal followers to the land of King Achish of Gath (1 Samuel 27). Although he is loyal to King Achish, he remains loyal to King Saul as well. Unlike Coriolanus, David is not rigid and is able to avoid fighting with the Philistines against Israel. This flexibility and human wisdom allows him to escape the dilemma he has been put in and become king of Israel. We will develop a clinical treatment plan deriving from this *David Intervention*.

Chapter 8 presents the story of the suicide of Narcissus. The terms "narcissism" and "narcissistic" have become almost bromides in modern society to describe people who are extremely selfish and self-involved. The actual story of Narcissus provides a much richer picture ending in his suicide. Strangely, the suicidal end of the story is largely ignored in modern psychology and psychiatry. In truth, Narcissus is a figure who cannot successfully integrate self and other. He is, in fact, the product of a rape and he is promised a long life only as long as he does not come to "know himself." In the first part of the narrative, Narcissus is totally self-involved at the expense of others. He is the prototype of "disengaged man." In the second part of the story, Narcissus falls in love with his reflection in a brook, and becomes the prototype of "enmeshed man." He is not able to integrate a healthy sense of self and with any healthy regard for another and ultimately takes his life, either actively or passively.

We will present real-life clinical examples of two patients (one man and one woman) we have encountered who have demonstrated this *Narcissus Syndrome*. We offer the biblical story of Jonah as a therapeutic alternative to this *Narcissus Syndrome*. The story of Jonah begins with him in a terrible conflict between his sense of self and what God asks for him: to go to warn the people of Nineveh. Jonah does not want to go. At the same time, he does not want to reject his relationship with his Creator. Although suicidal at several points in this story, Jonah does not kill himself. Rather, the story unfolds to provide a lesson of how to integrate a sense of self in relation to others. We will develop a clinical treatment plan deriving from this *Jonah Intervention*.

Chapter 9 discusses the Greek story of Oedipus from a different angle than one to which the reader may be accustomed. We compare him to Moses. Oedipus is a rather solitary figure when he reemerges in Thebes. When he is faced with the daunting tasks of first, solving the riddle of the Sphinx, and subsequently, of uncovering the source of the plague devastating Thebes, Oedipus is basically acting alone. He is surrounded by Sphinxes and oracles he must outwit and interpret. Yet the people around him don't really help, answering his requests for help in ambiguous riddles and incomplete information. He does not know whom to believe and whom not to, and pursues a path that ultimately leads to his self-blinding and the death of others close to him. Once again, we will present two real-life clinical examples of patients we have encountered (one man and one woman) who have demonstrated this *Oedipus Syndrome*. Moses, in contrast has significant help at various points in his life. We offer these stories as the basis for a clinical intervention to this *Oedipus Syndrome*. First. Moses, being a stutterer, has Aaron as a mouthpiece. Secondly, he is presented with the recommendation to establish a hierarchal judiciary system to help him delegate the burden of leading a growing society based on a moral and legal system. We will develop a clinical treatment plan deriving from this *Moses Intervention*.

In chapter 10, we compare the story of the Greek Phaedra to that of the biblical matriarch. Rebecca. Phaedra becomes hopelessly infatuated with her stepson Hippolytus. When her secret is revealed, she becomes despondent and kills herself, leaving a note falsely accusing him of raping her. This false charge leads to the death of Hippolytus at the instigation of his furious father, Theseus. Hippolytus too is flawed, expressing a vicious indictment of women, reflecting Greek misogyny. Once again, we will present two real-life clinical examples (one man and one woman) of patients we have encountered who have demonstrated this *Phaedra Syndrome*. Rebecca, in contrast tells her husband, Isaac, that she is weary of life because of her fear that her son Jacob will marry a daughter of Heth, the Canaanite. We offer this narrative as the basis for a clinical intervention to this *Phaedra Syndrome*. Rebecca is not being seductive towards her son, nor is she trying to block him from living his own life. What she wants is that Jacob marry a suitable partner. When Isaac listens to her, Rebecca's suicidal impulse is resolved. We will develop a clinical treatment plan deriving from this *Rebecca Intervention*.

Finally, we discuss in chapter 11 the tragic legend of the Greek Antigone. The product of incest—her father is also her brother—Antigone is unable to escape her dysfunctional family of origin to live any semblance of a normal life. She is enmeshed in her family pathology, though there is no indication that it was intentional, and is thus unable to develop a healthy sense of herself as a generative woman. Indeed, her name in Greek (*Anti-gone*) denotes a woman afraid of and against (*anti*) generativity (*gone*). She is hopelessly trapped by her dysfunctional family of origin and ultimately hangs herself. We will present real-life clinical examples of two patients (one man and one woman) we have encountered who have demonstrated this *Antigone Syndrome*. We counter this *Antigone Syndrome* with the story of Ruth the Moabites. Ruth is the descendant of an incestuous union between Lot and his eldest daughter.

Indeed, the word *Moab* in Hebrew denotes from (*mo*) the father (*ab*). Furthermore, this incest is not accidental but intentional. After the destruction of Sodom, Lot's daughters think that Lot is the last man alive. To preserve the human species, they get their father drunk, coerce him to have intercourse with them each individually on consecutive nights, and subsequently conceive what will become two distinctive nations. Ruth, several generations removed is not enmeshed in her family of origin, and in fact lives an exemplary life as a healthy, compassionate, daughter, wife, and mother, becoming in biblical narrative, an ancestress of the Davidic line. We will develop a clinical treatment plan deriving from this *Ruth Intervention*.

In each chapter, then, we will oppose the pathological Greek story with a healthy biblical antidote, in which the character does not commit suicide, and indeed thrives. We will examine factors lessening the vulnerability to the suicidal stressors for the biblical characters unavailable to the Greek figures (again, see Zubin and Spring, 1977). Chapter 5 counters Ajax with the story of Elijah; chapter 6, Zeno with the story of Job; chapter 7, Coriolanus with the story of David; chapter 8, Narcissus with the story of Jonah; chapter 9, Oedipus with the story of Moses; chapter 10, Phaedra with the story of Rebecca; and finally, chapter 11, Antigone with the story of Ruth. We will isolate what we feel to be the suicide-preventive and life-promoting element in each biblical narrative providing a reduced vulnerability for each of our Graeco-Rowman characters. Once again, we apply this to two patients illustrating each of our syndromes. Thus (1) Ajax will become *Patient Ajax*; (2) Zeno, *Patient Zeno*; (3) Coriolanus, *Patient Coriolanus*; (4) Narcissus, *Patient Narcissus*; (5) Oedipus, *Patient Oedipus*; (6) Phaedra, *Patient Phaedra*; and finally (7) Antigone, *Patient Antigone*. Contemporary cases will be presented, illustrating these seven syndromes. The names employed will, of course, be incomplete or completely fictitious.

We will offer as therapeutic antidotes the corresponding biblical narratives of (1) Elijah, the *Elijah Intervention*; (2) Job, the *Job Intervention*; (3) David, the *David Intervention*; (4) Jonah, the *Jonah Intervention*; (5) Moses, the *Moses Intervention*; (6) Rebecca, the *Rebecca Intervention*; and finally (7) Ruth, the *Ruth Intervention* to develop concrete hands-on working models of suicide-prevention and life-promotion. Each of these chapters will review the empirical literature underlying these seven respective issues and develop a treatment plan and provide a series of questions regarding this plan to the reader. Throughout, Dr. Kalman Kaplan will be denoted by *Dr. K* and Dr. Paul Cantz will be denoted by *Dr. P*.

NOTES

1. The authors would like to thank the *British Journal of Psychiatry* for permission to use the quote taken from your publication.
2. The authors would like to thank the American Psychological Association and the *Journal of Abnormal Psychology* for permission to use the quote taken from your publication.
3. The psychological autopsy is akin to the more common physical autopsy involving a post-mortem attempt to construct a psychological profile of the decedent.

Chapter Five

Elijah against Ajax

Constructively Dealing with the Experience of Being Isolated

Ajax: "Teucer, come—Where is Teucer, Will he never come back from cattle-raiding? While I perish?" (Sophocles, *Ajax*, 343–44)

And the angel of the LORD came again . . . and touched him (Elijah), and said: "Arise and eat." . . . and went in the strength of that meal . . . into Horeb the mount of God. (1 Kings 19:7–8)

There is little doubt that leaving a depressed and potentially suicidal person alone can be lethal and that the presence of responsive others can minimize this pressure. Both Ajax and Elijah find themselves at their wit's end and drained of emotional resources. Both express a wish to die. Ajax is allowed to go out alone from his tent, and falls upon his sword, killing himself. Elijah is provided food, water, and the chance to rest and recovers his strength. The common stressor is experience of persecution and humiliation. However, Elijah receives social support reducing his vulnerability while Ajax does not, leaving him even more vulnerable.

THE AJAX SYNDROME

Consider the Greek story of the great Greek warrior Ajax as portrayed in Sophocles' great play, *Ajax*. After the death of Achilles in the Trojan War, a contest was staged to determine which of the Greek heroes would inherit his arms. Ajax's leading competitor for this prize was Odysseus, who the Greek leaders chose over Ajax to receive Achilles' arms. Ajax feels his honor has been stained, and sets out at night to murder Agamemnon, the leader of the Greek forces in Troy and his brother Menelaus, whom he thinks are responsible for his misfortune. The goddess Athena, angry that he had previously exhibited excessive pride by not giving her sufficient credit for his military successes, and now because he was planning to do an act of violence against his leaders, makes him mad. In his frenzy, Ajax slaughters some of the sheep in the army's flocks, and leads others to his tent, thinking that he is actually killing and torturing the Greek leaders themselves. As his frenzied madness passes, Ajax realizes what he had done and retreats crushed and despondent into his tent, not at all disguising his suicidal thoughts due to his humiliation and loss of honor.

For the first time in his life, Ajax is portrayed as crying, something he had always refused to do as he had believed it "befitted cowards only" (320). Ah me, the mockery," he cries, and continues "To what shame am I brought low" (365). He shudders at the thought that Odysseus will laugh over his plight. Ajax says he will kill himself because his "former glory" is gone (406). He reveals that he has failed to live up to his father's "stern rugged code" that he be a hero and that he had been plucked early from his mother's warm embraces" (545–82). When Odysseus receives the prize of Achilles' armor that Ajax craves, he is absolutely crushed by the feeling that he is "second best": This feeling of being "second best" has now been compounded by becoming an absolute fool and a laughing-stock, a "sheep-killer." Ajax is overwhelmed by what has happened to him and calls desperately for his brother Teucer to come to his side: "Teucer, come—where is Teucer, Will he never come back from cattle-raiding? While I perish?" (Sophocles, *Ajax,* 343–44). But Teucer does not come and Ajax sees no way out other than suicide. Significantly, Ajax has not seemed to receive positive support from others in his tent including his woman Tecmessa and wanders outside, alone, in despair. His brother, Teucer, belatedly sends a messenger from the Greek chieftains ordering that Ajax not be allowed to leave his tent alone. The messenger arrives too late—Ajax has fallen on his sword (Sophocles, Ajax, ll.748–55, 848–49, 865).

The stressor for Ajax is his experience of humiliation, and his lack of social support leaves him vulnerable.

THE ELIJAH INTERVENTION

The biblical prophet Elijah represents a contrasting example of how to treat a depressed and suicidal person. As a result of his prophetic denouncement of Queen Jezebel, she sends Elijah a messenger announcing that she intends to have him killed (1 Kings 19:1–2). Elijah flees for his life into the wilderness and sits down under a broom-tree, and he requested for himself that he might

Figure 5.1. *The Suicide of Ajax the Great.* **Artist unknown (Etrurian red-figured calyx-crater) (ca. 400–350 BC). Said to be from Vulci. © The Trustees of the British Museum.**

die; and said: "It is enough; now, O Lord, take away my life; for I am not better than my fathers." Elijah is at the end of his rope and says he cannot go on, (1 Kings 19:3–4).

God is portrayed as listening to his prophet Elijah and taking his statement to heart, and sends an angel to him. Elijah lies down and sleeps under a broom-tree, and an angel touches him and says to him:

> "arise and eat": and he looked, and behold, there was at his head a cake baked on the hot stones, and a cruse of water. And he did eat and drink, and laid him down again. And the angel of the Lord came again the second time, and touched him, and said: "Arise and eat; because the journey is too great for thee." And he did eat and drink, and laid him down again and he arose, and did eat and drink, and went in the strength of that meal forty days and forty nights unto Horeb the mount of God. (1 Kings 19:5–8)

In summary, Elijah's plea is listened to and God has sent an angel to Elijah providing him with food and drink and allowing him to rest. On the basis of these life-promoting actions, Elijah recovers his strength and goes on to Mt. Horeb. God later raises up young Elisha to help the older prophet in his work (1 Kings 19:15–18).

The stressor for Elijah is his persecution by Queen Jezebel, but the support he receives from the angel sent by God reduces his vulnerability.

A contrast of these two narratives is presented in table 5.1. The common stressor is experience of persecution and humiliation. However, Elijah receives social support reducing his vulnerability while Ajax doesn't, leaving him vulnerable to suicide.

Consider the following two cases which illustrate well the *Ajax Syndrome* and the *Elijah Intervention*. First, we present Jack.

Case 5a. Jack: Male Ajax Syndrome (Dr. K)

Jack, a very vain man in his early 40s came into therapy with me (*Dr. K*). He presented as extremely depressed. Jack had been passed over for promotion at his law firm because the senior partners told him that he had not exhibited the proper deference to them. In response Jack wrote a public e-mail in which he lashed out wildly at members of the law firm who had had nothing to do with his non-promotion, compounding the damage. He reported feeling crushed and talked about "ending his life."

Jack told me he had been put on administrative leave by his law firm and has withdrawn from friends and even his relationship with his girlfriend Anne, who has always admired him. Jack had begun to spend more and more time alone, and as a result, he reported that Anne had become impatient, withdrew herself, and had begun to talk about ending their relationship. Jack's neighbor Joyce, who had initially brought Jack into my office, largely against his will, told me that she had noticed the change in Jack's previously friendly and active behavior, and had observed that he now rarely left his condo apartment and did not seem to change his clothes. Jack's previously impeccable dressing habits were gone and he now seemed to wear the same stained clothes for days. Further he seemed to shave only rarely, if at all, having a very rough stubble on his face. Joyce emphasized that she had insisted that Jack come into therapy.

Jack reported that he felt humiliated and could not bear to face his father, who had been a highly successful senior partner at a major law firm in the same city that Jack lived in. Jack insisted that he had only come into therapy at his neighbor's insistence, and that he had no intention of returning. Further, he explicitly stated that "his life was not worth living" as he was an absolute failure. He was behaving very much like the Greek Ajax.

Figure 5.2. *Elijah and the Angel* **(Published Date 1870). Gustave Doré.**

Dr. K's Elijah Intervention

My (therapeutic) intervention with Jack was as follows. First of all, I began to talk to Jack about what failure meant to him, and whether "failure at his

Table 5.1. Elijah against Ajax

Stage	Ajax	Elijah
1. Precipitating Stressor	Ajax is humiliated by both Agamemnon and the goddess Athena.	Elijah is overwhelmed and exhausted from his harassment by Queen Jezebel.
2. Reaction	Ajax says he wants to die.	Elijah says he wants to die.
3. Response of Others	Ajax is allowed to leave his tent alone.	Elijah is sent an angel who brings him food, drink, and companionship and lets him rest.
4. Effect	Ajax kills himself by falling on his sword.	Elijah recovers his strength and goes on to Horeb to continue his mission.

job" implied "failure as a human being." I asked him if he thought that the original criticism of him might have had some merit to it. After some reflection, Jack conceded that it might; that he had not always been as deferential to the partners at his firm as he might have been. He then conceded that he could understand how his e-mail had ruffled some feathers. Here we see Jack beginning to develop some perspective on his situation.

I then slowly began to explore with Jack how he defined himself as a human being and why he was so devastated by what happened. Jack was resistant at first to such self-examination, but over time began to explore the essence of his self-definition and whether it was overly dependent on somewhat transitory success or failure. I asked him to focus on what really gave his life meaning and provided him with a sense of self-worth. I also asked him to consider whether he had exaggerated the negative experience he had had at his law firm.

I then asked Jack why he was so afraid to face his father. What made Jack feel that his father would not support him in his failure? He did not give a direct answer in this regard. I urged Jack if he would be able to contact his father and asked permission from Jack to contact him myself if we deemed it necessary. Jack refused this request and I decided not to press this issue.

Parallel to this, I impressed on Joyce the danger in Jack being left alone in his state and that it was critical that he eat and drink regularly, that he have people to talk with on a regular basis, and finally, that any lethal weapons in his home be removed if possible, even if this involved calling in the police. I also arranged for social services to come in to address the following questions. (a) Is there food in the house? (b) Is Jack eating on a regular basis? (c) Is he getting sufficient rest? (d) Does he wash and shave? (e) Does he eat meals on time and is he eating meals on a regular basis? (f) Does he take necessary medications, if any?

At the conclusion of the therapy, Jack was continuing to make progress. My employment of the *Elijah Intervention* seemed to provide Jack with the hands-on attention necessary to alleviate his suicidal thoughts.

Now we present Amanda.

Case 5b. Amanda: Female Ajax Syndrome (Dr. P)

Amanda, a college freshman at a large state university, became disillusioned after struggling her first semester both academically and socially. Amanda had been the valedictorian of her high school class and well-liked amongst her peer group in the small Midwestern town in which she was raised. Suddenly, for the first time, she found classes to be increasingly challenging and also found it much more difficult to find the "right" group of friends. Amanda's self-esteem had been plummeting and she had never felt more alone and helpless in her entire life. Being somewhat embarrassed with her struggles she decided to keep them to herself, only reporting to her parents what she had thought they would want to hear: that she was adjusting well to her new surroundings and maintaining an impeccable academic record. However, this façade began crumbling at an alarming rate during her second semester. Now Amanda found it challenging to leave her dorm room to attend classes. Around this time, Amanda began depending on anti-anxiety pills that she was receiving from a male upper classman with whom she sometimes engaged in high risk sexual activities. Twenty pounds lighter, insecure, and exercising poor judgment—this was not the same Amanda who had left her parents' home with high hopes of college success.

After one particularly devastating mid-term exam result, Amanda—half drunk—confided in her roommate that she had lately been thinking about leaving school or even just "going away forever." Although Amanda's roommate was understanding and empathic, she felt unprepared to adequately help Amanda with her problems.

Dr. P's Elijah Intervention

My (*Dr. P's*) therapeutic intervention with Amanda was as follows: after Amanda had fallen asleep for the evening her roommate was concerned enough to alert the resident advisor, who in turn contacted the university counseling center's emergency number. The counselor on-call reached out to Amanda the next morning and promptly assessed her for risk of harm to herself. After concluding that indeed Amanda met criteria for a short-term psychiatric hospitalization, she was admitted to a good facility where she received not only stabilization and monitoring, but also encountered helping professionals who were truly invested in her safety and well-being. While at the hospital Amanda took full advantage of the clinical services available to her, deriving the most benefit from her individual therapist who she experienced to be a genuine presence who clearly cared to understand her circumstances and was able to provide her with a kernel of hope. Upon discharge Amanda decided to take a medical leave for the remainder of the semester, which was by this time approximately a month before summer break. Upon returning to her university, Amanda began regularly attending individual and group counseling sessions at the university counseling center. Amanda's parents and close friends were also involved in her aftercare, and frequently visited her on campus and spoke to her daily on the phone. On the recommendation of her therapist, Amanda also sought extra-curricular activities that helped counter-balance the rigors of her coursework and provide her with a sense of belongingness and fulfillment that she had not experienced since her senior year in high school. Additionally, as therapy progressed, Amanda began appreciating the benefits of sharing her burden with others. First it was her therapist, but as Amanda became more practiced in offering emotional disclosures, she found that her friendships became enriched. As a result, Amanda gained the ability to cultivate and maintain an effective support network.

LIFE LESSON

We end this chapter with an explication of the following life lesson. Do not leave a suicidal person alone! We must pay attention to suicidal cues and statements. Interventions do not have to be overly technical or sophisticated. In the case of Patient Jack, this involved his emphasis to his neighbor, Joyce, in the importance of her looking in on him, ensuring that he attended to rest, meals, hygiene, and medication compliance. In the case of Patient Amanda, she received clinical, familial, and fraternal care and attention that provided her with the necessary emotional and physical supports as she transitioned to independent living.

Oftentimes simple life-promoting gestures such as providing food, water, and companionship can be critical in promoting life and preventing suicide. In our society, short term psychiatric hospitalization can be helpful, but it does not replace interpersonal warmth and responsiveness.

Chapter Six

Job against Zeno

Constructively Dealing with the Need for Meaning

The manner of his (Zeno's) death was as follows. As he was leaving the school he tripped and fell, breaking a toe. Striking the ground with his fist, he quoted the line from the *Niobe*, "I come, I come, why dost thou call for me?" and died on the spot through holding his breath. (Diogenes Laertius, 1853, *Lives of Eminent Philosophers*, VII. 28)

Job: "Though He slay me, yet will I trust in Him" (Job 13:15)

There is no doubt that suffering great misfortune, or even continuing small setbacks, can create feelings of despair that some people seem to be able to overcome, while others cannot. Zeno the Stoic kills himself after the relatively minor mishap of stubbing (perhaps breaking) his toe. Job does not take his life, despite being totally unfairly and arbitrarily assailed with the loss of his fortune, his children, and his health. He complains mightily of his innocence, and certainly contemplates suicide. But in the end Job reaffirms the life force within him. The common stressor is experience of a sudden misfortune. However, Job is anchored in faith in God reducing his vulnerability while Zeno isn't, leading him to catastrophize in a search for meaning, leaving him vulnerable.

THE ZENO SYNDROME

The inability to create meaning in one's life often leads to feelings of utter despair. It can drive a person to very extreme, often destructive attitudes to try to artificially manufacture meaning and purpose in one's life through clinging to misguided "signs" or "omens." When in a state of despair, people are susceptible to engage in gross distortions of how they experience the world. According to the account of the ancient Greek chronicler Diogenes Laertius, Zeno, founder of the Stoic school of philosophy, wrenched his toe on the way home from lecturing at the *Stoa* (porch). He interprets this objectively minor mishap as a "sign from the gods that he should depart" and voluntarily holds his breath until he dies (Diogenes Laertius, *Lives of Eminent Philosophers*, 1925, VII. 28, 141).

The medically impossible depiction of his suicide begs further consideration. Zeno "holding his breath" until death defies the biological reality with regard to the involuntary aspect of breathing, and to the biblical conception that God breathes life into man and takes it away (Genesis 2:7). Zeno, like other Greek and Roman stoics, needs to control the conditions around his death, equating this control with a tragically tinged sense of freedom (Seneca, *De Ira*, 3.15.34).

Why should Zeno kill himself after so seemingly minor an annoyance as wrenching his toe while Job is able to withstand much greater stressors? Consider first Zeno. The leap from wrenching one's toe to killing oneself seems monumental. So why does he kill himself?

Understanding Zeno's actions necessitates examining more closely the Stoic school of thought. What the Stoics feared was loss of control, ultimately loss of control over life itself. For the Stoics, cheerfulness was a philosophical duty, not an indication of natural optimism. The Stoics did not accept the idea of a caring and loving deity, and they also were too deep as thinkers to place much permanent value on so limited a prospect as human success. They knew that they must fulfill their moral and social duty, but they could never even feel secure that their good acts would produce a good result.

Zeno defined the goal of life as living in agreement with nature (Diogenes Laertius, *Lives of Eminent Philosophers*, 7, 87). Suicide must not be undertaken frivolously, "but if he (god) gives the signal to retreat as he did to Socrates, I must obey him who gives a signal, as I would a general" (Epictetus, *Discourses*, 1.29).

In this quote, the contemporary writers Droge and Tabor (1992, 29–39), find a precedent for "rational suicide," in Greek and Roman Stoics which has provided the justification for physician-assisted suicide (PAS). Voluntary suicide is condoned when it is necessary (Greek: *ananke*) and rational; it is condemned when it is irrational. A rational suicide is preceded by an apparently divine signal that the time to die is at hand. In other words, Zeno killed himself by holding his breath, not because he broke his toe, nor because he was in pain, nor even because he was depressed, but because he bought into the notion that the event of stubbing his toe represented a divine signal to depart (Droge and Tabor, 1992, 31).

But this only begs the question. Why did Zeno interpret stubbing his toe as a signal from the gods to depart when Job did not similarly interpret his objectively far greater misfortunes? Droge and Tabor may be correct in citing Zeno's actions as a precedent for rational suicide. However, they may not be focusing on what is rational in Zeno's act. Zeno's rationality lies not in his interpretation that stubbing his toe represents a sign from the gods that he should depart, but rather in his need for the events in his life to have meaning. Zeno is aging and feels alone, and deludes himself into thinking that the act of stubbing his toe has cosmic meaning. Zeno becomes a hero, even if he dies in the process. Its inherent rationality is not that stubbing his toe is a sign to depart, but that it is better for Zeno to depart a world in which his actions are given meaning, even destructive meaning, than live in one in which they are not. In the absence of a meaning-giving system, Zeno is cast adrift, over-interpreting events in an attempt to feel less adrift and isolated. Zeno's over-interpretation may represent his attempt to find meaning and purpose in an otherwise hopeless and meaningless world.

The stressor for Zeno is the experience of stubbing his toe, and his lack of an inherent meaning structure leaves him vulnerable to his compulsive need to view his mild misfortune as a sign from the gods that he should depart.

THE JOB INTERVENTION

The biblical figure of Job, in contrast, does not commit suicide despite being assailed by far more serious misfortunes—the loss of his wealth, his family, and his health. First, Job is told by a messenger that his oxen and asses have been stolen from him (Job 1:15), then, that his sheep and his servants have been burned (Job 1:16), moreover, that he has lost his camels (Job 1:17), then that he has lost his children when the eldest brother's house fell upon them (Job 1:18–19). Finally, Job is covered with boils from head to toe (Job 2:7) and his wife tells him to "curse God and die" (Job 2:9).

His friends tell him to admit he deserves his punishment, but he refuses because he knows it is not true (Job 4–31). Job certainly complains bitterly but does not break his relationship with God. He is deeply grieved and indeed wrestles with suicide, stressing the same method of death, *strangling*, as did Zeno. "So, that my soul chooseth strangling, and death, rather than these bones" (Job 7:15). But Job does not act on this. As the story proceeds, Job reaffirms his relationship with his Creator: "Though He slay me, yet will I trust in Him" (Job 13:15). The work of Exline, Kaplan, and Grubbs (2012) points to the importance of being able to argue within a relationship with God without leaving it.

Strikingly, Job differs from Zeno in not seeing the act of holding his breath (strangling) as a voluntary act. He knows it is God Who breathes life

Figure 6.1. *Zeno of Citium*, Artist unknown. Marble bust. Farnese Collection, National Archaeological Museum of Naples.

into man (Genesis 2:7) and God Who takes it away (Job 34:13–15). The book of Job stresses that it is God himself that has given man the breath of life (Genesis 2:7, Job 33:4). "The spirit of God hath made me, and the breath of the Almighty giveth me life" (Job 33:4). And God that takes it away, man returns to the dust from which he sprung. "Thou withdrawest their breath they perish, and return to their dust" (Psalms 104:29). And when God restores the breath, man rises again and renews the face of the earth. "Thou sendest forth Thy spirit, they are created; And Thou renews the face of the earth" (Psalms 104:30).

Job, in contrast to Zeno, is anchored in a sense of a personal Creator who is with him from the moment of his birth and will be with him into his death and beyond. Thus, he can withstand far greater misfortune than can Zeno without the need to attribute cosmic meaning to it. This does not make Job less rational, but simply anchors his interpretive structure in his desire to live. Job follows the biblical injunction that one is born against one's will, and dies against one's will, and expresses his freedom in the way he lives his life (Job 4:29). He overcomes major losses in his life by deepening his faith in his Creator who provides him with an inherent meaning for his life.

Job's three "friends"—Eliphaz, Bildad, and Zophar—come to visit him, and say basically that he (Job) deserves what has befallen him. If Job is afflicted in this way, then he must have sinned. But Job maintains his sense of innocence and sarcastically unmasks his friends' pretensions of superior wisdom (Job 12) referring to them as "miserable comforters" (Job 16:2) and questions the morality of God's "justice." He simply does not comprehend it and will not pretend to understand something that he cannot understand. As the story proceeds, God appears in a whirlwind, describing Himself as an unquestionable power. Yet God punishes Job's three friends for presuming to say they understand His ways, and instructing them to offer burnt-offerings to His servant Job, who shall pray for them (Job 42:7–9). Then He turns to Job and tells him that he (Job) alone has spoken the truth, that God's ways are ultimately incomprehensible to humankind.

This is a very interesting response with double-edged implications. On the one hand God's response represents a strong rebuke to the friends of Job, who continually accuse Job of guilty behavior leading to his afflictions. On the other hand, God is rebuking Job himself for demanding tit-for-tat accountability. In other words, his afflictions are no indicator that he has sinned, nor does his just and righteous behavior ensure that he won't suffer afflictions. These of course are the two polarities of a simple-minded "just world hypothesis" in which the world is a just and orderly place where people always get what they deserve (Lerner and Miller, 1978). Under this view, if one suffers, one deserves it. Rather, God is communicating that His ways are beyond human understanding.

Only when Job accepts this more elevated conception of God does he become restored twofold, in everything. Job names his new daughter Yemima, meaning dove and deriving from the Hebrew word *yom* meaning day. (Job 42:9–17). The name Yemima has also been interpreted as meaning "day bright" or "being beautiful like the sun of the day" because Job has now emerged from the "night of his affliction."

Job does not need to continuously search for such meaning through catastrophizing and over-interpreting relatively minor misfortunes. Job's God gives and takes away life, but does not give signals that it is time for Job to depart. Job is not obsessed with death, nor does he need to control it, nor does he need to worry that it is timely. Job thus does not interpret each event as a signal to exit, but as a challenge to live the life that has been given to him in dignity (see Kaplan, 2007b). Life for Job has inherent meaning and purpose, and this represents the best alternative and antidote to the obsession of death with dignity and rational suicide so endemic to Zeno the Stoic and contemporary culture. Job, in contrast, is anchored in a sense of a personal Creator who is with him from the moment of his birth and will be with him into his death and beyond. Thus, he can withstand far greater misfortune than can Zeno without the need to attribute cosmic meaning to it. This does not make Job less rational, but simply anchors his interpretive structure in his desire to live.

The stressors for Job are the many physical and emotional assaults he is inexplicably bombarded with. His relationship with his God reduces his vulnerability, though he is understandingly questioning at times.

A contrast of these two narratives is presented in table 6.1. The common stressor is experience of persecution and humiliation. However, Job has an inherent meaning structure reducing his vulnerability while Zeno does not, making him vulnerable to the over-interpretation of negative experience (*catastrophizing*) in his desperate search for meaning.

Consider the following two cases depicting the *Zeno Syndrome* and the suggested *Job Intervention*. First, we present Sergio.

Case 6a. Sergio: Male Zeno Syndrome (Dr. P)

To the outside observer, Sergio—a 15-year-old Hispanic adolescent—was a typical teenager traversing the vicissitudes of teenage angst and high school romances (not to mention exams!). Indeed, despite having been bounced-around the foster care system most of his life, Sergio had many character strengths and intellectual abilities that served him well as he encountered the routine challenges of adolescent development. However, about half-way through his sophomore year, after failing to make his high school basketball team, he began spiraling into a serious depression that not only affected his academic performance and social life, but eventually led to a suicide attempt

Figure 6.2. *Job Speaks with His Friends* (Published Date 1870). Gustave Doré.

by overdosing on prescription medication that he had gained access to in his foster-parents' medicine cabinet. Thankfully Sergio had texted a friend short-ly before taking the pills, and that friend alerted Sergio's foster mother who in turn called 9-1-1. When Sergio's state-appointed case manager recom-mended that he begin seeing a therapist, Sergio was quick to identify the fact that he had been rejected to play basketball for his high school team as a sign

Table 6.1. Job against Zeno

Stage	Zeno	Job
1. Precipitating Stressor	Zeno the Stoic trips and stubs a toe on the way back from giving a lecture at the Stoa.	Job suddenly and unexpectedly loses his property, his children, and his health.
2. Reaction	Zeno interprets this as a sign from the gods he should depart.	Though Job complains, he maintains his innocent faith in God despite his misfortunes.
3. Response of Others	No mention made of reaction of others.	Job's wife tells him to curse God and die and his three friends tell him that he must be guilty.
4. Effect	Zeno immediately holds his breath until he dies.	Job steadfastly maintains his faith in God while proclaiming his innocence. God punishes Job's friends for saying they understand His (God's) ways and tells Job that he alone has spoken the truth, and restores him.

that he would never amount to anything, regardless of his efforts. More than that, he seemed to feel his life was not really worth living.

Although Sergio had been able to maintain a veneer of strength and positivity even while enduring an uncommonly stressful childhood, his personal tipping-point was reached when he had been cut from his high school basketball team. This insult had made a deep impact on his sense of self as well as his sense of universal justice and fairness. Up till then, Sergio explained, "things were bad, of course, but I didn't feel like I had much to do with the course of my future except try the best I could." When Sergio's "best" hadn't been good enough, his emotional house of cards imploded under its own weight.

Dr. P's Job Intervention

Sergio had been seeing me (*Dr. P*) twice a week and it didn't take long for a helpful measure of therapeutic rapport to be established. Understandably, upon beginning treatment Sergio was fixated on not making the team, but it soon became apparent that he had assigned an unusual amount of importance to this event, and his profound feelings of despair and rejection were exacerbated by a lifetime of unexpressed sorrow and frustration. Further, he expressed feeling great isolation and disappointment that some of his friends did not understand his despair over his sense of rejection.

As the sting of rejection from his high school basketball team began to wane, Sergio became able, for the first time in his life, to begin expressing the profound pain and anguish that he had been experiencing as a result of being taken from his parents and siblings when he was four years old, passed along from one household to the next, and from feeling generally disempowered to control the most important elements of his life.

I emphasized to Sergio that it was absolutely healthy and acceptable for him to feel this disappointment, and also to express his feeling of betrayal on the part of his friends. It wasn't until Sergio had an emotionally safe place to discuss these complicated feelings that he had successfully repressed for much of his childhood that he displayed movement away from a hopeless world view to that of a future full of possibilities.

As Sergio's treatment continued along the lines of the *Job Intervention*, he reengaged in many of his previous school and extracurricular activities with a newfound sense of confidence and zeal. Sergio joined a park district basketball league and was able to field athletic shortcomings without his disappointment cascading into a catastrophized distortion; Sergio began taking both his successes and failures in stride.

Case 6b. Charlotte: Female Ajax Syndrome (Dr. K)

Our second case here involves a woman of 73 named Charlotte (fictional name) who had recently undergone a hysterectomy (Kaplan, 2014). In the winter of 1996, I (*Dr. K*) was advising the *Detroit Free Press* on its study of the first 47 physician-assisted suicides conducted by Jack Kevorkian. I was writing frequently on this topic as well as teaching a graduate course in suicide and suicide prevention at Wayne State University in Detroit. In short, I was a semi-public figure in this regard in Michigan during this period. In December of that month I received an unsolicited duplicated copy of a letter from a person I did not know. It turned out to be the first of many letters and was written in impeccably neat, perhaps computerized handwriting. It was hand-addressed to me in the beginning and ended with her signature. As I discovered later, a number of other public figures, all in the psychological, medical, legal, or political realm received this and subsequent letters. In this first letter of December 2, 1996, Charlotte advocated for the legalization of state euthanasia clinics in Michigan.

> Dear Friend
> In matters pertaining to the euthanasia-assisted suicide issue, we have heard and read a thousand times that "Only God gives life and only He should take it away." True, God does give life and also takes it away gradually, by way of old age, disease, drugs, etc.
> When "life" (being able to do things for yourself and others) is taken away, unless a heart attack or accident strikes first, every human being usually

descends into the "miserable existence" stage (cannot do anything for yourself or others—totally helpless). This stage of that life-death cycle can last weeks, months or years and is the most dreaded of human experiences.

We also hear and read "the sanctity of life," "concern for human life," "we must protect life," etc. Everyone agrees that it is right, moral and proper to sanctify, protect and value "life." However, when "life" is taken away and we Elderly, terminally ill, Alzheimer's, etc. descend into the "miserable existence" stage, very few officials and medical personnel acknowledge that this stage is a special stage and should receive special treatment. In fact, many just say "if the heart is beating, then the patient is alive."

This refusal to divide the "life"—"miserable existence"—"death" cycle into distinct categories is causing most of the animosity in euthanasia discussions. Many deliberately use the word "life" when they know very well that they mean "miserable existence." (Kaplan and Leonhardi, 2000, p. 268)

Charlotte went on for three full pages, speaking about the suffering of those in the "miserable existence stage" which she also called the "other death row." She called for a state approved euthanasia clinic. Among the indignities of the "miserable existence stage" she included (1) nursing home or hospital tests and procedures, (2) living with children, (3) hospice, (4) in-home and visiting nurse arrangements, (5) living wills, and (6) committing suicide without the help of a doctor. She signed the letter "a still clear thinking 81 year old human being."

In March 1997, I received another letter. This time the tone had changed—ominously. Now Charlotte began to write of her own death and of using the money she would save through her death to buy her grandson (who was graduating from college) a car.

In April 1997, something new happened. I (and others) received a letter from Charlotte; this time from a hospital where she had undergone a hysterectomy after bouts with vaginal bleeding. She was doing fine and acknowledged that "she was getting stronger" but described the "torture" she was enduring. She specified: (1) "IVs with anesthetics, nutrients, etc.," (2) "tight rubber stockings that stretched from my toes to the crotch, and expanding and contracting legging attached to a motor for better blood circulation," (3) "tubes in my nose, for oxygen," (4) "breathing tubes to exercise my lungs," (5) "blood pressure and temperature checks every hour, an EKG, blood drawn for lab tests, etc.," and (6) "I was expected to walk alone from the bathroom, holding unto the IV pole one day after surgery."

All of us who have undergone surgery recognize the "tortures" that Charlotte had described as unpleasant but routine and temporary, but quite necessary to facilitate a quick and complete recovery. Charlotte's comments indicated that she also recognized the reason why these measures were taken. Yet she seemed to regard each of these measures as an assault on her dignity that made "life not worth living." She oddly claimed that in the absence of legalized euthanasia, she chose surgery "because the alternatives . . . such as living with children, in a nursing home, with hospice or home care arrangements were worse."

Charlotte spent three days in the hospital. Her surgery was successful and she returned home. Again, I tried to see her. Again, I was rebuffed, politely. I subsequently called her several times unsuccessfully over the net period. No one answered the phone. I received no more letters during this next period, and was away from Michigan over the summer months. I returned in September and was not successful in reaching her. I received no more letters from her.

On December 3, 1997, the newspapers, television, and radio in the Detroit metropolitan area reported that Jack Kevorkian had assisted yet another person to commit suicide in Oakland County, Michigan (a very wealthy county just north of Detroit). The name reported was Charlotte X, the very woman who had reached out to me. Charlotte was identified as having been aided to die by Kevorkian.

The autopsy indicated that the late Charlotte had no anatomical evidence of disease. She had stated elsewhere that she was not in pain, other than experiencing some mild age-related arthritis. Dr. Lubisoff Dragovic, the medical examiner of Oakland County, Michigan, at that time confirmed to me that he could find nothing anatomically wrong with Charlotte in her autopsy.

Charlotte exemplifies Zeno the Stoic, sadly hoping to find in her suicide a meaning to her life. Charlotte, like Zeno, was aging and felt alone. Zeno deluded himself into thinking that the act of stubbing his toe has cosmic meaning. Zeno becomes a hero, even if he dies in the process. Its inherent rationality is not that stubbing his toe is a sign to depart, but that it is better to have a world in which one's actions are given meaning, even destructive meaning, than one in which they are not. Charlotte behaved similarly, attempting to turn her death into a heroic martyrdom for the cause of euthanasia.

Dr. K's Failed Job Intervention

In retrospect, I (*Dr. K*) realize that I had attempted almost unconsciously to employ the narrative of Job in my attempt to dissuade Charlotte from taking her life. I tried to find a way of helping Charlotte give her life meaning.

I was concerned after receiving Charlotte's initial December 2, 1996, letter. I contacted her by telephone, though she was not my patient. Our conversation revealed that Charlotte had lost her husband to cancer three years previously and she was the mother of three grown daughters. She lived alone, and aside from some normal ailments associated with aging, was in reasonably good health. She was not terminal nor in acute physical pain. In fact, she seemed to be active in her community, had written three books, and had a very sharp mind.

Yet Charlotte advocated forcefully for a state-sanctioned clinic for "we terminally ill, Alzheimer's." Significantly, she was none of these except elderly, and by her own description "still clear thinking." Nevertheless, Charlotte insisted she wanted to die before she became incapacitated or terminally ill. I did not feel, after speaking with her, that Charlotte was acutely suicidal at this time. I was concerned, however, that her perception of her situation would lead to a more concrete death plan in the future, and also that she presented constricted thinking. I invited her to come into my university (Wayne State University) to talk with me. However she refused, politely.

When I received Charlotte's March 1997 letter, I immediately contacted her by phone. I stressed the hostility underlying committing suicide to save money to enable her grandson to buy a car, and the ambivalent feelings that he would have toward a gift brought about by her suicide. I stated that I thought her grandson would prefer a "live grandmother" to a car received as a result of her suicide. At this time, Charlotte told me about the death of her husband a few years previously. I acknowledged her loneliness and suggested she get involved in activities or even therapy. She rejected both of these options. I then stressed Charlotte's capabilities and how much she had to offer in the fight for better health care for the elderly.

I invited Charlotte to present her views in the class I was teaching on suicide. Charlotte declined but said she enjoyed our calls. I suggested that she go see a psychologist or a counselor to talk about her situation. She refused again politely; I offered to come visit her. Again she declined, but gave met the phone number of a speakers' bureau dealing with "problems of the elderly." Curious, I called the number. It was the law firm of Geoffrey Feiger, the lead defense attorney for Jack Kevorkian! Charlotte's legal knowledge and interests began to make some sense. Concerned, I resolved to keep in regular contact with her, though she was not my patient. As I mentioned previously, I attempted to call Charlotte several times before I left the area for the summer months, but I was unable to reach her nor did I receive any more correspondence from her. The next time I heard about her was on December 3, 1997 when I read in The Detroit Free Press that Charlotte had been the latest person Jack Kevorkian had helped to kill herself. When I heard her name, I felt as if I had been kicked in the head and resolved to investigate the case. Although Charlotte had not been my patient, I felt as if I had lost her. I wanted to know why she was so obsessed with wanting to die.

I did not need to wait long. That afternoon, I and others on her list received a neat suicide note from Charlotte insisting that she was rational and competent at the time of her death. "I am not stressed, oppressed, or depressed." she said. "I don't have Alzheimer's and am not terminally ill, but I am 82 years old and I want to die."

Let me repeat what I wrote earlier. The autopsy indicated that Charlotte had displayed no anatomical evidence of disease. She had stated elsewhere that she was not in pain, other than having some mild age-related arthritis. Let me reemphasize the medical examiner confirmed to me that he could find nothing anatomically wrong with Charlotte in her autopsy.

People who knew her said she had been active in her church in its fall cleanup. She had raked leaves, helped in painting a basement, and seemed to be in a generally cheerful mood. Why then did Charlotte kill herself, and what does this teach us about "rational suicide"? Why did my attempts at intervention fail so completely?

The key to Charlotte's logic can be found in the definition of life she offered in her first letter of December 2, 1996. To refresh our memories let us state Charlotte's reasoning in terms of premises and conclusions.

> "Life" (quotation marks, hers) is being able to do things for yourself and others.
>
> When this independence and self-sufficiency is taken away every human being usually descends into the "miserable existence" stage (cannot do anything for yourself or others—totally helpless).
>
> This "miserable existence stage" is a middle stage between life and death, which can last weeks, months or years and is the most dreaded of human experiences. It requires "special treatment," not just for Charlotte but for everyone, whether or not they share Charlotte's definitional scheme.
>
> Since this "miserable existence" stage is *not* "life," "euthanasia" of someone in this stage is "special treatment" and not "murder."

This argument is eminently logical and rational in the narrow sense of the term. First of all, life is defined in terms of independence and self-sufficiency and productivity. Second, and ominously, the taking away of this independence does not just make one feel miserable, but actually puts one into another, morally and legally unprotected, category": "the stage of miserable existence." The difference between "being a living person who feels miserable" and "being no longer a living person" but one who has entered a "miserable existence" category is monumental. The first category requires compassion. The second category requires "special treatment," a term which sends chills down the spines of anyone even remotely knowledgeable about the Nazi euthanasia program (cf. Lifton, 1986; Mitchell, 1999–2000). This "special treatment" ends in the euthanasia of the person in this "miserable existence" stage, whether he wants it or not.

But why did I fail so completely in addressing her misery? Why was I not able to implant in Charlotte any of the resilience so prominent in Job's life story? Why was I not able to demonstrate to Charlotte, really, to reach Charlotte, with the counter-narrative implicit and explicit in the Job story?

Why was Charlotte so focused on finding meaning in her death? What could I have done differently?

This case also raised broader issues for me: (1) With legalization of assisted suicide and euthanasia, there is more chance for abuse (both by the financially driven choices in health care, and also by families who wished their loved ones dead), (2) the extension of choice of assisted suicide to physically sound but depressed individuals, (3) the "quick" solution of death for the elderly when they feel useless (is there any relation between the rising rates of elderly suicide and he publicity related to assisted suicide and euthanasia?), (4) the substitution of "death with dignity' for "meaning of life," (5) the focus of death as a right rather than as a fact, and the over concern with the legal as opposed to the psychological and spiritual issues. [1]

The last point is worth reflecting on. The decriminalization of suicide in contemporary society does not mean that health care professionals should encourage it, and not try to prevent it. We need to explore the psychological reasons behind Charlotte's decision to kill herself. A number of general suicidal themes stand out in Charlotte's letters. They are: (1) black and white negative thinking (2) a counter-phobic stance toward dependency (rejection of all help or assistance), (3) insistence on a non-biological definition of life (as being able to take care of oneself), (4) use of euphemisms (she created a new life stage "miserable existence" rather than describing herself as feeling miserable), (5) unsolicited speaking for others (she advocated for a state-sanctioned euthanasia clinic for "we terminally ill, elderly, Alzheimer's," even though she personally fell into none of these categories, (6) an overly rational legalistic analysis of the problem of euthanasia and doctor-assisted suicide, (7) exaggeration of annoying but relatively minor and temporary discomforts, (8) an irrational tunnel vision behind her seemingly logical arguments, (9) an apparent blurring of her personal situation with the campaign to legalize euthanasia and the eagerness to make herself a martyr for the cause, (10) her plan to kill herself and to give her grandson a car with medication money she was saving, (11) reluctance to accept family support (she found death preferable to living with her children), and (12) her choice to die (and be in control) rather than accept her current relatively healthy though somewhat diminished state.

I have been haunted by the question of how to have better employed the biblical story of Job to help her. Charlotte was not formally religious, yet she was most likely aware of this story. De-situated from its theological context, the story of Job is one of a man who does not commit suicide despite being assailed by far more serious misfortunes. First Job is stricken by the loss of his great wealth, the deaths of all his children, and then his health. He reaffirms his faith in God:

Job knew that his God had created him uniquely in an act of living kindness. Why didn't Charlotte? Job knew his God gives and takes away life, but does not give signals that it is time for him to depart because of any imperfection or disability. Why didn't Charlotte know this? Job did not focus on the "quality of his life." Why did Charlotte?

Job did not focus on any particular attributes that make life worth living or not. Indeed, this is not even a question that even seemed to occur to Job. Why did it occur to Charlotte? Job was not obsessed with death, nor did he need to control it, nor did he need to worry if it was timely. Why was Charlotte? Job thus did not need to interpret each event as a signal to exit, in a fruitless attempt to find meaning in the heroic. Why did Charlotte? Job simply needed to live the life that has been given to him in dignity, and die when it was his time to die without wild over-interpretation. Why didn't Charlotte? These are questions which have continued to haunt me and have undoubtedly been a contributing factor in the writing of this book.

Though Charlotte was not my patient per se, she had reached out to me and I was unable, as much as I tried, to meet with her and attempt to de-valorize her idealized conception of suicide. I thought I knew how to apply what we now call the *Job Intervention*, but she did not make herself available, and I lost her to totally unwarranted physician-assisted suicide. Had she been my patient, I would have focused on Charlotte's cognitive style, employing the narrative of Job, and emphasizing that it was perfectly legitimate to complain without leaving life.

LIFE LESSON

We end this chapter with an explication of the following life lesson. We must offer an unassailable positive meaning structure to a depressed person who has been assaulted by a misfortune. With this meaning structure, he is able to feel cared for and thus can withstand the tendency to catastrophize his misfortune into an often melodramatic tragedy, over-interpreting events which need not be over-interpreted. Without such a meaning structure, a depressed person may exaggerate, personalize, and dramatize his misfortune in an attempt to find meaning, even with lethal consequences. Patient Sergio begins to recover from his despair over his being cut from his school's basketball team, and find meaning in his life in new activities. Charlotte, however, finds meaning only in her death (as a release from life), and becomes a poster child for physician-assisted suicide.

NOTE

1. The reader is referred to an excellent book on this topic by recently confirmed Supreme Court Justice Neil Gorsuch.

Chapter Seven

David against Coriolanus

Constructively Dealing with the Experience of Exile

Coriolanus: Cut me to pieces, Volsces: men and lads, Stain all your edges on me. Boy! False hound! If you have writ your annals true, 'tis there, That, like an eagle in a dove-cote, I Flutter'd your Volscians in Corioli: Alone I did it. Boy! (William Shakespeare, 1881, *Coriolanus*, Act V Scene VI)

And Achish, (King of Gath) . . . said to David: "I know that thou art good in my sight, as an angel of God; notwithstanding the princes of the Philistines have said: He shall not go up with us to the battle (against Israel)." And David rose up early, he and his men, to depart in the morning." (1 Samuel 29:9–11)

Becoming exiled or a refugee is an all too common experience in today's world. This chapter compares two prototypical stories in this regard, the beloved biblical warrior David and the Roman military hero Coriolanus. Both are forced to flee their homeland, David because of the paranoia of King Saul, and Coriolanus because he has angered the Roman senate through his provocative behavior. David thrives in his exile to the Philistines, and ultimately returns as King of Israel. Coriolanus, in contrast, swears vengeance on Rome and is ultimately murdered by the Volsces. David is flexible in personality, avoiding provocative behaviors thus reducing his vulnerability, and thrives, while Coriolanus, in contrast, is done in by his rigidity, creating a vulnerability leading to his death.

THE CORIOLANUS SYNDROME

Roman historians (Plutarch, 1909; Titus Livius [Livy], 1960) tell of Marcius whose military valor at Corioli against the Volsci, the enemies of Rome, won him the honorary name of Coriolanus. Shakespeare's (2014) great under-performed tragedy, *Coriolanus,* was brilliantly produced in a 2011 movie starring Ralph Fiennes in his directorial debut. Plutarch describes Marcius as a man of great energy and strength of purpose but combined with so violent a temper and self-assertion that he could not cooperate with people. Indifferent to hardship, pleasure, or money, he trained himself always for war. Honors in battle never satisfied him, fearful that he would fall short of what he had achieved before. His supreme joy was to please his mother Volumnia, a tough Roman matron of the old school. She glories in the battle scars her son bears. After his heroism and brilliance in defeating the Volsci, Marcius be-comes embroiled in angry arguments between the upper and lower classes of Rome, and his outspoken insults to the plebeians lead to his banishment and almost his execution, despite his glorious military services.

Infuriated and obsessed with wreaking revenge on Rome, Marcius (Cori-olanus) went to the Volsci and persuaded them to attack Rome. As Marcius's Volsci army sat encamped before Rome, two delegations came from the city but could not persuade him to desist. Roman women then came forth sponta-neously to the camp, accompanied by Marcius's mother (Volumnia), his wife, and children. Volumnia broke through Marcius's harshness by telling him, "You cannot attack Rome unless you trample on the body of the mother that bore you." Marcius broke down and withdrew the Volsci army. Plutarch writes that Coriolanus (Marcius) was murdered by the Volsci shortly after this withdrawal. In Shakespeare's play, Coriolanus is portrayed as goading on the Volsces to kill him. "Cut me to pieces, Volsces: men and lads. Stain all your edges on me. Boy! False hound! If you have writ your annals true, 'tis there That, like an eagle in a dove-cote. Flutter'd your Volscians in Corioli: Alone I did it. Boy!" (*Coriolanus,* Act V Scene VI, ll.130–35).[1]

Marcius, an intelligent, able man, was neither greedy nor petty, but his loyalty is focused to his own inhuman self-imposed code of behavior. Yet his behavior is rigid in the most self-destructive way. His actions show no love for Rome. He displays scars of his many battle wounds, but no sweetness in his manner or thought. Marcius is ultimately loyal neither to his gods nor his nation, nor even his own children. Rome is for him largely a vehicle to act out his powerful inner drives. Though not a suicide story *per se*, there is no question that the rigidity of Coriolanus was a factor in his death. He can be said to have provoked his death.

The stressor for Coriolanus is forced exile from his country, and his rigidity in character leaves him vulnerable.

THE DAVID INTERVENTION

Like Coriolanus, the biblical David was a war hero, but of a very different sort. He is described as playing the lyre for King Saul, and is loved by the people. He slew the Philistine giant Goliath not by brute strength but through agility and the use of a simple slingshot. Later, his life threatened because of the jealousy of King Saul, David fled his native Israel with a band of men to live under the Philistines, longtime foes of Israel (1 Samuel 27). Yet here the similarity to Marcius ends. David left not because he hated his countrymen but to save his life from King Saul's anger against him. Perhaps. Most important, David was no perfectionist but remained deeply human. Even in exile, David did not turn from his love of his king, his people, and of God, despite the king's anger at him.

Figure 7.1. *Death of Coriolanus*, H. C. Selous (1912). See the record for H. C. Selous' *The Death of Coriolanus* (1864), in Michael John Goodman, The Victorian Illustrated Shakespeare Archive.

Warmth is an existential element of David's being, and his loyalties were founded on love, not merely on his own rigid personal disciplines. In the period that David and his troop lived among the Philistines, he carefully avoided doing harm to Israel. Although David did lead his troops in war against common enemies of Israel and the Philistines, the lords of the Philistines remember that he is an Israelite who had fought against the Philistines and demand that he be sent away from the upcoming battle. Thus he is spared the conflict of having to fight for King Achish of the Philistines in a decisive battle against Israel. David responds to Achish when he is sent away: "But what have I done? . . . that I may not fight against the enemies of my lord the king?" Perhaps tellingly, David does not name the king he is loyal to. Is it Achish, Saul, neither, or both? In any case, Achish sends him away from the battle front with his blessing and David is spared being part of the battle in which Saul and his son Johnathan are both killed (1 Samuel 29). And as a result, David's hands are clean and he ultimately became King of Israel after the death of both Saul and Jonathan in battle at the hands of the Philistines (1 Samuel 31).

As king, David (2 Samuel 6:12–23) does not show contempt towards the common people as Coriolanus did to the plebeians in Rome. Rather, David danced with the people when the ark is brought into Jerusalem, even though this earned him the contempt of his wife Michal.

The stressor for David is forced exile from his country, but his flexibility of character provides a buffer of invulnerability.

A contrast of these two narratives is presented in table 7.1. The common stressor is the experience of being exiled. However, David demonstrates a flexible personality structure, reducing his vulnerability while Coriolanus is rigid to a fault, leaving him vulnerable.

Consider the following cases which illustrate well the *Coriolanus Syndrome*. The following two cases do not deal with refugees per se, but they illustrate well the *Coriolanus Syndrome* and the *David Intervention* with regard to the above issue.

Case 7a. Ken: Male Coriolanus Syndrome (Dr. K)

Ken, a divorced male with a son, was 39 years old when he entered therapy with me (*Dr. K*). His presenting symptom was inability to get along with others at a prestigious interior design firm. Ken was artistically very creative, extremely honest, and strongly principled and had brought the firm considerable business through his innovative approaches. Nevertheless, colleagues typically shied away from him. They seemed to find Ken inflexible, intolerant of criticism, and critical to a fault. When any of his ideas for the firm, typically far-reaching and innovative, were ignored, Ken exhibited outbursts

Figure 7.2. *David Playing the Harp ahead of the Ark*, Scuola Napoletana (Neapolitan School) (18th century). Artgate Foundazione Cariplo.

of anger, which further alienated others in his firm which tended to provoke greater outbursts of anger on Ken's part, and so on.

In short, Ken became perceived in his firm as a person who could not get along with others. Over the course of therapy, the source of Ken's outbursts became clearer. When he applied for a partnership in his firm, he was turned down, despite his obvious talents. This made matters even worse, and Ken became even more aggressive, resulting in his being asked by the senior partners to leave the firm.

Enraged, Ken joined a competitive firm with a history of shoddy work and hostile competition with Ken's original firm. Ken quickly rose to the top of the new firm which seemed less concerned about interpersonal relations. He won several contracts for them because people were so impressed with his obvious talents in interior design.

Shortly thereafter, Ken's new firm found itself in fierce competition with his old firm over a contract which had the capacity to "make or break" Ken's original firm. Though Ken might well have been excused from this conflictual situation, he engaged in it with a relish and led a vicious attack on his original firm, besmirching them in a much-exaggerated fashion. One day, one of Ken's only friends from his original firm came to him and told him

Table 7.1. David against Coriolanus

Stage	Coriolanus	David
1. Precipitating Stressor	Coriolanus, a Roman military hero, antagonizes his countrymen and is exiled from Rome.	David, a military hero in Israel, flees from Israel to escape Saul's murderous jealousy and wrath.
2. Reaction	Coriolanus joins with the Volsces, the enemy of Rome.	David joins with the Philistines, the enemy of Israel.
3. Response of Others	The Romans fear Coriolanus will lead the Volsces in battle against Rome. His mother, his wife, and his children come to him to try to dissuade him.	David attacks common enemies of Israel and the Philistines.
4. Effect	Coriolanus stops the Volsces from attacking Rome but remains condescending, provocative, and insulting to the Volsces and is subsequently killed by them.	David is spared fighting against the Israelites and is thus able to remain loyal both to King Achish of the Philistines and to Israel. David becomes King of Israel after Saul's death.

that he (the friend) would lose his job and begged him not to act in such a vicious manner.

At first, Ken disregarded his friend's plea, but ultimately was moved in his words "on principle," and unilaterally withdrew the proposal of his new firm from consideration. He was immediately fired by his new firm and was not rehired by his old firm, is presently without a job, and has become quite despondent and embittered, drinking heavily and stating specifically that people are without any courage or moral principle and are not worth anything, and that "leaving this world" would represent a welcome escape from people's hypocrisy. Tellingly, though his father lives in the same city as Ken, he seldom has any contact with him.

Dr. K's David Intervention

I (*Dr. K*) became quite concerned over Ken's suicidal thoughts. I immediately tried to determine if he had an actual plan or was just venting his frustrations. The latter seemed to be the case, but still he needed to be watched. I immediately focused on Ken's rigidity and harshness that seemed to ruin everything for him. I complimented Ken for his sense of principle but attempted to show him that his rigid adherence to it made him act precipitously and harshly in a way that antagonized people he encountered; that he seemed unable to relate to them as human beings.

Ken was highly resistant at first, stressing that people around him were weak, without backbone, and hypocritical. I acknowledged he was very creative in interior design, but asked why he felt that he could not be more lyrical and creative in dealing with people. As therapy proceeded, it became increasingly clear that when Ken was growing up, he felt that his father had wanted Ken to play competitive sports in high school, especially football.

Ken reported that he had no interest in playing football and chose to join the high school band instead, where he played the clarinet. Ken reported his mother was very supportive but his father did not seem very proud of this, and several times he smirked to a friend within Ken's earshot about "Ken being on the sissy's football team."

Ken's mother supported him to some extent, but her support made him feel infantilized and girlish. Ken reported that his father's comments hurt him very much, and that he vowed not to act "girlish" when he went out on his own. Ken reported he felt inadequate in his marriage and had serious questions about his masculinity. On the one hand, he scoffed at the macho male image; on the other, he did not have full confidence in his own, more artistic temperament.

My therapeutic approach was to use the "David story" to try to show Ken a softer, more flexible way to assert himself. His talent as an interior designer was evident. And Ken's creativity was manifest. Yet he was terribly rigid in his interpersonal dealings. I suggested this rigidity represented a distorted masculinity, rather than a healthy manifestation of self-assertiveness and strength. Ken began to "loosen up" in his interpersonal relationships and found a position in a more boutique interior design firm in another city. I lost contact with Ken at this time, but some six months later, I received a holiday card from Ken on which he wrote that he had begun dating someone seriously. In this letter, he mentioned how relieved he was to get away from his father.

Now consider a second case, Kristen, illustrating the *Coriolanus Syndrome*.

Case 7b. Kristen: Female Coriolanus Syndrome (Dr. P)

Kristen was a 13-year-old girl from an upper middle class neighborhood who seemed a few years more mature than her chronological age would indicate, and who, upon meeting her therapist for the first time, flatly exclaimed that, "I don't need to be here; this is complete bullshit." Despite her initial protests, Kristen agreed to discuss why her parents brought her to see me (*Dr. P*) explaining that her parents were concerned that she had fallen in with a "bad" crowd of girls. Kristen admitted that she had recently left the social clique that had composed most of her friends through elementary and middle school in favor of running with the more popular girls. This social switching happened relatively abruptly, and it reached a tipping point when Kristen's new group of friends plotted to plaster with eggs the house of one of Kristen's former friends. Although Kristen went along with these plans, she decided not to actively participate but denied feeling too much remorse for the actions of those friends with whom she currently associates.

When asked about her view of her "former friends," Kristen shared that they lacked class, and were not very attractive people. When asked whether she would ever do something to hurt or embarrass her former friends she responded with an underwhelming: "hmmmm . . . probably not." However, Kristen did not seem to be very satisfied with her newer group of friends either. She described one person as having terrible manners, another being too short, and a third not being as smart as she thought she was. It began to seem no group of friends would satisfy Kristen, nor would she show much loyalty to any such group.

Dr. P's David Intervention

After Kristen developed a good measure of trust in the therapeutic relationship, much of her treatment focused on issues relating to her identity and personal values which, understandably, where all rather fluid since she was only a young adolescent. Nevertheless, Kristen was able to gain a much-needed perspective on her choices and actions, and eventually decided to work on salvaging many of the important friendships that she had been quick to distance herself from only a few months earlier. Kristen realized that her social allegiances carried great weight in shaping the person whom she desired to become, which when explored in greater detail, helped her in articulating and identified what she valued the most and how she was seduced away from the loyalty and friendship that she had enjoyed since childhood.

Responding to the *David Intervention*, Kristen's self-esteem as well as her cognitive flexibility and social problem-solving skills improved and she became able to shed her previous rigid style and capitalize on the hope that she achieved through therapy, consequently avoiding draconian social ultimatums with her peers. Although Kristen was unable to regain the trust of all her previous friends, she nevertheless enjoyed a good measure of social success by exhibiting an admirable degree of loyalty towards her new friends, supporting them when they needed support, comforting them when they needed comfort, and standing up for them when they needed an advocate.

LIFE LESSON

We end this chapter with an explication of the following life lesson. We must offer a way of expressing strength and integrity that is not rigid. A person may show integrity in a friendly non-aggressive manner. One can show strength in a non-hostile manner. In short, one can disagree without being disagreeable. Patient Ken learns this lesson the hard way, after suffering a number of rebuffs at work. Patient Kristen also learns this lesson with regard to her relationships with friends.

NOTE

1. Livy in his history of Rome tells of another report that Coriolanus in fact lived on for many years and endured the miseries of exile.

Chapter Eight

Jonah against Narcissus

Becoming Oneself with Others

Narcissus had played with her affections, treating her as he had previously treated other spirits of the waters and the woods, and his male admirers, too. Then one of those he had scorned raised up his hands to heaven and prayed; "May he himself fall in love with another as we have done with him! May he too be unable to gain his loved one!" Nemesis heard and granted his righteous prayer. He was enchanted by the beautiful reflection (of himself) that he saw. . . Alas, I am myself the boy I see. (Ovid, *Metamorphoses*, 3: 366–475)

"Woe is me for the boy I loved in vain" and the spot re-echoed the same words. When he said his last farewell. "Farewell!" said Echo too. (Ovid, *Metamorphoses*, 3: 407–502)

Nothing seemed to have any meaning to the Greek unless it included the defeat of another. (Slater, 1968, *The Glory of Hera*, 36)[1]

Now the word of the LORD came onto Jonah, the son of Amitai, saying: "Arise, go to Nineveh, that great city and proclaim against it: for their wickedness is come up before me." But Jonah rose to flee unto Tarshish from the presence of the Lord . . . and found a ship going to Tarshish. . . But the LORD hurled a great wind into the sea, so that the ship was likely to be broken. . . . And the mariners were afraid. . . . So they took up Jonah, and cast him forth into the sea; and the sea ceased from raging. . . . And the Lord had prepared a great fish to swallow up Jonah. . . . Then Jonah prayed unto the Lord his God out of the fish's belly . . . and the Lord spake unto the fish, and it vomited out Jonah upon the dry land. (Jonah 1–2)

"If I am not for myself, who will be for me? If I am only for myself, what am I? If not now, when?" (BT, Avot 1:14)

Greek thought sees self and other as fundamentally opposed. One wins at the expense of another losing. In fact, almost all of Greek life was seen as a competition. Finley (1959, 128–129) argued that this sense of competition was extended from simply physical prowess to all areas of life. Huizinga (1955, 73) argued that nothing seemed to have meaning to the Greek unless it involved defeat of another. In a brilliant book, Gouldner (1965, 52–57) emphasizes the Greek contest system as a zero-sum game; simply a redistribution of assets without any increase in their total.

The Apollonian side of Greek culture relies totally on a walled-off and disengaged intellect. The Dionysiac side of Greek culture portrays an enmeshment which destroys individual boundaries. Narcissus is unable to integrate self and other, and ultimately kills himself. The biblical world, in contrast, does not see self and other in contradiction. Jonah does learn to express his own personality in his relationship with others and overcomes his suicidal impulses. As Rabbi Hillel taught, "If I am not for myself, who will be for me. If I am only for myself, what am I?" (BT, Avot 1:14).

The inability to integrate sense of self with needs of others is a potentially dangerous stressor and is common to both Jonah and Narcissus. However, Narcissus, emerging from a culture that views everything as a contest, is unable to resolve this conflict, leaving him vulnerable to suicide. Jonah in contrast, is reflective of a culture that does not view self and other as contradictory, thus reducing his vulnerability to any self-destructive behavior.

THE NARCISSUS SYNDROME

Sigmund Freud developed the term "narcissism" in his seminal 1914 published work (Freud, 1914). The term "narcissistic" is usually used to describe a person who is very self-involved and cannot truly relate to others. In other words, narcissism usually is used to refer to someone who is full of oneself. However, examination of the story of Narcissus illustrates a far more complex, fascinating, and lethal pattern.

The earliest sources of the myth of Narcissus have long since been lost. Our most complete account from antiquity is in Ovid's *Metamorphoses* (c. 43 B.C.E. to 17 C.E.). The broad outlines of the story are simple to recount. Narcissus is born out of a rape of his mother Lirope by a river god. When his mother enquires from the Greek seer Tiresias about whether her son will live to a ripe old age, she receives a strange answer: "He (Narcissus) will live a long life as long as he doesn't come to know himself" (*Metamorphoses*, 3: 343–50).

Narcissus grows to be a vain young man, so physically beautiful that many fall in love with him by simply looking at him (*Metamorphoses*, 3: 359–78). Narcissus seems to be completely self-absorbed, treating his lovers of both sexes as mere extensions or *mirrors* of himself. Echo, the nymph who loves Narcissus in vain, is transformed, left merely repeating the words he says—as an *echo* (*Metamorphoses*, 3: 379–82). One would-be lover who feels scorned prays to the god of fate, Nemesis, and asks that Narcissus too fall hopelessly in love and be unable to achieve his desire (*Metamorphoses*, 3: 405–6). Soon, Narcissus sees a beautiful youth in a brook, not realizing it is his own reflection. Narcissus is obsessed with the image in the brook, and looks at it night and day (*Metamorphoses*, 3: 414–454).

Ultimately, however, Narcissus recognizes the face in the brook is his (3: 463–73). The reflection becomes simultaneously an ideal and a mirror (see Kohut, 1971, and his distinction between *mirroring* and *idealizing* narcissism [2]). He is not self-invested, but self-empty, driven to grasp his self, which has now been projected onto the outside world. Such a psychotic juxtaposition rips Narcissus apart. As Ovid expressed it, "How I wish I could separate myself from my body" (*Metamorphoses* 3: 470–71). Narcissus finally becomes aware of the unobtainability of the figure he sees in the pond- it is his own reflection. He pines away until he dies, mourning the youth he loves in vain. "'Woe is me for the boy I loved in vain' and the spot re-echoed the same words, When he said his last farewell, 'Farewell!' said Echo too" (*Metamorphoses*, 3, 497–502). Conon goes further, actually portraying Narcissus as actively stabbing himself to death (Conon, *Narrationes*, 24).

The suicidogenic element in the myth of Narcissus is the inability of Narcissus to successfully integrate his individuation and attachment behaviors. First, he is individuated at the expense of attachment (i.e., egoistic); then he is attached at the expense of individuation (i.e., altruistic). Finally, he is overwhelmed by the irreconcilable confusion between his individuation and attachment issues (i.e., anomic) and resolves the conflict through self-murder. Narcissus represents the extreme example of the inability to integrate one's personal self and one's social self. One can only be obtained at the expense of the other. Narcissus cannot be said to show any sort of healthy development, simply cycling back and forth, and finally self-destructing. Much of this pattern of course, is present throughout Greek tragedy. The myth of Narcissus simply presents this dilemma in its most graphic, elemental, and lethal form.

The stressor for Narcissus is his experience of not being able to possess the object of his love (himself) and a disconnect between self and other. His vulnerability lies in his inability to grow, and thus to come to know himself.

THE JONAH INTERVENTION

The story of Jonah begins with Jonah placed in an essentially similar individuation-attachment dilemma to that of Narcissus. God calls on Jonah to go to

Figure 8.1. *Echo and Narcissus*, **John William Waterhouse (1903). Image courtesy of the Art Renewal Center® www.artrenewal.org.**

Nineveh to warn the people to repent of their wickedness. Jonah does not want to go, but he is too God-fearing to defy the command. On the other hand, Jonah is too strong-willed to submit. In desperation, Jonah boards a ship to flee to Tarshish to run away from this individuation-attachment dilemma, and hides from God in the innermost part of the ship and falls deeply asleep. However, God sends a great storm after Jonah and the ship is in danger of being broken apart and capsizing.

Jonah continues to sleep throughout this calamitous situation until he is angrily awakened by the shipmaster who demands to know Jonah's identity, which Jonah in fact has been fleeing from. His shipmates cast lots to determine the cause of the storm, and the lot falls on Jonah. Only now, upon being questioned, does Jonah reveal his identity as a Hebrew, and admits that he has fled from the Lord. And only now, in response to his shipmate's questioning of how to bring calm, does Jonah advise them to throw him overboard to bring calm, which they do (Jonah 1:1–12).

The story could thus end in Jonah's drowning, which, if he died, could be looked at as a voluntary though belated altruistic suicide—he finally admits that his running away from God's command to go to Nineveh was the cause of the storm, and tells his shipmates to throw him overboard to save themselves. However, God does not want Jonah to die, and prepares a great fish to swallow up Jonah and protect him as a loving parent until he can recover his sense of self. Jonah prays to God from the safety of the belly of the fish until he becomes stronger. Unlike Narcissus, he comes to "know himself." Only then does the fish vomit him out on dry land (Jonah 2).

This same pattern repeats itself. God again asks Jonah to go to Nineveh. This time Jonah goes and gives the people God's message. They repent and are saved (Jonah 3:1–10). Jonah becomes angry and again expresses the wish to die and leaves the city to sit on its outskirts (Jonah 4:1–3). Again, God intervenes, sheltering Jonah with a leafy bush from the burning sun (Jonah 4:6).

After a worm destroys the protective bush, Jonah once again expresses suicidal thoughts (Jonah 4:7–8). God once again intervenes, this time engaging Jonah in a mature dialogue to teach him the message of *teshuvah*, repentance or return and divine mercy and that he can reach out to another without losing himself (Jonah 4:9–11). As Jonah is strengthened in his identity, he is able to show more compassion to others, and not feel he will be swallowed up in their quicksand.

In other words, biblical thinking sees self and other in complementary harmony. Jonah avoids both the polarities of disengagement and enmeshment. In the words of the biblical sage, Hillel, "If I am not for myself, who will be for me? If I am only for myself only, what am I? If not now, when?" (Avot 1:14). As Jonah becomes more himself, he is able to give more fully to others (see Kaplan, 1998a).

The stressor for Jonah is being commanded to do something he does not agree with, but his ability to grow and mature enables him to become less vulnerable.

A contrast of these two narratives is presented in table 8.1. The common stressor is the experience of conflict between self-desires and demands of others. However, Jonah demonstrates a humility in his world view and an openness to change, reducing his vulnerability. Narcissus, in contrast, is hampered by a culture viewing everything as a contest, leaving him vulnerable to suicide.

In the process of developing a workable approach to therapy with *Patient Narcissus*, we will develop the lessons of the positive way in which Jonah is treated in contrast to the way in which Narcissus remains untreated. Let us first present the case of Robert.

Case 8a. Robert: Male Narcissus Syndrome (Dr. P)

Robert was a 31-year-old junior marketing executive and a former college athlete who described himself as "very extroverted" and "super casual." Robert initially sought-out psychotherapy services because he had been dating Gail for a little over a year and was beginning to feel pressure from both his girlfriend and his family to settle down and get married. Although Robert loved his girlfriend and expected to eventually propose to her, he didn't feel

Figure 8.2. *Jonah Leaving the Whale*, **Pieter Lastman (1621). Museum Kunstpalast—Walter Klein/ARTOTHEK.**

that he was yet "ready," so to speak, to get married because he had always envisioned himself having attained a specific level of financial success before getting married. In fact, Robert felt that getting married to Gail would slow him down and be a detriment to his personal advancement. Consequently, Robert broke up with her and began to play the field, engaging in a number of unsatisfactory short term relationships. He became infatuated with a model he had met on a singles' cruise and showered her with gifts. However, his feelings were totally unrequited and he was quite miserable.

Simultaneously, Robert had been struggling to find his vocational niche, hopping from one job to the next in hopes that he would eventually find a position where his talents could be fully expressed and where he could subsequently build the foundation for a good career. Robert's sense of identity was still strongly linked to his role as a college athlete—an accomplishment that was hard fought; however, unfortunately his prowess on the field was not matched by his success in business. This led to profound despair and an impoverished sense of hope about his future. Perhaps Robert's previous successes had interfered with his ability to update his sense of self to extend beyond that of an aspiring professional athlete. In essence, he "peaked" in his early twenties and had been trying to recapture the glory of his youth while the rest of the world moved on without him.

Table 8.1.   Jonah against Narcissus

Stage	Narcissus	Jonah
1. Precipitating Stressor	Narcissus is born of a rape of his mother. He is prophesied to have a long life as long as "he does not come to know himself." In other words, Narcissus cannot know his identity.	God asks Jonah to go and warn the wicked people of Nineveh to repent lest they avoid great punishment. Jonah does not want to go and tries to flee on a ship to Tarshish to avoid the conflict.
2. Reaction	The beautiful Narcissus heartlessly exhibits *hubris* by rejecting would be lovers of both genders.	God sends a great storm after Jonah but he initially hides until confronted by the shipmaster demanding to know his identity. Only after a lot falls on him does Jonah admit that he is the cause of the storm, and altruistically advises his shipmates to throw him overboard to save the ship. However, rather than let him drown, God sends a big fish to swallow Jonah and protect him, and allow him to recover his strength, and grow and come to "know himself."
3. Response of Others	Narcissus is brought down by *Nemesis* and becomes completely infatuated with a face he encounters in a brook.	After the fish vomits out the restored Jonah unto dry land, God again asks him to go to Nineveh to warn its inhabitants to repent and change their ways. This time Jonah goes.
4. Effect	Narcissus realizes the face in the brook is his, and thus unobtainable. He is without an identity that self-knowledge makes possible. He commits suicide, either in a passive (pining away) or active (stabbing himself) manner, depending on the source. Narcissus continuously looks to the outside world for his own missing identity. Yet, per prophesy, if he finds it, he will die.	Jonah warns the people of Nineveh but becomes suicidal again and sits outside the city walls under a hot sun. God again protects Jonah through shielding him from the sun with a large gourd. Ultimately God removes the gourd, and in addressing Jonah's complaint, strengthens Jonah's identity and teaches him the lesson of mercy and compassion—and that reaching out to others does not mean that he must lose himself.

Dr. P's Jonah Intervention

Much of Robert's treatment focused on the need to both mourn an ideal self-image that had not followed the trajectory that he had forged in his mind while he was in college. Assisting Robert identify and appreciate the man that he had become rather than the man that had hoped he would be represented a formidable task in therapy, one for which Robert—to his credit—was fully engaged in.

Robert became more comfortable being himself, accepting some poor life choices that he had made after finishing college and also, and more importantly, acknowledging the many character strengths and other positive attributes that have led him to a place in his life where he was on the precipice of marrying a lovely young lady and beginning a family, regardless of whether he had yet become partner in his firm or whatever other arbitrary financial benchmarks he had made for himself.

As his treatment continued, Robert became more confident in himself—the evolving self that he had become and continued to refine. He became open to new experiences, less self-conscious about his financial situation (which objectively could have been considered firmly middle-class). Robert was able to get over his unrequited infatuation and reconnect with Gale. He subsequently decided to "take the plunge" and become engaged to her. At the conclusion of treatment Robert had achieved a greater sense of inner congruence with his sense of self and his life choices, and he reported feeling a greater sense of personal fulfillment and hope about his future.

Case 8b. Nina: Female Narcissus Syndrome (Dr. K)

This second case involved a beautiful woman named Nina who was a moderately successful abstract painter. She came into therapy sobbing that she was "crazy in love" with another woman painter Dana, who Nina felt was "just like her" but who did not even seem "to know that she was alive." Nina sobbed that all her advances were rebuffed, and that each time, she tried to approach Dana, Dana would withdraw. When Nina withdrew, Dana seemed to come back into the picture. This pattern was paralyzing Nina who reported she felt like dying.

Nina revealed that she had had been married unsuccessfully two times and that neither marriage lasted. She admitted that she had not loved either husband though she felt that each was "crazy about her." She did not have children nor had she wanted them. She reported becoming increasingly restless, bored, and unfulfilled in the marriages and unable to express her true self. Nina reported feeling relieved when both marriages ended, though both husbands seemed to take the break-ups very much to heart. She reported that her second husband loved her most deeply, and begged her to stay. He seemed resigned to a loveless and sexless marriage with her as long as he could be with her. Nina expressed contempt for such weakness, and the more he begged her to stay, the more determined she was to leave.

After the dissolution of her second marriage, Nina embarked on a number of short-lived affairs, including one with a woman (Nina now identified herself as bisexual), but she left every one precipitously, reporting that at least several of these people were deeply hurt and one expressed the wish that she, Nina, also experience unrequited love. Now the tables were turned and Nina herself was hopelessly infatuated.

Dr. K's Jonah Intervention

Over the course of therapy, Nina revealed that she had been adopted and had been unable to find out the identity of her natural mother or father. Her adopted parents were now dead, and their surviving friends tried to dissuade Nina from her search for her biological parents. But Nina felt lost, reported not knowing who she was, and moreover felt trapped by her infatuation with Dana, and kept repeating that she wanted to die.

We attempted to treat Nina with lessons derived from the *Jonah Intervention* to enable Nina to express who she was in a relationship without the stark alternatives of heartless rejection or mindless infatuation. Doing this, we felt, required that Nina come to know who she was and thus avoid the trap Narcissus found himself in. We encouraged Nina to not be swayed by her relatives' advice, and begin to find out who her biological parents were, and who she was, and the story of her adoption.

As therapy proceeded, Nina did establish contact with her birth mother, and wrote her. It took some time for her mother to answer, and Nina felt she was wasting her time. But eventually, Nina's mother did respond. She lived in a nearby state. The two began to make plans for a meeting which took place at a neutral site, midway between their two homes.

Nina came back to therapy after the meeting and began to cry. Although she naturally had a host of conflicting feelings, including why her birth-mother put her up for adoption to begin with, she began to see her mother's situation in a fuller context—her mother was unmarried and struggling to make a living and find her own way in life. Nina began to forgive her mother and learn more about herself and a family she never knew she had. As a result, Nina's unrequited infatuation with Dana began to naturally dissipate.

LIFE LESSON

We end this chapter with an explication of the following life lesson. We must encourage lost people to find out more about themselves and to show them a means and method of integrating self and other. In other words, we must guide our patients to connect to others in a healthy way, without losing themselves in the process. We must present a model to such people of how to help others in a self-expressive way which does not involve "losing oneself," but in fact "finding oneself." Otherwise, a person may cycle in a borderline fashion between destructive and lethal polarities, destroying relationships in an attempt to find freedom and denying oneself in an attempt to find love and meaning in life. A healthy person needs to learn to love another as a defined self and not as a stick-figure, but as a whole living vital personality (Kaplan, 1988; 1990b; 1998a; 1998c; Kaplan and O'Connor, 1993; Kaplan and Worth, 1993). Patient Robert learns he can form a close relationship without losing himself. Patient Nina learns to forgive her mother and thus becomes less rejecting to people who care about her.

NOTES

1. The authors would again like to thank Ms. Dashka Slater for permission to use the quote taken from her father's (Philip Slater's) publication "The Glory of Hera."

2. For Kohut (1971), unlike Freud, narcissism is defined not by the target of the instinctual investment (i.e., whether it is the subject himself or other people) but by the "nature or quality of the instinctual charge" (p. 26). Therefore, Kohut sees an idealizing configuration whereby one invests his energy in the "omnipotent other" as narcissistic, as is the withdrawal of psychic energy inward into the "grandiose self" (i.e., the mirroring configuration). The intent behind the idealizing position is as inherently self-serving (you are perfect, but I am part of you) as is that behind the mirroring position (I am perfect). Narcissus cycles between Kohut's mirroring and idealizing narcissistic positions and ultimately commits suicide.

Chapter Nine

Moses against Oedipus

Constructively Obtaining and Accepting Help in One's Life Mission

O wealth, and empire, and skill surpassing skill in life's keen rivalries, how great is the envy that cleaves to you (Teiresias), if for the sake, yea, of this power which the city hath put into my hands, a gift unsought, Creon the trusty, Creon mine old friend, hath crept on me by stealth, yearning to thrust me out of it, and hath suborned such a scheming juggle as this, a tricky quack who has eyes only for his gains, but in his art is blind! . . . And it is I whom thou art trying to oust, thinking to stand close to Creon's throne. Methinks thou and the plotter of these things will rue your zeal to purge the land. Nay, didst thou not seem to be an old man, thou shoudst have learned to thy cost how bold thou art. (Sophocles, *Oedipus Rex*, ll. 380–97)

I (Moses) am not able to bear all these people myself alone because it is too heavy for me. . . . And the Lord said unto Moses: "Gather unto Me seventy men of the elders of Israel, whom thou knowest to be the elders of the people, and officers over them; and bring them unto the tent of meeting, that they may stand there with thee. And I will come down and speak with thee there: and I will take of the spirit which is upon thee, and will put it upon them, and they shall bear the burden of the people with thee, that thou bear it not thyself alone." (Numbers 11:14–17)

We focus in this chapter on Oedipus acting alone in trying to uncover the reason behind the plague infesting Thebes. And we compare this with the story of Moses. Both are sent away from their natural parents at birth, but with different intent: Oedipus to die and Moses to live. Yet both are saved: Oedipus is adopted by King Polybus of Corinth, and Moses comes to live in the palace of Pharaoh in Egypt. But this is where the similarity ends. Oedipus ultimately behaves like an unwanted child, while Moses does not. Oedipus finds it very difficult, if not impossible to solicit, trust, and accept aid from others, while Moses is able to do so. Throughout his life, Oedipus is confronted with misleading oracles, maddening riddles, and incomplete entrapping information. Moses is portrayed as receiving a direct message from God.

The experience of being expelled as an infant from one's parental home can be lethal. This is a stressor shared by Moses and Oedipus, both being sent away from their parental home as infants. However, Moses has a social support system lessening his vulnerability, and he thrives. Oedipus, in contrast, lacks this support, indeed is done in by it, and remains vulnerable, misled into patricide, incest, and ultimate self-blinding.

THE OEDIPUS SYNDROME

Our contemporary understanding of Oedipus has been so shaped, indeed somewhat misshaped, by Freud's postulation of the *oedipus complex* (Freud, 1923a, 1924) that we reflexively think of Oedipus as a man who knowingly killed his father to possess his mother. Indeed, that he was motivated to do so. However, close examination of Sophocles' play *Oedipus Rex*, suggests that it represents a serious misreading of the story of Oedipus.[1] In fact Oedipus seems to be doing everything possible to avoid this fate, but is done in by being surrounded by figures who taunt and entrap him with misleading riddling information, rather than give him usable information in a clear manner. Perhaps his earliest experience as an unwanted child (however unconscious) leaves him unable to trust.

Sophocles' version of the story begins as follows. Laius, King of Thebes, hears from an oracle that his newborn son Oedipus will murder him and marry his wife Jocasta when he grows up. Laius orders Jocasta to pierce the infant's ankles (Oedipus meaning "swollen foot") and give him to their servant to abandon in the fields to die. However the servant takes pity on the infant and gives him to the herdsman in the adjoining pasture, who saves Oedipus and takes him to the childless King Polybus and Queen Leirope of Corinth where he is raised. As a young man, he hears his identity questioned by a drunk at a dinner party that they are not his natural parents. He becomes insecure and goes to his Polybus and Meirope to ask them if what he has heard is true. They deny it, angrily, but Oedipus does not seem to fully believe them and goes to the Oracle of Delphi (The Pythia) to try to confirm what they are saying.

The Oracle maddeningly does not answer his question as to the identity of his biological parents (who's my mama, who's my papa?) but instead warns Oedipus that he is destined to kill his father and marry his mother. However, the Oracle withholds the critical information as to the identity of who Oedipus' biological parents are. Oedipus, thinking that Polybus and Meirope are his biological parents, runs away from Corinth to Thebes in order to avoid this terrible prophecy. On a crossing on the road to Thebes (where three roads meet), Oedipus encounters an old man on the road in a coach. The older man attempts to proceed along the road and to clear his path strikes Oedipus on the head with a club knocking him to the ground. Oedipus responds angrily and in the quarrel, kills the older man. The slain man, unbeknownst to Oedipus, turns out to be Laius, Oedipus' biological father. As Oedipus continues on his way, he encounters The Sphinx who is terrorizing the people of Thebes with a vicious riddle, killing those who cannot answer it. Oedipus is able to answer her riddle and the Sphinx plunges to her death. Oedipus continues to Thebes where he is rewarded with the widow of King Laius, Queen Jocasta, in marriage. Oedipus does not realize Jocasta is his natural mother. He begets four children with her (*Oedipus Rex*. ll. 775–834).

Oedipus, seemingly is a kind and responsive ruler, concerned about the plague infesting Thebes, and tries vigorously to find its cause, not realizing it was engendered by his own act of patricide. However, he engages in this search largely alone, his life riddled with misleading, false, and even taunting answers to questions he legitimately raises, by a drunk at a dinner party, his "parents," Polybus and Meirope, and by the taunting prophet Teiresias when he tries to get at the truth, and by entrapping riddles from the Sphinx and the Oracle of Delphi. Moreover, Oedipus does not fully trust his brother-in-law Creon whom he accuses of treason, so he is basically alone in his quest for the source of the plague.

Despite warnings from both Teiresias and his wife-mother Jocasta to desist in his quest, Oedipus plunges compulsively and blindly ahead. His quest ends in the most dreadful destruction for Oedipus and his family. Jocasta hangs herself, Oedipus blinds himself, their two sons, Eteocles and Polyneices kill each other at the Seventh Gate of Thebes, and his daughter Antigone hangs herself before the state could execute her for defying Creon and burying Polyneices who fought against Thebes, by sealing her into a cave. Nowhere does Oedipus receive any real help he can fully trust. He is acting largely alone in his quest to uncover the truth (Sophocles, *Oedipus Rex*; Aeschylus, *The Seven Against Thebes*).

The stressor for Oedipus is his experience of being cast out of his biological parents' home (to be left to die on mountain top) and his vulnerability is his inability to find others he can trust.

THE MOSES INTERVENTION

For Moses also, birth brought danger of death, but from different sources. Moses' life is threatened by Pharaoh's decree to throw all males born among the Israelites into the Nile. Oedipus's life is threatened by his own father, Laius, who perceives his son's life as a threat to his own and therefore orders Oedipus to be killed at birth. Whereas Oedipus is sent out from his natural home in order to be killed, Moses is sent away by his natural family to be saved.

As infants, both Moses and Oedipus end up in the house of a king. But the differences are more telling: King Polybus is a good man who takes in the baby Oedipus, whereas Pharaoh is the villain of the piece. In fact, were it not for Pharaoh's decree, Moses would never have had to be sent away from his parents' home. In the Oedipus narrative, it is Laius himself who orders his son Oedipus killed and causes his infant son's exile to save his life.

Significantly, Moses' biological parents are aware of his whereabouts, and Moses' mother and sister conspire to save the boy's life, and he is raised in the house of Pharaoh himself. Moses' helpers include the two Israelite midwives, Shifrah and Puah, who by attending his mother Jochebed when

Figure 9.1. *Oedipus and the Sphinx*, **Francois-Xavier Fabre (ca. 1806–1808). Image courtesy of the Art Renewal Center® www.artrenewal.org.**

she gives birth to Moses, defy Pharaoh's order at considerable risk to themselves. The network of assistance also includes Miriam who arranges for Jochebed to nurse Moses (Exodus 2:1–10).

Moses is portrayed in a quite different manner than Oedipus. He seems guided by his conscience and circumstances and does not consciously attempt to seek clues about his destiny. From the account of Moses going among his Hebrew "brethren" one can see his latent identification: he kills an Egyptian attacking a Hebrew (Exodus 2:11–12). Moses subsequently chances upon the burning bush and encounters the Hebrew God, who informs him of his mission to save the Children of Israel from Pharaoh. Yet Moses has a speech impediment—he stutters—and is genuinely helped in his mission by his older brother Aaron who does the public speaking for him (Exodus 7). Despite Moses' misgivings as to his own abilities, he does ultimately agree to God's call and leads the Children of Israel out of slavery.

Yet he subsequently does feel overwhelmed by his task and unable to go on, crying to God in his despair:

> Wherefore hast Thou dealt ill with Thy servant? And wherefore have I not found favor in Thy sight, that they layest the burden of all this people on me? Have I conceived all this people? Have I brought them forth, that Thou shouldest say unto me: Carry them in thy bosom, as a nursing-father carrieth the suckling child, unto the land which thou did swear unto their fathers. (Numbers 11:12)

The demands are too great and Moses feels inadequate to the task. He doubts that all the people can be provided for. "Whence should I have flesh to give unto all this people?" (Numbers 11:13, 21–23). Moses blames himself for not being up to the task. "I am not able to bear all these people myself alone because it is too heavy for me" (Numbers 11:14). And then challenging, indeed imploring God to kill him, Moses cries out: "If thou deal thus with me, kill me, I pray Thee, out of hand, if I have found favor in Thy sight; and let me not look upon my wretchedness" (Numbers 11:15). God responds and provides him with the help of seventy people, a Sanhedrin, to share Moses's burden:

> And the Lord said unto Moses: Gather unto Me seventy men of the elders of Israel, whom thou knowest to be the elders of the people, and officers over them; and bring them unto the tent of meeting, that they may stand there with thee. And I will come down and speak with thee there: and I will take of the spirit which is upon thee, and will put it upon them, and they shall bear the burden of the people with thee, that thou bear it not thyself alone." (Numbers 11:16–17)

This intervention overcomes Moses' suicidal despair and allows him to go on. While similar to the previously discussed help received by the prophet Elijah, this comparison involves not so much an antidote to being physically alone, but more as a life-lesson as to the importance of receiving help in pursuing one's life-mission.

The stressor for Moses is his experience of being cast out of his biological parents' home and his; however, his ability to trust others and both seek and accept help from them enables him to reduce his vulnerability and survive, and even thrive. Moses is able to solicit and accept help from Aaron (and others) throughout his journey (see figure 9.2).

A contrast of these two narratives is presented in table 9.1. Being sent away from one's parental home as an infant is a stressor common to Moses and Oedipus. Moses has a social support system lessening his vulnerability, and he thrives. Oedipus, in contrast, lacks this support, indeed is ultimately done in by his inability to know whom to trust.

How can the Moses narrative help us treat *Patient Oedipus*? Given the theme of the Oedipus narrative presented in this chapter, how can we apply the lessons of the positive way that Moses is treated? In other words, how can we alter Oedipus's feeling of lack of support in his life mission and the resultant self-destructive actions such lack of social support engenders? (See the work of Halevy and Kaplan, 1968; Selinger, 1998).

Let us begin with Harry, the first *Oedipus Syndrome* case.

Case 9a. Harry: Male Oedipus Syndrome (Dr. K)

At the time he entered therapy with me (*Dr. K*), Harry, an osteopath in his late 60s who owned a chain of nursing homes in the northern suburbs outside of Detroit, was going through a bankruptcy and a bitter divorce. He came in highly agitated and suicidal. He reported being depressed, but was also quite angry and aggressive. He had threatened legal authorities who had been coming after him, and was generally very antagonistic. He needed to have the last word about everything.

As therapy began, Harry reported he had been raised during "the depression" (the 1930s) by a rejecting and ineffective father for whom he had no respect. He reported feeling that his father resented him for succeeding in school and was terrified that Harry would surpass him, and constantly undercut him. Harry reported his mother as ineffective in keeping his father from belittling him.

Harry reported being a self-made man who had done everything on his own. He had practiced as a physician for several years, and married a girlfriend from his college days whom he reported feeling was "totally ineffective" like his mother. She gave birth to three children. Harry was very dissatisfied with his marriage and could not wait for his children to leave the

Figure 9.2. *Victory O Lord*, John Everett Millais (1871). Manchester Art Gallery.

family home so he could file for divorce. And so he did during a period in which he was doing very well financially. He had opened up a chain of nursing homes, as mentioned above, and married a considerably younger

Table 9.1. Moses against Oedipus

Stage	Oedipus	Moses
1. Precipitating Stressor	Oedipus's mother sends the infant Oedipus away to be exposed on mountain top and die.	Moses' mother sends the infant Moses away to save him from being killed by Pharaoh.
2. Reaction	Oedipus is rescued by a kindly shepherd and raised by the king of a neighboring state, Corinth.	Moses is rescued and raised by the daughter of Pharaoh.
3. Response of Others	Oedipus's identity is questioned and he has no one to talk to. He attempts unsuccessfully to gain usable information from the Oracle of Delphi, who speaks in riddles and entraps Oedipus into patricide and incest.	Moses sees an Egyptian mistreating an Israelite and kills him with a rock. He flees Egypt but God appears to Moses and chooses him to lead the Israelites out of slavery from Egypt. He is helped by a number of people along the way, including his sister, his mother, and Shifrah and Puah.
4. Effect	Oedipus attempts to save Thebes from a plague but is undone by misinformation and riddles from others. This results in Oedipus's self-blinding as well as many killings and suicides of others.	Moses seeks and receives necessary help at various times in his mission (Aaron, a Sanhedrin, etc.) and is able to carry out his mission.

woman who was working for him at one of his homes. Harry was flying high, made a good deal of money, and accrued considerable power. He was subsequently nominated to head an important county-level health department in a Midwestern state. Yet Harry felt he was really alone and did not know whom to trust.

At the zenith of his career, Harry found himself charged with a number of allegations that he had violated a number of requirements regarding poor staffing and unsanitary conditions at one of his nursing homes. Many of his friends, including some with considerable influence, offered to help Harry but he rejected all their help, and accused them of siding with his enemies. Rather than attempt to achieve some conciliatory resolution with the prosecutors, he dug in his heels and made matters worse rather than compromise, leading to his losing his homes and filing for bankruptcy. His appointment to the County position was also scuttled on the grounds that he was not responsible in handling his personal business affairs and could or would not follow basic health standards.

He became angry and abusive and drove his second wife Roberta away when she tried to help him. Roberta reacted bitterly and wrote him a letter which he showed me in which she blamed him for being dishonest with her before they were first married and highly manipulative. In this letter, she reported telling him she wanted children, and accused him of having undergone a vasectomy without informing her of his decision in advance while they were still dating. Harry admitted that this was true, because he was determined not to father any more children. He had already fathered three in his first marriage. When Harry did tell Roberta he had undergone a vasectomy, she was furious but decided to marry him anyhow. However, Harry felt she carried a resentment into the marriage. Specifically, Harry complained that Roberta spent more time with her sister's children than she did with him, which Harry became intensely jealous about. Harry told me that he felt Roberta was more married to her sister than to him. She said she "wanted out" because he was making impossible demands on her.

Shortly after entering treatment, Harry first threatened and then attempted suicide by overdosing, but survived. When he was released from the hospital, he brought in a letter from his son Richard from his first marriage, also a doctor, from whom he was at least partially estranged. His son seemed to question the sincerity of his attempt. Specifically, Richard's note had contained the phrase, "your suicide attempt, if it was one."

Harry seemed more indignant than hurt over this note, and insisted to me that he was a doctor and that he had taken enough pills "to kill three people." Puckishly, I asked: "which three people were you trying to kill?" He responded immediately the names of three people that had led to the charges of violation of nursing home standards. I too had my doubts that his action represented a full suicide attempt rather than a parasuicidal gesture. He was a doctor himself and in all likelihood knew how many pills to swallow, to leave a trace in his blood and yet not run the risk of death or serious complications. Yet medicine is inexact and people can and do die from parasuicidal gestures.

Harry's problem seemed to be that he always felt he was on his own. He felt rejected by his father (as perhaps Oedipus did unconsciously with regard to Laius) and thus was never able to trust anyone, or be sufficiently honest with anyone to allow a real relationship to develop. He had to keep all his doubts to himself, and through a false bravado appeared stronger and more completely self-reliant than he needed to be or indeed could be.

Dr. K's Moses Intervention

My *(Dr. K's)* therapeutic intervention with Harry began with my trying to impress on Harry the impossibility of doing everything on his own. I impressed on him that he was making impossible demands on Roberta. I raised the possibility with Harry that he might be able to repair his relationship with her by acknowledging how badly he had hurt her with the lack of trust he had exhibited to her. He approached Roberta but she was not very receptive.

I suggested they take a trip together and they decided to drive together from Michigan to New Mexico to try to patch things up. However, this plan did not work out very well, the blame for this not all falling on Harry. On the one hand, Roberta complained that Harry was imposing his itinerary on her for the trip. On the other hand, Harry reported that Roberta had showed no sign of taking any initiative at all in planning the trip. The trip ended explosively, with Roberta flying back home alone from Albuquerque, leaving Harry to drive their car back alone. This seemed to be the last straw for both, and Roberta filed for divorce.

Harry was furious and decided to swear off relationships. I pointed out to Harry that his very domineering attitude had inhibited Roberta from helping arrange the trip and indeed participating fully in the marriage. I suggested that Harry did not know how to ask for help. Further, I stressed that his inability to ask for and accept help had been at least partially responsible for the failure of his nursing home empire as well as his marriage. And it didn't seem to endear himself to his son either.

I stressed to Harry that it would be okay to ask for help, and that it would drop his false sense of bravado, he would be better able to make friends that he could trust. That his father's attitudes towards him when he was growing up had fixated him emotionally in not trusting anyone, and thus not being able to reach out.

Harry did not make any more suicide attempts during the time he was seeing me. He took my thoughts to heart and brought in a book. which argued that if your business fails, that did not mean that you have failed as a person. He even worked with me to make a film on forces leading to his crisis, and began to practice medicine again in a limited fashion, despite losing his nursing home empire. Harry was beginning to learn how to solicit and accept help. I have lost touch with Harry over the years, but I am hopeful that this process continued for him and he was able to build back a more balanced and less grandiose life.

Now let us turn to as second case illustrating the *Oedipus Syndrome* and the *Moses Intervention*.

Case 9b. Kelly: Female Oedipus Syndrome (Dr. P)

Kelly was a 25-year-old young lady of Puerto-Rican descent who was adopted shortly after birth, joining two other adopted siblings, all from different families of origin. Although Kelly was raised in an upper-middle-class socioeconomic class with all of the privileges and benefits that go along with that, she paradoxically sought out emotional support from a clinical professional erstwhile staunchly refusing to accept help from family and friends who she acknowledged loving. As a young child Kelly became the primary target of her older brother's rage-filled tantrums, often enduring almost unbearable emotional and physical abuse on a regular basis. She felt alone in dealing with this.

Although Kelly's parents were somewhat aware of this sibling dynamic, they were also mindful of keeping up appearances, and therefore minimized Kelly's experiences and discouraged her from talking about them with others, especially other people who were outside the family. A tipping point was reached when Kelly was in high school and made an attempt on her life, slashing her wrists and ingesting a fistful of prescription medications. Even then, after being psychiatrically hospitalized for suicidality, her parents failed to follow through with meaningful and appropriate after care services. Kelly was left to fend for herself emotionally. The culture of the family was implicitly clear: what happens in the family stays in the family. Compounding this message was the dynamics among the siblings, who had their own private, perhaps even collusive, understanding that nobody could be trusted to look after their best interests except each other. Kelly, therefore, learned to suppress the expression of her sadness and despair and finished high school and college having only developed superficial, stagnant friendships to complement a long series of sexual relationships that left her temporarily satisfied but emotionally unfulfilled. Kelly had become professional artist who specialized in sculpting and who used this creative medium as a way to express her inner pain that she has been carrying around since childhood.

Dr. P's Moses Intervention

Seeking out a psychotherapist at the behest of her eldest brother, Kelly had already made an important first step to take responsibility and secure support for her emotional distress from a qualified professional. Although much of Kelly's treatment focused on her troubled past and the resultant trauma reactions which had been formative in shaping her personality, a competing clinical priority consisted of helping her identify and then utilize those people in her life who were currently in a position to relieve her emotional burden through love, support, and perhaps most importantly of all, acceptance.

As Kelly's treatment continued along the lines of the *Moses Intervention*, she became more comfortable taking advice and counsel from her friends and family around important decisions in her life. The level of trust that Kelly developed with her friends and family served her well as she worked to regulate her mental welfare. She furthermore relied on the love and trust of these confidantes as traversed the vicissitudes of career advancement, and a serious romantic partnership.

LIFE LESSON

We end this chapter with an explication of the following life lesson. We must offer suicidal people a means and method of learning to reach out to others for social support regarding their life mission. Oedipus is a solitary figure when he returns to Thebes. When he is faced with the daunting tasks of first solving the riddle of the Sphinx and, subsequently, of uncovering the source of the plague devastating Thebes, Oedipus is basically acting alone. He does not know whom to believe and trust and whom not to, and pursues a path that ultimately leads to his self-blinding and the death of others close to him. Moses, in contrast has significant help at various points in his life. First, Moses, being a stutterer, has Aaron as a mouthpiece. Secondly, he is presented with a Sanhedrin to help him, when he complains to God that he cannot shoulder the burden of leading the Israelites alone. Patient Harry shows signs of learning to accept help in his less grandiose life. Patient Kelly also seemed to be learning how to accept and utilize help from others.

NOTE

1. There are certainly other characters in Greek mythology that display this pattern. For example, Cronus castrates his father Ouranos on behalf of his mother Gaia. Cronus himself kills many of the offspring he has with his wife Rhea (Hesiod, *Theogony*, ll. 533–615; *Works and Days,* ll. 53–105). Zeus alone is saved through a ruse. These figures have "oedipus complexes." But does Oedipus? The esteemed classicist, E. R. Dodds (1970), insists that the warning of the oracle to Oedipus was unconditional. It did not say, as might the biblical prophet "If you do so-and-so, you will kill your father. But if you do not do it, you won't. The warning "if X, then Y" implies that "if *not* X, then *not* Y." For example, God sends Jonah to warn the people of Nineveh to change their ways to avoid calamity. They do listen to him and change their outcome, at least temporarily. The case of Oedipus is very different. This oracle simply pronounces to Oedipus: "You will kill your father; you will sleep with your mother." In other words, the oracle presents Oedipus with the fatalist doctrine, "Y will occur"—and there is nothing Oedipus can do about it, as hard as he tries, and he does. "There is no X that can prevent Y from occurring."

Chapter Ten

Rebecca against Phaedra

Constructively Dealing with Feelings of Possessiveness toward One's Offspring

Phaedra: What is it they mean when they talk of people being in "love"?
Nurse: At once the sweetest and the bitterest thing, my child.
Phaedra: I shall only find the latter half.
Nurse: Ha! My child, are thou in love?
Phaedra: The Amazon's son, whoever he may be—
Nurse: Means't thou Hippolytus?
Phaedra: Twa's thou, not I that spoke his name. (Euripides, *Hippolytus*, ll. 347–53)

And Rebecca said to Isaac, "I am weary of my life because of the daughters of Heth. If Jacob takes a wife of the daughters of Heth, like these who are the daughters of the land, what good shall my life be to me?" (Genesis 27:46)

And Isaac called Jacob . . . and said unto him: "Thou shalt not take a wife of the daughters of Canaan. Arise. Go to Paddan-aram . . . and take thee a wife from thence of the daughters of Laban, thy mother's brother. (Genesis 28:1–2)

Parents can have strong feelings of possessiveness toward their opposite sex children, stepchildren, and even younger siblings of their partners. Yet these feelings must loosen to allow and even support these younger people to lead their own lives. Phaedra is hopelessly enmeshed with her stepson Hippolytus, and cannot let him lead his own life. When the secret of her hopeless infatuation is revealed, she hangs herself. Rebecca, in contrast, is concerned that her son Jacob will marry a woman from a family she cannot abide and that this provokes her to say that she does not want to live. When her husband Isaac sends Jacob away to marry the daughter of her brother Laban, Rebecca no longer speaks of suicide.

The common stressor is the experience of facing an empty nest. Rebecca is anchored in the biblical idea of family and intergenerational continuity, allowing her to redirect the effects of any vulnerability she may feel with regard to loss into appropriate mothering behavior concerned for the next generation. Phaedra does not have this sense of intergenerational continuity and thus remains vulnerable to depression caused by the loss of her stepson, and kills herself.

The stressor for Phaedra is being rejected by her stepson; her vulnerability is her lack of any sense of parenting (in her case stepparenting) and intergenerational continuity.

THE PHAEDRA SYNDROME

Here we contrast the story of the Greek Phaedra with that of the biblical matriarch, Rebecca. In Euripides' *Hippolytus,* Phaedra, the wife of King Theseus of Athens, is caught in a miserable family situation, and at the same time she has unrealistic expectations of herself. Phaedra suffers under the burden of a family background that rivals that of Oedipus. Her mother had slept with a white bull, her sister had been raped by Dionysus, and she herself is the "third to suffer" (ll. 337–40): "That 'love' has been our curse from time long past" (l. 343). Phaedra struggles to free herself and her children from her family pattern, but she is too enmeshed to succeed and destroys both herself and Hippolytus.

The goddess Aphrodite plots to destroy Hippolytus for living in chastity: she has filled his stepmother, Phaedra, with passion for him. Though Phaedra resists her passion, with great misery to herself, her servant betrays her secret to Hippolytus. She fears most that her passion for Hippolytus will become known and that she will be seen as a traitor to her husband and children. She would rather die: "This it is that calls on me to die, kind friends, that so I may ne'er be found to have disgraced my lord, or the children I have borne" (ll. 426–27). Phaedra hangs herself (ll. 776–79), leaving behind a note that falsely accuses Hippolytus of raping her (ll. 882–98). Theseus believes the note and pronounces a curse of death on his son. The curse is soon fulfilled—Hippolytus is torn apart by the horses pulling his chariot running amuck (ll. 1170–1256)—and the truth of his innocence is revealed too late.

Phaedra mixes an exaggerated sense of honor and guilt with a tendency toward self punishment: "My hands are pure, but on my soul there rests stain" (l. 317). She must hide her passion to save her honor: "Alas for thee! My sorrows, shouldn't thou learn they would recoil on thee" (l. 327)—even if it means suicide: "Out of shame I am planning an honorable escape" (l.

331). The nurse accuses her of trying to be better than the gods: "O cease, my darling child, from evil thoughts, let wanton pride be gone, for this is naught else, this wish to rival gods in perfectness" (ll. 474–75). There is no stopper in Phaedra's rush toward suicide. She is too overwrought to remain silent, Aphrodite works against her, and her nurse betrays her by spilling the secret of her passion to Hippolytus.

When discretion and good sense fail, death seems to be the only cure: "And last when I could not succeed in mastering love hereby, me thought it best to die; and none can gainsay my purpose" (l. 397). As she expresses it with finality, "I know only one way, one cure for these my woes, and that is instant death" (l. 599).

Phaedra's punitive conscience is accompanied by low self-esteem engendered by her fears of misogyny and her unhappiness and helplessness at being a woman. This view is echoed by the chorus and by Hippolytus, who delivers a particularly sharp attack on women. Women are vile and filthy: "I can never satisfy my hate for women, no! Not even though some say this is ever my theme, for of a truth they always are evil. So, either let someone prove them chaste, or let me still trample on them forever" (ll. 665–67).[1]

In his last breath, Hippolytus also laments that he is bound by a miserable family past that cannot be expiated: there is neither repentance nor forgiveness. The gods remain unhelpful to the end. Hippolytus is special to Artemis, but she cannot help him in his final pains. She leaves before his death, the sight of which would be a pollution to her: "And now farewell! Tis not for me to gaze upon the dead, or pollute my sight with death scenes, and e'en now I see thee nigh that evil" (ll. 1432–33).

Phaedra lives in a world in which her gods and her family have been at best uncaring, in which her individuality and womanhood are despised, and in which error cannot be corrected. Caught in a conflict between the goddesses Aphrodite and Artemis, Phaedra sees no way out but suicide. The revealing of Phaedra's passion for her stepson leads to her suicide and his death.

THE REBECCA INTERVENTION

The story of the biblical matriarch Rebecca is very different. After orchestrating the deception by which Jacob has received Isaac's blessing, Rebecca tells Jacob to go away to her brother Laban, so that he won't be killed by his brother Esau who feels that Jacob has stolen his father's blessing that rightly belongs to him (Genesis 27:42–45). But as can be seen in the next passage, Rebecca's request is motivated by a second perhaps even more pressing concern. Rebecca tells Isaac that her life has been made miserable by Esau's Hittite wives, and she worries that Jacob may similarly marry a daughter of Heth, the Cannanite:

Figure 10.1. *Phaedra*, **Alexandre Cabanel (1880). Image courtesy of the Art Renewal Center® www.artrenewal.org.**

And Rebecca said to Isaac, "I am weary of my life because of the daughters of Heth. If Jacob takes a wife of the daughters of Heth, like these who are the daughters of the land, what good shall my life be to me?" (Genesis 27:46)

Although this has been read as a "suicidal ideation" narrative, such an interpretation may be somewhat overdrawn. Rebecca's words seem more like a message to her husband: "Please fix this situation because I can't stand it!" In any case, the tactic works, and Isaac commands Jacob to not marry one of the daughters of Canaan, who are so offensive to Rebecca and instead tells him to go to Laban and marry one of his daughters. Rebecca is relieved, and there is no more mention of her "suicidal" musings (Genesis 28:1–4). Rebecca is not being seductive towards her son, nor is she trying to block him from living his own life. What she wants is that Jacob marry a suitable partner. When Isaac listens to her, Rebecca's suicidal impulse is resolved.

The stressor for Rebecca is being frightened that her son will choose an unsympathetic and hostile mate; however, her maternal sense of responsibility in helping him find a suitable mate overcomes her sense of loss, and mitigates against any vulnerability.

A contrast of these two narratives is presented in table 10.1. The common stressor is the experience of facing an empty nest. Rebecca is anchored in the

Figure 10.2. *Rebecca and Eliezer*, Bartolome Eseban Murillo (1650). Image courtesy of the Art Renewal Center® www.artrenewal.org.

biblical idea of family and intergenerational continuity and moves into the role of choosing an appropriate wife for her son Jacob. Phaedra does not have this sense of intergenerational continuity and thus remains vulnerable to depression caused by the rejection and loss of her stepson, and kills herself.

How does the Rebecca story help us treat Patient Phaedra? In other words, how can we alter Patient Phaedra's pathological need to seduce and enmesh her son, and triangulate her family situation, playing him off against her husband?

Consider first Gary, the first case exhibiting the *Phaedra Syndrome*.

Case 10a. Gary: Male Phaedra Syndrome (Dr. P)

Gary is a 52-year-old Caucasian real estate broker who came into my office. He had been married to his wife, Beth, for 10 years. Although Gary would likely characterize his marriage as "happy," he has never felt the sense of romantic reverie that is so often portrayed in the movies. For as long as Gary has known Beth, he had been smitten with Beth's younger sister, Sally, and had continual sexual fantasies about her. Gary and Sally had always gotten along well together, shared a similar sense of humor, and maintained a rela-

Table 10.1.   Rebecca against Phaedra

Stage	Phaedra	Rebecca
1. Precipitating Stressor	Phaedra falls passionately in love with her stepson Hippolytus, wanting him for herself.	Rebecca is concerned that her son Jacob will marry a totally unsuitable Hittite woman.
2. Reaction	Phaedra attempts to resist her passion but becomes very depressed.	Rebecca tells her husband Isaac that "her life will not be worth living" if Jacob marries a Hittite woman, like his brother Esau did.
3. Response of Others	Phaedra's servant betrays the secret of her infatuation to Hippolytus.	Isaac sends Jacob away to marry a daughter of Rebecca's brother Laban.
4. Effect	Phaedra hangs herself and leaves a note to her husband Theseus falsely accusing Hippolytus of raping her. This leads to the death of Hippolytus.	Rebecca is satisfied and does not speak of suicide again.

tionship that had a playful dynamic which, to an outside observer, may have been interpreted as being flirtatious. Gary has been well aware and reconciled to the fact that his sexual interactions with Sally would have to perpetually remain in the realm of fantasy, but lately he has begun the habit of writing short stories about his secret feelings for Sally, which he had kept in the desk drawer of his home office. Gary had decided to disclose these secret feelings to a longtime friend of his who was unable to provide Gary with satisfying advice on how to handle his feelings.

Gary's despair increased and he began experiencing serious doubts whether he could continue to stay married to his wife, Beth, or risk everything and pursue Sally, fully knowing that his chances would be slim to none, aside from creating an irreparable upheaval within his family. Yet the thought of Sally dating men her own age filled him with jealousy which he found very difficult to control. He reported he began to have thoughts of suicide.

All this led Gary to become more emotionally distant from his wife and children, and less satisfied and productive at work. It had reached the point where his supervisor had noticed his work had been suffering and he was consequently forced to go on a performance improvement plan. After consulting with a counselor through his EAP (Employer Assistance Program), he decided to seek out intensive psychotherapy.

Dr. P's Rebecca Intervention

After meeting with Gary for a few sessions it became clear that he had always found it challenging to directly communicate his relationship needs to his wife, experiencing shame intensified by his fear that his desires would be viewed by her as selfish and overly indulgent. This, perhaps more than his actual attraction to his sister-in-law, motivated his rich fantasy life until these psychological maneuvers began competing with his existential angst: was he "meant" to be with his sister-in-law and only settling for his wife? Questions like this had been haunting Gary, but were finding expression for the first time with his therapist, who was able to help Gary clarify what he really wanted in a romantic partner, most of which he already had!

After approximately 8 months of individual work Gary felt more grounded, oriented, and optimistic about his marriage than he had ever remembered feeling. Although not without a couple of setbacks, Gary was able to regain perspective on his marriage and, more importantly, focus on understanding the feelings he had been harboring toward his sister-in-law. After relinquishing his desire to be with Sally, appreciating that this fantasy was motivated by his need to be more intimate with his wife in order to satisfy his emotional needs, Gary was able to realize a path towards marital happiness. He found that his wife welcomed and did not shame him for being more expressive about his desires, and in turn Gary became less inhibited and more "alive" in his marriage, exclaiming towards the end of his treatment that he had only wished that he had sought help 20 years earlier! At the same time, Gary reported that Sally had begun to seriously date a young man, and that although this was difficult for him, Gary had begun to accept this development.

Now let us tune to a second case illustrating the *Phaedra Syndrome*.

Case 10b. Carol: Female Phaedra Syndrome (Dr. K)

Carol came into my office clearly distraught and suicidal over a deteriorating relationship with her son. The mother of two children, Carol has been widowed for over 20 years. Her husband Dick had been a highly successful attorney who died in his 50s. Carol had never remarried nor for that matter had ever had a serious romantic relationship. She was now in her mid-60s. Her older son was already in his 20s when Carol's husband Dick died and was now married himself with two children and lived out of state.

However, her younger son Benjamin had still been a child when his father died. Over the years, Carol reported raising him as a single parent, feeling that she was both father and mother to Ben. She would take trips with him, and really treated him as a companion. Though he had moved out to be on his own in his early 20s, he could not settle upon a career though he was highly intelligent with a very engaging and warm personality. At the time of Carol's therapy, Ben had returned to school to obtain a master's degree and, for financial reasons, had returned to temporarily live at his mother's home.

This adjustment was proving difficult both for Ben and his mother. He was used to being on his own, and she had adjusted to living alone as a widow and had filled her life with activities with friends, including trips, charity events, plays, and political action groups. She even had begun to take up bridge. Suddenly, this adjustment to an empty nest was shattered, as Ben reentered her home, and her life, albeit temporarily. Many of the previously unresolved separation issues began to resurface, coming to a head when Ben began to date someone whom his mother strongly disapproved of.

Dr. K's Rebecca Intervention

Carol reported that Ben had had girlfriends in the past but they had not proven to be serious. Now, however, he seemed to be deeply involved with a woman towards whom Carol expressed strong disapproval, both to me and to her son. Carol reported feeling that the woman came from a different background and conflicted with the values with which Carol insisted that she and her late husband Dick had tried to raise Ben.

Ben was invited into one therapy session. He complained that his mom was "insanely jealous" and had tried to break him up with every girl he had dated and that she wanted him as a life partner, which was stifling him. He claimed he loved his mother but that he "couldn't take it anymore." Carol vigorously denied this and insisted that it was his choice of girlfriends she disapproved of and that would not fit into the friendship circle that she and Dick had developed.

This all came to a head at one very intense family session. Ben accused his mother of never having built her own life after the death of her husband, and of wanting to make him into a surrogate husband. Carol vigorously denied this and responded that he had not shown good taste in girlfriends and that this one was the worst.

Ben became enraged and called his mother "sick" and that she didn't want him to have any girlfriend or wife, and that she would not accept anyone as suitable, and that she wanted to keep him for herself. Carol responded that he was behaving like a child, and he didn't know how difficult marriage was even if the two partners came from similar backgrounds. Carol related how difficult it was when her husband and Ben's father, Dick, became ill. Ben claimed that his mother was critical of every girlfriend he ever had and didn't want him to get married. Carol vehemently denied this and retorted that these girlfriends were not good enough for him. Ben became furious, called her a liar, and stormed out of the session.

I (*Dr. K*) had the feeling Ben himself shared some of his mother's reservations about his girlfriend but that her stance was driving him away and pushing him to defend his girlfriend despite his doubts. As the session ended, Carol cried and said she wanted to kill herself; that she couldn't live if Ben married somebody whom Carol felt opposed the very values with which she and Dick had attempted to raise Ben.

I attempted to settle Carol down and scheduled a follow-up appointment later in the week. I stressed how important it was for Carol to let Ben know that she was *not* opposed to him having a girlfriend or getting married, but that her objections were to this particular girlfriend. And that she express her blessing that he would find a good mate, but that he find a woman who would share his values and make him happy. I asked her in the meantime to list qualities she would want and accept in a daughter-in-law.

During the next session I concretized the *Rebecca Intervention* to Carol, asking her to outline criteria for a woman whom she would think would make a good partner for her son in contrast to those she thought would pull him down and away from her. As she began this list, I stressed how important this exercise potentially was in restoring relations with her son, and that I would, with her permission, see Ben separately to learn what he thought about it. She seemed happier, and I stressed that it was in her interest to get along with the woman Ben would marry. I asked her to try to start seeing his getting married as a gain rather than a loss, that she would be a mother-in-law, ushering in future generations.

I emphasized to Carol that she had a right to offer suggestions, but that she had so alienated her son that he felt she was trying to block him from living his own life. As she articulated this list for a suitable mate for her son, Carol seemed to become much less depressed. Discussion of suicide completely disappeared.

This case remains very much in the air, and it is unclear whether Ben will continue his relationship with his present girlfriend whom Carol finds so inappropriate.

LIFE LESSON

We end this chapter with an explication of the following life lesson. We must offer parents a means of dealing with the empty nest syndrome and fear of abandonment. They need to build their own lives and to differentiate themselves from their children to encourage them to pursue their own journeys. Phaedra becomes infatuated with her stepson Hippolytus. Phaedra must learn to apply her love for her stepson to encouraging him to choose a mate wisely and live his own life. Rebecca, in contrast tells her husband, Isaac, that she is weary of life because of her fear that her son Jacob marry a daughter of Heth, the Canaanite. Rebecca is not being seductive towards her son, nor is she trying to block him from living his own life. What she wants is that Jacob marry a suitable partner. When Isaac listens to her, Rebecca's suicidal impulse is resolved.

Patient Gary began to become more emotionally expressive towards his wife and thus had less need to look outside the marriage. Patient Carol's depression seemed to lift some as she also began to accept that her son Ben would ultimately marry someone, albeit a partner she found more suitable.

NOTE

1. Note how different this situation is from that described in the biblical narrative of Joseph resisting the advances of Potiphar's wife (Genesis 39). Joseph does not commit adultery with Potiphar's wife out of a sense of loyalty to him rather than as a result of misogynistic attitudes such as those displayed by Hippolytus.

Chapter Eleven

Ruth against Antigone

Constructively Dealing with a Dysfunctional Family of Origin

From what manner of parents did I take my miserable being? And to them I go thus, accursed, unwed, to share their home. (Sophocles, *Antigone*, l. 869)

The husband lost, another might have been found, and child from another, to replace the first born: but, father and mother hidden with Hades, no brother's life could ever bloom for me again. (Sophocles, *Antigone*, 907–13)

Entreat me not to leave thee . . . for whither thou goest, I will go, and where thou lodgest, I shall lodge . . . (Ruth 1:16) . . . So Boaz took Ruth, and she became his wife; and he went in unto her, and the LORD gave her conception, and she bore a son. . . . And he shall be unto thee (Naomi) a restorer of life, and a nourisher of thine old age; for, thy daughter-in-law, who loveth thee, who is better to thee than seven sons, hath borne him. (Ruth 4:13–15)

Both Antigone and Ruth are products of enmeshed and dysfunctional families of origin and, to be more precise, scions of incestuous relationships. Antigone is the daughter of Oedipus and his mother-wife Jocasta; Ruth, the product several generations back, is a descendant of the incestuous union of Lot and his eldest daughter.

In one way, Ruth's family background is even more dysfunctional: Lot's daughter *intentionally* gets him drunk and sleeps with him and she produces a son Moab (derived from the Hebrew *mo-ab,* meaning "from the father"). Antigone, in contrast, is the product of an *unintentional* incest based on the seeming ignorance on the part of both Jocasta and Oedipus as to their mother-son relationship. The case is more complicated with regard to Ruth's

167

Moabite ancestors, as the thrust of Lot's daughter is to preserve the species as she thinks her father Lot is the last man alive after the destruction of Sodom. It is true that Ruth is not the direct product of incest, being several generations removed. Nevertheless, her designation as a *Moabitess* reflects awareness of the incestuous nature of her family. The comparative outcomes are highly instructive. Ruth frees herself from the effects of any dysfunction and goes on to lead an exemplary life as daughter, wife, and mother. Antigone cannot free herself from her enmeshment from her family of origin and ultimately leads a frustrated life, eschewing an imminent marriage, and ultimately taking her own life.

The common stressor for Ruth and Antigone is being the product of incest, either directly or several generations back. However, the vulnerabilities are different, the Greek culture viewing Antigone's situation as untenable. She is fixated on the past and cannot get beyond it to live her own life as a wife and mother. Ruth, on the other hand, is portrayed as a healthy daughter, wife, and mother, able to place the event which she inherited from her ancestors in a larger healthier biblical context of intergenerational continuity.

THE ANTIGONE SYNDROME

Greek thought posits that one is doomed when born of a dysfunctional family. Oedipus expresses this succinctly: "For now I am forsaken of the gods, son of a defiled mother, and successor to his bed who gave me my own wretched being" (Sophocles, *Oedipus the King*, ll. 1359–61). This is played out in the tragic story of Antigone, the daughter (and half-sister) of Oedipus.

Oedipus kills his biological father Laius in an altercation on the road and equally unknowingly marries his biological mother, Jocasta. They have four children. When Oedipus discovers his incest, a tragic sequence of events evolves: his wife/mother kills herself, he blinds himself, and he curses his two sons to kill each other (Sophocles, *Oedipus at Colonus*, ll. 1386–94; Aeschylus, *Seven Against Thebes* ll. 878–924), which they do at the Seventh Gate of Thebes (Aeschylus, *The Seven Against Thebes* ll. 803–21). He is fulfilling the Greek tragic view of life.

This sense of doom is continued in the story of Antigone, the daughter of Oedipus. "From what manner of parents did I take my miserable being? And to them I go thus, accursed, unwed, to share their home" (Sophocles, *Antigone*, l. 869). Antigone (*anti-gone* which in ancient Greek literally translates to "opposed to semen" or "anti-generative") is unable to separate herself from the incestuous nature of her birth and hangs herself after being buried alive for trying to bury her dead brother Polyneices, a rebel against Thebes, against the order of Creon, the ruler of Thebes. Strikingly, Antigone says she values her brother more than a husband or a child because the latter can be replaced with another while the former cannot.

> Never, had I been a mother of children, or if a husband had been mouldering in death, would I have taken this task upon me in the city's despite? What law, ye ask, is my warrant for that word? The husband lost, another might have been found, and child from another, to replace the first born: but, father and mother hidden with Hades, no brother's life could ever bloom for me again. (Sophocles, *Antigone*, 907–13)[1]

The stressor for Antigone is her being the product of incest; the lack of cross-generational continuity leaves her vulnerable. Let us reemphasize that the very name *Antigone* in Greek may be seen as a rejection (*anti*) of motherhood (*gone,* denoting semen or generativity). How different this is from the name of the first woman in biblical accounts (Eve or *Chava* in Hebrew, denoting the giver of life).

THE RUTH INTERVENTION

Biblical thought offers a hopeful alternative for overcoming the effects of a dysfunctional or even an abandoning family. "Cast me not off, neither forsake me, O god of my salvation. For though my father and mother have forsaken me, the Lord will take me up" (Psalm 27:9–10). When the sinful people of Sodom are destroyed, Lot and his two daughters escape. Under the [false] impression their father is the last living man, Lot's two daughters get him drunk on successive nights and each lie with him in order to become impregnated. The male offspring of the union of Lot and his older daughter is named Moab (Gen. 19:30–38), *mo-ab* literally meaning "from the father" in biblical Hebrew.

Although the Israelites have their problems with the Moabites, Ruth the Moabitess, a descendant of this incestuous relationship, does not remain a victim of historical circumstance, but progresses to becoming a survivor and an important figure in the history of Israel. This despite the fact that Ruth, her mother-in-law Naomi, and her sister-in-law Orpah all are widowed at approximately the same time while "strangers in a strange land." As widowed women, away from home, and without male relatives to protect them, they are among the most vulnerable people in society. Indeed, Orpah abandons Naomi and returns home. However, Ruth does not abandon her, and in one of the most moving of all speeches in the Hebrew Bible she pledges her loyalty to her mother-in-law, saying: "Whither thou goest, I will go" (Ruth 1:16–17).

Nevertheless, upon her return to Judah, Naomi tells her relatives not to call her "Naomi" which connotes "pleasant" but "Mara" for the bitter turn her life has taken (Ruth 1:19–20). Yet despite her losses and despite her

Figure 11.1. *Antigone in Front of the Dead Polyneices*, **Nikiphoros Lytras (1865). The authors would like to thank The National Gallery of Greece for permission to use this painting from its collection.**

dysfunctional family history several generations earlier, Ruth, unlike Antigone, is not suicidal, and does not reject motherhood. Rather Ruth maintains her hope, and is steadfastly loyal to Naomi who advises Ruth on how to meet and marry Boaz, a suitable and significant kinsman. This enables both Naomi and Ruth to find their way back to experiencing their lives in a meaningful and hopeful way.

The triptych below (figure 11.2) shows three central moments in the story of Ruth. From right to left: Ruth's adherence to Naomi; Ruth's meeting with her kinsman Boaz whom she later marries; and Ruth gazing at Naomi holding Obed, her baby son who would become the grandfather of King David and the Davidic/Messianic line. In other words, Ruth is described as an exemplary figure, who, widowed herself, is loving toward her widowed mother-in-law, a faithful wife and a loving mother, herself becoming the ancestress of the Davidic line (as King David's great-grandmother).

The stressor for Ruth is her being the product of purposeful incest several generations back. The name of the product of the incestuous union between Lot and his daughter is Moab (again, "from the father"). Ruth's description as a Moabitess reflects awareness of this act. However, she is anchored in a sense of intergenerational continuity, prodded on by Naomi, which renders her invulnerable to the stressor.

A contrast of these two narratives is presented in table 11.1. Both Ruth and Antigone are confronted with the stressor of incest, though Antigone's is certainly more generationally direct. However, the rigidity of the Greek culture in this regard and the lack of a sense of intergenerational continuity leaves Antigone quite vulnerable in this regard. Ruth, in contrast, is surrounded by a strong social support system and a sense of historical continuity that protects her against any negative effects.

Consider the following two cases which illustrate well the *Antigone Syndrome* and the *Ruth Intervention*. First, we will present Phil and then Dominique.

Case 11a. Phil: Male Antigone Syndrome (Dr. P)

Phil, a Caucasian 35-year-old accountant, was never married and had difficulty maintaining long-term romantic relationships, subsequently leaving him feeling lonely and even resentful. Most of his close friends had already gotten married and started families—life events that appealed to Phil but for which he felt undeserving of achieving. Although likely over-determined, his feelings of inadequacy were likely compounded by his parents' harsh criti-

Figure 11.2. *The Story of Ruth* (1876–1877). Thomas Matthews Rooke; Ruth and Naomi; © [Trustees of the Chantrey Bequest 1877] Photographic Rights © Tate (2017), CC-BY-NC-ND 3.0 (Unported), http://www.tate.org.uk/art/artworks/rooke-ruth-and-naomi-a00839.

Table 11.1. Ruth against Antigone

Stage	Antigone	Ruth
1. Precipitating Stressor	Antigone is enmeshed with incestuous family of origin. Unable to separate self as a mature woman to marry and become a mother..	Ruth is unaffected by history of incest in her ancestors. Goes on to be loyal daughter-in-law, wife and mother.
2. Reaction	Though raised in a seemingly secure home, Antigone does not seem to be able to separate from her family of origin.	Though Ruth is widowed at an early age and away from her native land, she does not seem to be enmeshed and indeed is able to bond to her also widowed mother-in-law Naomi.
3. Response of Others	Antigone is over-identified with her family of origin and winds up being buried alive because she will not leave her brother fighting against Thebes to remain unburied.	Naomi accepts Ruth as her daughter and brings Ruth back with her to Judah and facilitates Ruth's marriage to Boaz, the kinsman of Naomi.
4. Effect	Antigone hangs herself, rejecting her wood be lover. Antigone means in Greek against generativity (semen).	Ruth thrives and becomes a mother of Obed, and ancestress of King David and the Davidic line. She integrates Naomi into her family in a beautiful way.

cism as well as their frequent habit of comparing him to his older, more successful brother, with whom they clearly favored and even lived through vicariously to a noticeable degree. Adding to Phil's stressors, as a young man he had learned that he possessed an unusually low sperm count and that his chances of conceiving naturally were close to non-existent. Phil later discovered that his condition was the result of a genetic abnormality, and while he knew it wasn't his parents' "fault," *per se*, he nevertheless harbored bitterness towards them for bequeathing to him compromised genes.

Invariably, Phil's relationships crumbled when he disclosed his infertility problems to his girlfriends, though it was unclear whether this was simply the consequence of the fact of Phil's sterility, or the result of unconscious efforts to self-sabotage his happiness. The therapist suspected the latter. Phil's despondency over his infertility and lack of a romantic partner and a family of his own reinforced in his own mind that he must be "cursed" to traverse life alone. Phil couldn't help but compare himself to his older brother whom he at once admired and resented, sometimes feeling as if his parents and perhaps even the world has written him off as a loser. During one of the early sessions Phil sarcastically reflected that, "since I'll be alone forever, perhaps I should start collecting dogs. I'll be one of those 'crazy' people you see on the ten o'clock news who is found dead in a house full of dozens of animals . . . if I'm lucky!"

Dr. P's Ruth Intervention

My (*Dr. P's*) approach to treating Phil was to first explore with him issues of his childhood, focusing on the latent attitudes and beliefs that motivated him to think that he was fated to be alone and unhappy. Relationship issues likewise played a central place in his treatment, and by working through and articulating the shame and despair that Phil experienced while engaged in relationships with women—the emasculation and masochism that fueled his sense of emotional insecurity as well as his underlying resentment towards his parents. We also reviewed several instances in his past where he encountered relational distress with his romantic partners, typically resulting from his inability to contain his frustrations after he was triggered by decidedly benign behaviors from his girlfriends. These patterns in his own life were linked to the marital conflict that he observed with his parents and his nagging feeling that he was an unwanted child.

As his self-esteem increased, so did his ability to become more self-aware of his own actions and choices. He cultivated a greater degree of responsibility for his own future, and became less preoccupied with the weight of his past mistakes and the accident of his genetic make-up. Predictably, the quality of his relationships also improved and by the time treatment concluded he had begun seeing a lovely woman to whom he intended on proposing marriage. Phil was able to come to the realization that history is not destiny, and while it is certainly healthy to have compassion for one's own situation in life and the events that led to them, this had to be balanced with respecting the agency and responsibility that he had over shaping the course of his life and the future that he desired.

Case 11b. Dominique: Female Antigone Syndrome (Dr. K)

Dominique is a stunningly beautiful and vibrant woman in her late 40s. She immediately impressed me (*Dr. K*) with her warmth and kindness, her intellectual curiosity, her courage, and her love of language—she was multilingual. She was born in Belgium to a downwardly mobile French family who had descended from aristocracy but who had fallen upon hard times financially. Her early childhood was quite traumatic, with her being left alone for significant periods while quite young, resulting in a very strong fear of abandonment. At the same time, Dominique may have had something of an enmeshed relationship with her father, and after her father's death her mother treated her older brother as "her little man," liking to go out with him and his friends. Though she had been married, she was adamant about not having children, a stance which may have been instrumental in the breakup of her marriage.

At the time she began to see me, she had just gone through a divorce. She had moved to America alone in her early 20s and made a highly successful career for herself, both in business and in law. Although Dominique was exceptionally biblically literate and creative, she seemed to herself more as a tragic heroine, along the lines of Anna Karenina (Tolstoy, 2000), and very misused and unappreciated in her life. What was interesting about her home was that it was quite tasteful and elegant downstairs but quite chaotic upstairs. Dominique once remarked that this seeming anomaly was like her personality, organized on the outside but chaotic on the inside.

Several things became apparent over the course of my interactions with Dominique, illustrating each of the problems outlined above.

1. Dominique had a severe fear of abandonment, terrified that people who left would not return. This fear was manifested in her compulsive non-stop talking, which while initially fascinating, tended to bombard people and not give them a chance to leave, which seemed to be Dominique's underlying unconscious intent. This stemmed from her early history of abandonment. She told me that she had become emotionally paralyzed and even sometimes suicidal when she was left alone for long periods of time. In this way, she was like the Greek Ajax.

2. Dominique tended to search for hidden meanings in seemingly random events. For example, she would interpret a minor car accident or the flooding of her house as a sign that she should not go to an appointment, or lightning hitting a tree near her house as a sign that she was cursed, or her failure to find a suitable job as a sign that she was evil and never should have been born at all—that suicide would not be sufficient, but that she wanted her birth annulled. In this way, Dominique behaved very much like the Greek Zeno rather than the biblical Job.

3. Despite her fear of abandonment, Dominique was reported being very stand-offish at parties, feeling she could not express herself in relationships, especially with men. She would tend to become very quiet. Yet as mentioned above, she tended to become very enmeshed in the relationships she did have, demanding a great deal of undivided attention, and becoming hurt and resentful when she did not receive it.

4. Dominique spoke many times about her dysfunctional family of origin. She felt her parents in post–World War II Belgium were not ready to be parents. She felt they did not provide her with a secure sense of parenting and left her fending on her own. Moreover, they often went out their own leaving her as a young child to care for a younger sister.

Her unwillingness to become a mother may have been instrumental in ending her marriage. Yet this is something she seemed to come to regret and lavished a great deal of love and concern for her dog, towards whom she was extraordinarily attentive and nurturing. She became a great lover of the Hebrew Bible, the Jewish people and of Israel, and learned some Hebrew. Thus, I used biblical imagery to compare her to Ruth.

Dr. K's Ruth Intervention

My (*Dr. K's*) approach towards Dominique was to stress that many of her attitudes and feelings were coming from a Greek tragic view of her life, and to emphasize the hopeful, anti-tragic and life-affirming stories of the Hebrew Bible, which she loved. I would tell her, God puts before us life and death and enjoins us to choose life!

1. I tried to address Dominique's fear of abandonment as manifested by her compulsive "stream of consciousness" non-stop talking, pointing out that that this drove people away. That she had to give people a chance to separate from her without interpreting this as abandonment and that people needed their own space in relationships. I stressed the biblical adage that God never abandons us, and that in the service of keeping people close to her she was driving them away. I also to tried to model to Dominque ways to reach out to people when she needed company, without making them feel trapped. She brought in a roommate and this made her feel better, and more like Elijah receiving food and drink and having a chance to rest.

2. I focused on Dominique's tendency to overcome her need to catastrophize and exaggerate the purposive meaning behind seemingly random events. This was difficult as Dominique was so brilliant and perceptive in her tendency to see malevolent intent behind every random action. I stressed that the Greek Zeno needed to search for the divine sign behind his stubbing his toe, as a call to die, because he did not feel he had a solid and unconditional relationship with his Creator as did the biblical Job. I stressed that she as a Judeo-Christian (which is how Dominique regarded herself) had a secure sense of a loving Creator and thus could withstand life stressors and did not need to over-interpret events in a desperate attempt to find meaning.

3. I stressed to Dominique ways she could express herself to others. To reach out to others, but not bombard them with excessive talking. I stressed the kabalistic concept of *tzimtzum*[2] which involved contracting to make room for the other. I again stressed the concept of I and Thou: to learn how to be herself and let other be themselves, in this way to behave like the biblical Jonah rather than the Greek Narcissus.

4. I emphasized to Dominique that she was not done in by her dysfunctional family of origin like Antigone. I stressed that her love for the Hebrew Bible, the Jewish people, and Israel was following the path of Ruth who herself overcame the incestuous nature of her own Moabite ancestry, and became a daughter to Naomi, a wife to Boaz, and a mother to Obed. The lack of having a child of her own was a sore spot for Dominique. I stressed to her

that she could reach out to younger people in so many ways, and also to older people, and had so very much to give, and what a wonderful woman she was. She joined a foster-parent program for an orphaned child in a developing country.

Since my meetings with Dominique, she experienced what we used to call a nervous breakdown and now call a psychotic episode, and was hospitalized. She is doing better now and trying to find some employment. She has also applied for social security disability. She has several friends who are helping her out to some degree and is now under psychiatric care which manages her medication. Her family in Europe helps her out minimally, though they could do much more. They say they feel drained. I hope she will be able to apply the techniques of biblical living that I tried to express to her. She is truly a wonderful and gifted woman and person.

LIFE LESSON

We must offer people from a dysfunctional family the means of righting themselves. Nothing is more important that instilling a hope rather than a fear regarding the future. People can overcome a dysfunctional and traumatic beginning and go on successfully and happily with their life if their sense of identity does not preclude openness to the future rather than simply fixate on the past. One does not have to negate and ignore his past. Indeed, such repression is an impediment to growth in the long run, and when it occurs, it can lead to fixation. Having an accepting relationship with one's past, in contrast, can free one to move on to the future. Patient Phil showed signs of coming to grips with his past and thus freeing himself from it. There is reason for optimism in the case of Patient Dominique. Much depends on whether she is able to find a way of living on her own in a healthy manner.

NOTES

1. It should be noted that the veracity of this line has been disputed in some quarters, specifically by the translator R. C. Jebb.

2. The reader is referred to the classic work of Isaac Luria (see Fine, 2003) and the contemporary ingenious application of this idea to clinical psychology by Mordechai Rotenberg (1993, 2004a, 2004b, 2005, 2016).

Conclusion

What, then, Glaucon, would be the study that would draw the soul away from the world of becoming to the world of being? (Plato, Republic, 7. 521d)

Pray thou no more; for mortals have no escape from destined woe. (Sophocles, *Antigone*, l. 1336)

Ehiyeh asher ehiyeh. (I will be what I will be). (Exodus 3:14)

Even if a sword's edge lies on the neck of a man he should not hold himself back from prayer. (Berachot, 10a, Babylonian Talmud)

This book has presented a biblical approach to psychotherapy, which we have developed in response to the implicit and even explicit Greek bias in mental health that has led to a limited and narrow view of psychological health (e.g. Oedipus, Electra, Narcissus, the split between the *soma* and the *psyche*). Nowhere is the Greek sense of the tragic more dangerous for psychotherapy and counseling than in dealing with suicidal patients and people generally. Biblical narratives provide an absolutely necessary alternative world view, providing a therapy that facilitates healthy resolutions of real-life dilemmas.

STRESSORS AND VULNERABILITIES

In chapters 5 through 11 we have described seven stressors empirically related to suicidal behavior: (1) Feeling isolated and ignored; (2) Feeling one's life is without meaning; (3) Feeling exiled from one's homeland as a refugee; (4) Feeling unable to express one's own needs with others; (5) Feeling as an adopted child that one is unable to trust enough to seek or accept help; (6)

Feeling abandoned by one's child leaving the family nest and building his or her own life; and (7) Feeling doomed by a dysfunctional (incestuous) family of origin.

We have matched each of these stressors in parallel narratives from the biblical and Graeco-Roman worlds. What is fascinating is how similar the biblical stories are to the Graeco-Roman stories in terms of stressors. This squares with the approach of the historian Cyrus Gordon in viewing both Hebrew and Greek stories as deriving from a common Ugaritic source (Gordon, 1965). Other interpreters of myth such as Claude Levi-Strauss (1970) and Joseph Campbell (1969) also point to the universality of mythic themes.

However, this is where the similarity ends. Although the stressors are similar in the biblical and Graeco-Roman worlds, these two foundation cultures offer different protections against vulnerability. Thus, the Graeco-Roman characters are highly vulnerable and overcome by the stressors they encounter, leading them to self-destructive behaviors and even suicide; the matched biblical figures, however, are not vulnerable in this way. They may bend, but they do not break in the face of similar stressors. The biblical context in which these characters live offers protection and indeed antidotes, unavailable to the characters in the seven matched stories from the ancient Greek and Roman worlds. We have desituated biblical narratives from their formal religious context to offer respective blueprints for how to treat people exhibiting each of these seven respective risk factors. In chapters 5 through 11, we have drawn the clinical lessons from biblical narratives and shown how they can be used clinically to help people experiencing the seven above stressors. Thus, for example, we have employed an *Elijah Intervention* to treat a patient exhibiting an *Ajax Syndrome*.

Let us summarize and review the contrasts we have presented in chapters 5 through 11 in table C.1.

Table C.1. Stressors and Vulnerability in Seven Biblical versus Graeco-Roman Narratives

Common Stressor	Graeco-Roman Figure	High Vulnerability Tragic Character Flaw	Response	Outcome	Biblical Figure	Low Vulnerability Hopeful Character Strength	Response	Outcome
Experience of persecution, exhaustion, and humiliation.	Ajax	The crumbling of an overly grandiose self-image heightened by his experience of punitive gods.	Ajax's brother Teucer does not respond in timely manner to Ajax's call for help.	Ajax flees alone from tent and commits suicide by falling on his sword.	Elijah	A healthy degree of confidence stemming from his experience of help from a loving God.	Angel provides Elijah with food, water, and the chance to rest.	Elijah overcomes suicidal thoughts and continues with his mission.
Experience of sudden misfortune.	Zeno the Stoic	Exaggerates relatively minor misfortune of stubbing toe as a sign from the gods that he should depart.	None of which we know.	Zeno commits suicide by holding his breath till he dies.	Job	Insistence to God that he is innocent of any wrongdoing, but yet he maintains his relationship with God.	Blaming interpersonal responses from wife and friends mitigated by Job's faith in a loving God.	Job overcomes suicidal thoughts. He maintains his sense of innocence but accepts that he cannot understand all of God's ways. All is restored to him.
Experience of exile/flight from home	Coriolanus	Rigidity and arrogance with fellow Romans	Roman senate exiles Coriolanus	Coriolanus murdered by the Volsci after	David	A flexible world view toward his fellow Israelites.	Saul's jealousy forces David to join and fight	David ultimately rejoins his

Common Stressor	Graeco-Roman Figure	High Vulnerability Tragic Character Flaw	Response	Outcome	Biblical Figure	Low Vulnerability Hopeful Character Strength	Response	Outcome
country: being a refugee.		despite being lauded as a military hero.	from Rome who then joins the Volsci foes.	aborting his mission to attack Rome and then insulting Volsci.			along side of the Philistines, whom he is pleasant with, though does not fight against Israel.	people, is embraced by them, and ultimately becomes King of Israel.
Experience of inability to integrate sense of self with needs of others.	**Narcissus**	A lack of self-knowledge. Promised a long life as long as he does not come to "know himself."	Vacillates between self-absorption and infatuation with his reflection in brook. Does not realize that it is his own.	Narcissus dies, either by passively pining away or actively stabbing himself in the chest.	**Jonah**	An openness to self-knowledge and personal growth.	God does not give up on Jonah but protects him from suicide and facilitates his integration of self and other.	Jonah overcomes his desire to kill himself and learns to understand why God wants to give the people of Nineveh the chance to repent.
Experience of being sent away as an infant from the	**Oedipus**	Oedipus becomes uncertain as to his identity.	Oedipus receives riddling and entrapping information	Oedipus unknowingly commits patricide and incest with his	**Moses**	Moses comes to realize slowly that he is an Israelite and not an Egyptian.	God facilitates Moses receiving help from Aaron, his sister Miriam,	Moses slowly finds his identity as an Israelite and leads his

Common Stressor	Graeco-Roman Figure	High Vulnerability Tragic Character Flaw	Response	Outcome	Biblical Figure	Low Vulnerability Hopeful Character Strength	Response	Outcome
home of his biological parents. Later searches for his identity.			from Oracle. Does not trust either the soothsayer Teiresias or his brother-in-law Creon.	mother. He becomes humiliated in his native Thebes and takes out his eyes and curses his children.		Slays an Egyptian who is mistreating an Israelite.	and the Sanhedrin.	people out of Egypt.
Experience of being abandoned, having an "empty nest."	Phaedra	Depressed as a function of incestuous passion for her stepson Hippolytus.	Phaedra confides her passion to her nurse and hopes to endure. Nurse betrays Phaedra's secret.	Phaedra hangs herself out of shame, leaving a note to her husband Theseus, falsely accusing Hippolytus of raping her.	Rebecca	Rebecca expresses a wish to die if her son Jacob should marry a Hittite. She asks her husband Isaac for help in preventing this.	Isaac agrees to send Jacob away to Rebecca's kinsman, Laban.	Rebecca's fears are allayed and her suicidal thoughts dissipate.
Experience of being the offspring of an enmeshed	Antigone	Enmeshment with family of origin (her father was her half-brother) and is	Antigone's uncle does not understand her need to	Antigone hangs herself after being buried alive for refusing to	Ruth	Ruth can live unconcerned about the fact that she had been the product	Ruth is unconditionally accepted into the family of Israel.	Ruth proves to be a loyal daughter-in-law, wife, and mother in Israel.

Common Stressor	Graeco-Roman Figure	High Vulnerability Tragic Character Flaw	Response	Outcome	Biblical Figure	Low Vulnerability Hopeful Character Strength	Response	Outcome
(even incestuous) family history.		unable to separate herself from her family of origin. Her name denotes "against generativity."	bury her unburied brother and orders her buried alive.	leave her dead brother, a rebel, unburied.		of a known incest of her ancestor (Lot) with his eldest daughter.		and becomes the ancestress of the Davidic/Messianic line.

In chapter 5 we have compared the stories of Ajax and Elijah. Both are overwhelmed by a stressor and feel emotionally exhausted. Yet one dramatic difference emerges in these two narratives. Ajax is basically ignored and abandoned (high vulnerability) while Elijah is tended to (low vulnerability). This is a seemingly small difference, yet it changes the entire focus of the respective life-situations. This points to the absolute importance of human contact and concern. Did the Greeks not recognize this, and if they did, why did they fail to take this factor into account? Does this point to a different view of community in the Greek and biblical cultures and caring for people in distress?

Both personalities in chapter 6 encounter misfortune. Zeno over-interprets a relatively minor stressor (stubbing his toe) which leads to his death. Why does he do this? Was the Greek society so devoid of normal meaning (high vulnerability) that one had to catastrophize the meaning of events to feel noticed? This may represent very much the psychodynamic of a paranoid personality structure. Job, in contrast, is assailed with overwhelming misfortunes (a major stressor), but he has no need for this over-interpretation. He is anchored in his relationship with God (low vulnerability) and thus knows he is of intrinsic value. He can thus experience even great misfortunes without disintegrating. This does not mean that Job doesn't complain—of course he does—but this does not break his basic relationship with his creator (see Exline, Kaplan, and Grubbs, 2012). Do the two civilizations differ in their attribution as to the source of a misfortune and what does this imply for doing psychotherapy with people who experienced a trauma in their lives?

Chapter 7 contrasts the stories of Coriolanus and David. These two figures share the stressor of having to flee into exile after initially being lionized in their respective societies. But the reasons for this exile are entirely different, reflecting their different vulnerabilities. Coriolanus is banished from Rome because of his own arrogance and rigidity (high vulnerability); the flexible David (low vulnerability) because of the jealousy and paranoia of King Saul. Both go to fight for the enemies of their people, Coriolanus to the Volsci and David to the Philistines. Coriolanus is obsessed with a need for revenge against Rome. David is not described as having vengeance towards Israel, but rather as simply trying to survive. Coriolanus's rigidity leads to his rejection by both the Romans and the Volsci and his demise; David's flexibility is instrumental both in him being trusted by King Achish of the Philistines and also in his ultimately becoming King of Israel after Saul's death. What does this teach us as to how to deal with the conflicting identities and loyalties inherent in being a refugee or an immigrant?

The two figures in chapter 8 experience the common stressor of conflicting pulls between self and other. Narcissus, reflecting the ancient Greek culture, is not able to navigate the vagaries of reconciling self and other. One is attained at the expense of the other, leaving him highly vulnerable to any stressor. Jonah, in contrast, is helped by his biblical God to learn how to integrate the two and how to express his self in the context of interaction with others (low vulnerability). What does this teach us with regard to doing couple or family therapy, or even individual therapy in situations where people feel their identities may be compromised by their relationships?

Chapter 9 describes the importance of being able to ask for help from others and accept and trust it when it is offered. Oedipus and Moses share the stressor of being sent away as newborn infants from their parents' homes. Oedipus receives taunting riddles and misleading information, and winds up trusting no one (high vulnerability). This leads to his destruction. Moses is able, in contrast, to ask for help when he needs it (low vulnerability). He receives fairly straightforward answers and this is essential in his completing the life mission entrusted to him. Being able to seek, receive, and accept help when one needs it is essential to completing one's task. One can pay a huge price if one always tries to tough it out alone. One need not be compromised by seeking and accepting help.

Chapter 10 compares the stories of Phaedra and Rebecca. They can be said to share the common stressor experiencing an empty nest. Phaedra has no sense of being a stepmother (high vulnerability) and is thus unable to overcome her infatuation with her stepson and allow him to live a normal life. Rebecca, in contrast, is anchored in the biblical idea of family and thus has a strong sense of being a mother and of intergenerational continuity (low vulnerability). She is thus able to allow her son to choose a woman to marry, given that she comes from an appropriate family and culture. This speaks to the importance of teaching a parent how to give advice to his or her children without suffocating them. Specifically, it addresses the need to provide a parental blessing to a child to live his/her own life.

The stories of Antigone and Ruth in chapter 11 illustrate dramatically the importance of being able to overcome trauma and pathology in one's personal or family life. They share the common stressor of being born into an incestuous family structure. Antigone cannot overcome her incestuous beginnings (even though it was unintentional) and never seems able to enjoy her life as a woman or, as her name (*anti-gone*) denotes, accept motherhood (high vulnerability). Ruth, in contrast, is able to overcome an incestuous familial history, initiated intentionally by her ancestor Lot's daughters (albeit for positive reasons to preserve the human race) and thrive in her role as role as a daughter, wife and mother. She is anchored within the biblical sense of intergenerational continuity which reduces her vulnerability to trauma. How does one deal with a traumatic family history and how does one overcome it without being entrapped by it, on the one hand, or denying it on the other?

THE IMPORTANCE OF HOPE

We have discussed in chapter 2 the critical role of hope in developing a positive psychology in the face of distressing and overwhelming life situations. As bad as circumstances seem, things can get better. People can, and sometimes do, change. It is difficult to see how a person can have a genuine sense of hope in the absence of a meaning structure in which to anchor it, and vice versa. See the classic work on meaning by Frankl (1962), and more recent works on hope by Kaplan and Schwartz (2008) and Scioli and Biller (2009) and on resilience by Cyrulnik (2011). A sense of secure parenting (Ainsworth, 1972; Bowlby, 1969; 1973; 1978; Main, Kaplan, and Cassidy, 1985) may also be intimately involved as well.

This absence of hope, lack of a meaning structure, and sense of helplessness can be seen to pervade the seven Greek narratives we have developed in this book. There is no stopper when one's life begins to unravel. In contrast, each of the biblical narratives contain important elements of hope. Let us consider the role of hope in our comparisons in chapters 5 through 11 of ancient Greek and biblical narratives.

In chapter 5, Ajax's upbringing can be said to have left him without hope. Once he has humiliated himself, his suicide seems to be the only way out. He cannot face his parents nor his countrymen. This hopelessness intensifies his desolation and sense of abandonment. Ajax has no hope of change or any sense that he is cherished for who he is rather than his accomplishments which are now tarred irretrievably. His only "out" is an honorable death through suicide. Elijah, in contrast, feels he has been singled out to fulfill God's mission. This represents a secure attachment and a formidable meaning structure. He is able to stand up to King Ahab and Queen Jezebel when he feels they are acting in an unconscionable way which violates God's commandments. He does this at the risk of his life. Although he is exhausted and says he cannot go on, one does not sense that he is devoid of hope. He needs help, and he receives it. Once this happens, Elijah is able to pick himself up and go on with his mission, which is filled with meaning.

In chapter 6, Zeno over-interprets a relatively minor annoyance which leads to his death. Why does he do this? He is aging and may feel isolated and hopeless. His future may look bleak and hopeless to him. His sense that his stubbing his toe is a sign from the gods that he should depart implies that the gods are noticing him. In the absence of any genuine hope with regard to the future, Zeno's over-interpretation and catastrophizing of a relatively minor mishap may be the best he can do. It provides a meaning structure, as lethal as it may be and thus in a strange way a hope-substitute for him. The absence of any genuine hope in his life for having a dignified old age may lead him in his quixotic and lethal search for meaning. Job, in contrast, finds intrinsic meaning in his relationship with his Creator. This represents a secure attachment that sustains him and gives him his hope and resilience. He has no need to engage in a meaning-making narrative which will exaggerate his misfortune, nor does he need to choose between a false acceptance of his guilt and rejection of his Creator. He can argue with his Creator, proclaiming his innocence without resorting to a damaging meaning-making structure.

Chapter 7 has described the bleak situation that Coriolanus comes to be in. His own rigidity has brought about his exile from Rome and he has no real hope of escaping it. Banished from Rome, and swearing vengeance upon it, he is confronted by his mother and others in his family to desist in leading the Volsci against Rome. What is he to do? He is truly in a hopeless situation, with no way out. The unyielding brittleness of his personality and his inhuman standards may be the only means of maintaining any meaning structure, even though they lead to his exile and his death which he has provoked. David's situation, though objectively similar in some ways, is decidedly very different. He is very beloved by his people but has had to flee for Israel to escape the jealousy and wrath against him on the part of King Saul. His sense of being part of Israel never leaves him, nor the hope that springs from this certainty. David knows that he is God's anointed, loved by God, and this provides him with the sense of secure attachment and an unassailable meaning structure to withstand the life stressor he finds himself in. He is resilient and never gives up hope. Though he has had to flee Saul, he never turns against Israel and at the same time is loyal within limits to his temporary Philistine hosts.

Chapter 8 finds Narcissus in a truly hopeless situation. Teiresias the taunting soothsayer has told his mother Lirope that he (Narcissus) will die if he comes to know himself. Yet if he doesn't, he is absolutely at the prey of outside forces. Where will he find his meaning structure? He desperately tries to find his missing sense of self through destructive and lethal cycling between disengagement and enmeshment. He cycles destructively rather than grows.[1] He finally finds his reflection, but it is unobtainable to him and the very quest leads to his death. Jonah is the reluctant prophet, *par excellence*. He discovers he may try to run away from God, but he will be found and restored without being rejected. God will find him and not reject him. This is a very heady realization indeed. God provides Jonah with hope and the help to grow into his role and gives him the time and support to do so. Slowly Jonah matures into being able to fulfill God's mission to go to warn the people of Nineveh to change their ways. This sense of secure attachment and hope must make Jonah feel he is loved by his Creator, and this allows him to grow, and even change.

Hope is essential in chapter 9 to enable Oedipus to try to turns his life situation around. But he has no access to it. He has been a conscientious ruler and a good father and husband, but none of this means anything to him, as his life unravels. His life is a hopeless riddle and he is obsessed to get at the "truth," no matter what the consequences. He is driven to find meaning in his life. His situation is truly hopeless. Once his situation is revealed, there is no possibility of change or redemption, and he takes out his eyes because of his great shame. Moses, in contrast, is described as actually seeing God. Although he is raised in the court of Pharaoh, Moses identifies with an Israelite he sees being beaten. He has a God he can ask help from and indeed argue with. He almost has more meaning than he can handle. He feels God is asking too much from him and he complains. And his complaint is answered! If this does not provide a meaning structure and a sense of hope, what does?

Chapter 10 depicts hopelessness *par excellence*. There is no hope for Phaedra to overcome her mad infatuation with her stepson Hippolytus. She lies paralyzed by her depression and sense of shame. She seems completely unable to get out of her situation. Her life is meaningless without her consummating her forbidden love. Yet her sense of shame, and perhaps her conscience, tells her that she can't. Perhaps holding on silently to her forbidden passion, even though she suffers greatly for it, provides some meaning in her life. When her secret is revealed by her nurse, her accommodation is exposed and demolished. Phaedra's suicide seems to come as the only relief she has. Rebecca, in contrast, is understandably concerned that her son Jacob marry an appropriate woman. She has already experienced disappointment in the choices of her other son Esau in this regard. But she has hope that things can change. She complains to her husband, Isaac, to prevent this from happening. She must feel secure in her wifehood and motherhood to do this, and it this sense of purpose and hope which provides her the meaning structure and resilience to go on and the hope that Isaac will listen to her, and even more, that her two sons will reconcile after the elaborate mummery she has orchestrated to provide Jacob with his father's blessing.

The sad account of Antigone in chapter 11 represents an excellent example of the role of hopelessness and the importance of being able to overcome trauma and pathology in one's personal or family life. Antigone cannot overcome her incestuous beginnings and therefore never seems hopeful. She seems totally unable to enjoy her life as a woman or, as her name in Greek (*anti-gone*: against generativity) implies, against motherhood. How different this is from the name the Hebrew Bible gives to the first woman Eve (*Chava*: mother of life, in Hebrew). And as we emphasized before, prayer itself is blocked as a means of both meaning-making and hope. There is no underlying source in which she can ground her life to allow her to recover from her upbringing. She is more fixated on the past than on the present. Ruth in contrast shows as much resilience as any character in the Hebrew Bible. Though she is the product several generations removed from purposeful incest, she never seems phased by this, as is Antigone. Moreover, she is not done in by her early widowhood. Her sense of purpose, her loyalty to her mother-in-law Naomi, and her hope in the future are rewarded in her remarriage and her becoming the ancestress of the Davidic line.

Critical to this, it seems to us, is an intrinsic "hope for" rather than a "fear of" the future (Schwartz and Kaplan, 2013). But how can this hope, the hope that things can change, be instilled in a person? One way is to proceed on the behavioral route. Change a person's experiences and his ability to control his outcomes, and you will instill in that person a sense of efficacy and the sense that he is not helpless and hopeless. But yet we know from experience that this is not always true. Some people cannot give up their inherent pessimism no matter what their successes in life. We have presented the ancient Greeks as a case in point in this regard. No matter what their success, a sense of pessimism and hopelessness remained.

We have previously cited several studies that even the *search*—not necessarily the *presence*—for meaning in life predicted decreased suicidal ideation. This line of research has been supported by findings by Kleiman and Beaver (2013) and Heisel, Neufeld, and Flett (2015), who concluded that there is a growing body of knowledge suggesting that establishing a personal meaning in life contributes not only to general mental wellness, but also decreases future incidents of suicidal contemplations later in life.

However, the case may not be so simple. The inability to create meaning in one's life often leads to feelings of utter despair. It can drive a person to very extreme, often destructive attitudes to try to artificially manufacture meaning and purpose in one's life through clinging to misguided "signs" or "omens." We have also cited several studies of the negative effects of the catastrophizing personality style in an exaggerated search for meaning, with regard to predicted mortality, especially accidents and violent deaths, especially for males (Peterson et al., 1998). Kaplan et al. (2003) found that in the absence of an inherent meaning structure of life, undergraduate students tended to catastrophize and generalize singular negative hypothetical events with which they were presented. Further, this tendency tended to be linked with greater levels of clinical depression and hence more positive attitudes towards suicide, and physician-assisted suicide for both men and women.

In a state of despair, people are susceptible to engage in gross distortions in their experience of the world. We have described the account of the death of Zeno, founder of the Stoic school of philosophy, who wrenched his toe on the way home from lecturing at the *Stoa* (porch). He catastrophizes this objectively minor mishap as a "sign from the gods that he should depart" and voluntarily holds his breath until he dies (Diogenes Laertius, *Lives of Eminent Philosophers*, 7.28).

In contrast to this is the sense that another person may have that against all odds, and even with personal experience of helplessness, that things may change for the better. We have presented the story of Job, perhaps the very prototype of biblical man in this regard. No matter what misfortunes Job experiences, and no matter how great his despair, a sense of optimism remains.

It seems to the authors that one's sense of optimism or pessimism is not simply derivable from personal experience with efficacy or helplessness. True, personal experience plays a role, sometimes a critical role, but yet there is more. One might respond that people differ in moods, some are pessimistic and others are optimistic, and this may be, no, is somewhat autonomous from personal experience.

However, in this book, we have argued that this sense of hope is rooted in something deeper than behavioral experience and deeper than personality traits. We have argued for what Jung would have called a collective unconscious that Athens and Jerusalem (Shestov, 1966) have provided contrasting motifs, perhaps unconscious, which are at war in modern human beings, and the modern personality. One can think of the biblical and Jewish holiday of Chanukah as being paradigmatic in this regard. People may carry mythic structures which battle in their own personalities. On a superficial level, the story of Chanukah is about the fight of the Jews against the Assyrians to preserve their religious tradition. Closer examination indicates the story is a bit more complicated than this. It is also about those Hebraizing Jews who follow the Maccabees and those Hellenizing Jews who are in league with the Syrian Greeks. Yet there is a third level at which this story can be understood. The fight within each person, each individual personality between these two tendencies, the Hebraic and the Hellenic (see Cantz, 2012; Kaplan and Markus-Kaplan, 1979; Markus-Kaplan and Kaplan, 1979).

DIFFERENTIAL ORIENTATIONS TOWARD THE FUTURE

Perhaps central to the difference between Israel and Hellas lies in the different way they view time, stasis, and change. It can be argued that Greek society fears change and the future. Plato experienced a number of changes that may have been quite devastating to him, including the breakdown of the Athenian state, and specifically the trial and execution of his mentor Socrates. Perhaps this is why Plato elevates *being* over *becoming* a higher form of knowledge (Republic, 7.514a–7.521d). As being is to becoming, so knowledge is to opinion.

Biblical society views time very differently. It embraces change and the future. God's response to Moses asking for His name is *ehiyeh asher ehiyeh* (Exodus 3:14). This answer is given in first person singular imperfect form, ancient Hebrew lacking a future tense, but is probably best translated as "I will be what I will be" or perhaps "I will become what I will become," given the context of God promising to be with his people through their future troubles. The glue of the Greek political world then is stasis (always in an uneasy battle with chaos). Change is a threat to this equilibrium. The glue of the biblical world is the Creator. Thus, change is not threatening, and the future need not be dreaded.

With this in mind, let us return to discuss the incest stories of Antigone and Ruth, and then one we have not yet discussed, the biblical stories of Tamar and Judah, her father-in-law, and finally the story of Miriam, the sister of Moses. Recall the beginning of the story of Oedipus. An oracle warns King Laius of Thebes that there is danger if his newborn son should reach manhood, for the son will kill Laius and marry Laius's wife Jocasta. This warning leads Laius to hand his infant son over to a herdsman to be left to die. However, the herdsman gives him to a fellow herdsman who brings him to the childless King and Queen of Corinth.

Many years later, when Oedipus grows up, he hears his identity questioned at a dinner party, and goes to another oracle to ascertain his heritage. The oracle does not answer Oedipus's question but prophesies that Oedipus will cause the death of his father and will marry his mother, neglecting to inform him that King Polybus and his wife are his adoptive rather than biological parents. Oedipus, who has known Polybus (with whom he has a good relationship), as his only father, takes the oracle to mean that he will kill Polybus.

To avoid killing the man he believes to be his father, Oedipus departs from Corinth. Along the way he encounters an older man on a narrow road. Unknown to Oedipus, the man is Laius, Oedipus's biological father, who is heading to Delphi. A quarrel breaks out, and Oedipus does indeed kill the man (unbeknownst to Oedipus, Laius) in self-defense—as well as all but one of his attendants.

Shortly after, Oedipus encounters the Sphinx, a monster part woman, part lion, and part eagle, which has been terrorizing Thebes, devouring all those who cannot guess her riddle. "What walks on four legs in the morning, two legs in the afternoon and three legs in the evening?" Oedipus correctly answers "man" resulting in the suicide of the Sphinx. In gratitude for their deliverance, the Thebans make Oedipus their king and give to him in marriage their queen—Laius's widowed wife and Oedipus's biological mother, Jocasta. They have four children together: two daughters (Antigone and Ismene) and two sons (Eteocles and Polyneices), and Oedipus seems to be a kind and concerned ruler.

Despite this confusion in identities, there is no indication of evil intent. We might look at this and say: "All is well that ends well" and move on. The Greek mind, however, won't let this rest. In Sophocles' *Oedipus Rex*, a great plague falls upon Thebes, and Oedipus is told by his brother-in-law Creon that the gods have sent the plague due to a "defiling thing, which hath been harbored in this land" (ll. 98–99). Oedipus innocently and conscientiously asks how Thebes can be cleansed. Creon responds "By banishing a man, or by bloodshed in quittance of bloodshed, since it is that blood which brings the tempest on our city."

In the process of trying to uncover the reason for the blood-curse, Oedipus uncovers the facts that he has killed his biological father, Laius, and married his biological mother, Jocasta. The uncovering of these facts leads inexorably not only to his own undoing, but to his mother Jocasta's, his two sons', and his daughters'. Oedipus is filled with shame and self-loathing. "So, had I not come to shed my father's blood, not been called among men the spouse of her from whom I sprang; but now am I forsaken of the gods, son of a defiled mother, successor to his bed who gave me mine own wretched being; and if there be yet a woe surpassing woes, it hath become the portion of Oedipus" (ll. 1348–52).

Reflecting these feelings of shame and rage, Oedipus rushes to confront and most likely kill Jocasta: "To and fro he (Oedipus) went, asking us to give him a sword,—asking where he should find the wife who was no wife, but a mother whose womb had borne alike himself and his children" (l. 1256). Seeing that his mother has already hung herself, Oedipus takes out his eyes with the golden brooches on her dress out of shame, as he does not want to face his biological parents in the next world.

As the story of Oedipus proceeds, more tragic events unfold consequentially. Aeschylus described it thusly in *The Seven against Thebes*. After his blinding, Oedipus feels mistreated by his two sons and curses them to kill one another. "A curse prophetic and bitter (of Oedipus on his sons)—the glory of wealth and pride, with iron, not gold, in your hand ye shall come, at the last to divide" (ll. 785–86). One brother, Eteocles, becomes king of Thebes and exiles his brother Polyneices, a rival for the kingship. Polyneices enlists the aid of Argos and leads an army against Thebes to seize the throne. The two brothers do slay each other at the Seventh Gate of Thebes, fulfilling the curse of Oedipus: "And both alike, even now and here have closed their suit, with steel for arbiter. And lo, the fury-fiend of Oedipus, their sire, hath brought his curse to consummation dire. Each in the left side smitten, see them laid—the children of one womb, slain by a mutual doom!" (ll. 879–924).

Creon, who has now assumed the vacant throne of Thebes, issues a proclamation that the body of Eteocles, the defender of Thebes, be given the full funeral honors due a hero, while the corpse of Polyneices, the attacker, be left unburied, without proper funeral rites, a punishment and a slight the Greeks viewed with horror. Antigone, their sister, refuses to follow Creon's order and attempts to bury her brother (Sophocles, *Antigone*, ll. 406–18). Creon responds by ordering her buried alive (ll. 891–96). Antigone subsequently hangs herself while in the vault below (l. 1223).

This is a powerful story, and it is easy to be carried away by it. But one must ask why such a disastrous outcome? Why does Oedipus's unknowing killing of his father in self-defense and unknowing begetting children by his mother lead to such terrible consequences for his mother, himself, his two sons, and his daughter? Oedipus is a very decent man, a compassionate king, and probably a good father and husband as well. Why then doesn't the Greek mind possess a psychological, legal, and political stopper?

It is the Greek obsession with abstract pollutants that makes the Oedipus story end so tragically. Oedipus finds out Jocasta is his mother as well as his wife. She hangs herself, he puts out his eyes, curses his sons to kill each other at the Seventh Gate of Thebes (which they do), and Antigone is buried alive because she refuses to leave her dead brother unburied. And the very idea of pollutant is perhaps rooted in the concept that things cannot change, and man cannot be redeemed.

Compare this to three biblical stories illustrating hope for the future in the most difficult of situations. First, let us reexamine the incest between Lot and his daughters. After the miraculous destruction of Sodom in which their fiancés have been killed, the two daughters of Lot get their father drunk and lie with him because they believe he is the last man left in the world. "And the first-born said unto the younger: 'Our father is old, and there is not a man in the earth to come in unto us after the manner of all the earth. Come let us make our father drink wine, and we will lie with him, that we may preserve the seed of our father'" (Genesis 19:31). Both daughters conceive, and two boys are born.

As we have stressed numerous times in this book, the son of the elder daughter is named Moab deriving from the Hebrew words *mo-ab* (from the father) and is the ancestor of the Moabites; the son of the younger daughter called Ben-Ami (son of my people) is the father of the Ammonites (Genesis 19:36–30), neither people friendly to the Israelites.

Israelite women are forbidden to marry Moabite and Ammonite men not because of the incestuous origin of the people, but because their nation did not show hospitality to the Israelites in the Sinai and also because they hired the sorcerer Balaam son of Beor to curse Israel (Deuteronomy 23:4–6). Female Moabites and Ammonites, when converted to Judaism, were permitted to marry with only the usual prohibition against a convert marrying a *kohen* (high priest). As discussed previously, the shining example of this is the Moabitess Ruth. After her husband's death, Ruth chooses to remain with her mother-in-law Naomi, and joins the Israelite nation. In a very moving speech, Ruth says to Naomi "Whither thou goest, I will go; whither thou lodgest, I will lodge; thy people shall be my people and thy God my God" (Ruth 1:16). The incestuous nature of the origin of Ruth's family is never mentioned, and subsequently, Ruth marries Boaz (Ruth 4:13). Through their union, Ruth becomes the ancestress of King David (Ruth 4:17) and in Christian tradition the ancestor of Jesus of Nazareth (Matthew 1:1–17).

Another story supports this view—the sexual encounter between Judah and his former daughter-in-law Tamar. Judah, Jacob's fourth son, is a leader among his brethren; indeed the royal family of David and Solomon will stem from him. In Genesis 38, Judah separates himself from the society of his brothers and goes into business with Hirah the Adulamite, a Canaanite merchant. He marries a local woman, the daughter of Shua the Canaanite (that is, someone outside the family) and the couple eventually raise three sons. Er, the eldest, marries; but God slays Er for an unspecified wickedness, and his widow Tamar is left with no children.

Levirate law requires that the brother (or close relative) of the deceased marry his childless widow to try to have a son with her—a son who would be an heir to the deceased. So, Judah instructs Onan, his second son, to take this responsibility with Tamar. But Onan does not want to "give seed to his brother." Pretending to consummate his legitimate (but unwanted) marriage to Tamar, he allows his seed to fall to the ground rather than produce a son to carry on his brother Er's heritage (thus the term *onanism* denotes male masturbation). Onan's behavior is displeasing to God, and like his older brother, he also dies. Judah then tells Tamar to return to her father's house and live as a widow while she waits for his third son, Shelah, to reach the age when he will be able to marry her and fulfil the levirate requirement. But in point of fact, Judah, seeing that his two older sons have married Tamar and died shortly after, fears that he will be sending Shelah to the same fate. Time passes, and Tamar, who is no fool, realizes that Judah does not intend to send his third son to marry her; but she is determined to bear children for Er's sake—as well as to accept and participate in the God-given mission of Jacob's family.

In the meantime, Judah's wife dies. After his period of mourning, Judah goes to Timnah with his business associate Hirah for the annual shearing of the sheep, an important event that is celebrated with feasting and drinking. Tamar hears of this and is determined to practice a deception of her own, a lie whose purpose is honorable and will be, in Scripture's terms, "eye-opening." Dressed as a prostitute and with her face covered, Tamar approaches Judah at a crossroads as he is returning from the shearing. Though it is proscribed by everything in his upbringing, Judah decides to have relations with this prostitute and begins to negotiate a price. We should note that Tamar, in her deception of her father-in-law, is sitting at a *petach anayim*, which is generally translated as "crossroads"; but the Hebrew term, taken literally, would mean "opening of the eyes."

By deceiving Judah, Tamar opens his eyes and reveals to him what was best in himself. When Tamar is threatened with death for adultery, Judah assumes responsibility for his act and says "She was righteous (because I did not give her to Shelah). It is by me." In impregnating Tamar and acknowledging the act, Judah himself will beget twin sons, Perez and Zerah to replace the dead Er and Onan. Perez will become an ancestor of Boaz and of King David and his dynasty.

Let us contrast these Greek and biblical narratives. Each of these stories relates an act of incest. Yet the story of Oedipus and his mother ends in disaster while that of Lot and his daughters and of Judah and his daughter-in-law Tamar ends happily. Why? The real difference lies in the underlying attitude towards the future and how that impacts society. The very beginning of the Oedipus legend reflects the Greek distrust of the future. Oedipus is seen as a threat to displace his father Laius, and thus must be destroyed. The father, *afraid of the future*, has the power of infant exposure and uses it. This is the act which precipitates the later incest, unaware as it may be, and the entire tragic events of the house of Oedipus.

However, this is a view foreign to a biblical view of society. Why doesn't Laius glory in the arrival of a new son who hopefully will surpass him? In the biblical view, the father is not the owner of his son as with the Roman *patria potestas,* nor does he hold the power of infant exposure. The Bible sees the relationship between father and son in terms of the fulfillment of the covenant. Indeed, this is what the ceremony of the covenant of circumcision (*brit milah*) represents. The urge of father to destroy his son is superseded by the command to the father to teach his children thoroughly (Deuteronomy 6:7; *Kiddushin,* 30a). The father's identity is not threatened by the son; he wants to see his son develop and surpass him.

The incest stories of Lot and of Judah reflect this biblical *hope in the future*. Lot's daughters get their father drunk and lie with him because they think he is the last man left in the world. Tamar plays a prostitute with her widowed father-in-law Judah to carry on the tribe of Judah. These three women do not fear the future, but create it.

No biblical story illustrates a faith in the future more than Miriam's calling on her parents to remarry to have more children, even in the face of Pharaoh's decree to murder all the newborn boys of the Israelites. The Talmud (*Sotah,* 12b) fills out the rather cryptic account in Exodus 1–2 by telling how, when Pharaoh decrees that all Israelite infant boys be killed, Amram and Jochebed separate in despair over the doom that would fall on any male child they would bear. Miriam, still a very little girl, goes to her father and argues: "Pharaoh's decree affects only the sons; your act affects daughters as well." Amram accepts his daughter's advice and her sense of faith, and he and Jochebed remarry (Miriam dances at their wedding). In due course, this reunion produces Moses.

As Franz Rosenzweig argues in *The Star of Redemption* (1971, 1985), history has a meaning, proceeding from creation to revelation to redemption (see figure C.1): (1) God creates the world. (2) God reveals to the human being. (3) The human being redeems the universe. He/she does this by his closeness to God and by his resultant moral creative behavior. The Star of

David presented below illustrates these relationships in visual form (see also de Tocqueville's distinction between the relationship of religion and freedom in France and America (de Tocqueville, 2000, 282) and Buber's distinction between European and Hebrew humanism (Buber, 1938/1963).

This indeed is a beautiful vision. Yet there is much to be done to apply it to everyday psychotherapy with troubled individuals. We have applied the life-saving lessons of seven biblical narratives to real people demonstrating the destructive patterns and pathways of seven tragic Greek characters. Biblical psychology attempts to go far beyond many modern attempts to integrate religion and psychology. This biblical psychology will encompass the very best parts of positive psychology without lapsing into a Pollyanna-like view of life. "Bad things do happen to good people," and the question becomes how to use biblical narratives to help people deal with these misfortunes in a helpful way. How can biblical psychology help a patient presenting with the plight of Ajax? How can it help a patient behaving like Zeno, Coriolanus, and Narcissus? How would it benefit an Oedipus, Phaedra, and Antigone? How would it help patients presenting with all the myriad of problems illustrated in Greek mythology and history? How can a civilization so brilliant in

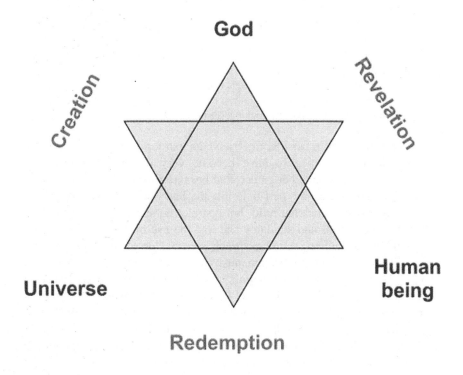

C.1. A Representation of Franz Rosenzweig's *Star of Redemption*.

its ability to analyze dysfunction appear so powerless in alleviating it—other than through magical potions and amulets?

As we have argued previously, the Greek mind has created an antithesis between mythos and logos. Henri Frankfort and his group at the Oriental Institute of the University of Chicago published a number of fascinating books on this topic in the 1940s through the 1970s (Frankfort et al., 1964). The essence of this work is that philosophy and later Greek history was in many ways opposed to the earlier mythic structure. Not so for the Hebrew Bible, where earlier legends blend into later history in a relatively non-antagonistic seamless way, making it difficult to exactly pin down where legend ends and history begins. Perhaps this was one of Freud's great insights, expressed so well in Euripides' great drama "The Bacchae" and Thomas Mann's novella, *Death in Venice* (1925) regarding the return of the repressed (see also the comments of Yerushalmi, 1991).

The senior author would like to share a personal experience in this regard. I have a friend who is a great lover of the Hebrew Bible, and of Israel, both biblical and modern. She always has sung the song that Jews sang when they were exiled in Babylon.

> By the rivers of Babylon, there we sat down, yea, we wept, when we remembered Zion.
> We hanged our harps upon the willows in the midst thereof.
> For there they that carried us away captive required of us a song; and they that wasted us required of us mirth, saying, Sing us one of the songs of Zion.
> How shall we sing the Lord's song in a strange land?
> If I forget thee, O Jerusalem, let my right hand forget her cunning.
> If I do not remember thee, let my tongue cleave to the roof of my mouth; if I prefer not Jerusalem above my chief joy. (Psalm 137:1–6)

At a certain point in her life, my friend, an extraordinarily intelligent and sensitive woman, seemed to have become very disconnected from her roots—she lost her home, her career, and became financially destitute. And on her first days on a new part-time job she had obtained, she was struck down by a stroke, somewhat mild, but a stroke nonetheless. It affected the left side of her brain, and suddenly she lost the use of her right hand (her right hand lost its cunning) and her speech became slurred and she reported it feeling like she was talking through mush (her tongue clove to the roof of her mouth). Thankfully, she is recovering, slowly, but recovering. But what do we make of an experience like this? Does this biblical passage describe a psychosomatic understanding of how a disconnection from one's life meaning can lead to a physical stroke? And is this question not true of so much of modern mental health? What is the effect of being disconnected from our life message on both our psychological and physical health?

What do all our diagnostic categories really tell us? Do they in themselves really deal with the fundamental issues of psychopathology other than through often unnecessary and sometimes harmful "medications" (a different pill for every disorder)? And how does this fundamentally differ from the Greek solution of offering amulets and potions to alleviate various problems people find themselves in rather than attempt to get to the psychological and spiritual heart of their dilemmas? Don't these solutions ring of a "*deus-ex-machina*" approach to psychopathology rather than any truly humanistic and serious psychiatric attempt to treat people as human beings?

This question in the past has been raised by the brilliant psychiatrist Thomas Szasz, and has been more recently examined by Robert Whitaker (2010) in his work "Mad in America" arguing that many patients are over-medicated. The ongoing prospective 20-year Chicago Follow-Up study of psychiatric patients by Martin Harrow and his associates, as well as the work of other researchers points to the ineffectuality of many antipsychotic medications after the initial phase of a disorder (Harrow, Jobe, and Faull, 2012; 2014; Wunderink et al., 2013; Mollanen et al., 2013). Our point here is not to argue for the complete abolishment of psychiatric medications—they can be helpful and even necessary at times—but to argue that medication in itself does not and cannot replace "talk-therapy" whereby the therapist listens with a "listening heart" to the patient in distress (c.f. Pargament, 1997; Pargament and Mahoney, 2002; Reik, 1948).

The field of biblical psychology is slowly emerging and is absolutely unique in being driven by patients or consumers rather than simply by professionals. In addition, it has the potential of transcending the limitations of earlier waves of psychology. As mentioned before, biblical psychology differs from earlier waves of psychology in being driven by clientele who feel increasingly adrift and dissatisfied with mental health treatment. Specifically, it transcends both psychodynamic theory and behaviorism in its emphasis on the integration of inner processes and outer behavior. It is more inclusive than humanistic psychology, in being more open to the spiritual concerns of faith communities. Finally, it transcends multi-cultural psychology by trying to identify the universal processes intrinsic to human life itself as they are manifested in particular culturally specific areas of behavior. It can employ many of the methods of cognitive behavioral therapy, specifically by replacing a fatalistic and tragic ancient Greek way of thinking with a hopeful biblical one. Yet it probes more deeply into psychodynamic issues freed from the fatalism and the Greek narratives underlying Freudian theory.

This book has specifically presented a biblical approach to psychotherapy, which we have developed in response to the implicit and even explicit Greek bias in mental health that has led to a limited and narrow view of psychological health (e.g. Oedipus, Electra, Narcissus, the mind-body split). Nowhere is the Greek sense of the tragic more dangerous for psychotherapy and counseling than in dealing with suicidal patients or clients. Biblical narratives provide an absolutely necessary alternative world view, providing a therapy allowing healthy resolutions of real-life dilemmas.

Positive versus Negative Freedom

The Hebrew Bible is not obsessed with the sense of heroism so endemic to the Greek world; nor is there the Greek dualism between body and soul. The biblical God is a strong and nurturing parent, not a capricious deity. The highest goal of humans is thus to be obedient to God's will rather than to liberate the soul from the body. Freedom is a movement *toward* something (*positive freedom*) rather than merely *away* from something (*negative freedom*).[2]

Humans do not have to earn love through fame or achievement, for it comes unconditionally from God, nor is there the same sense of the tragic that exists in the Greek world. Humans are free to choose good over evil. There is no belief in doom, and there is always the possibility of prayer, repentance, atonement, and genuine change. A person's life is not warped beyond cure or without hope.

BIBLICAL VERSUS GREEK VIEWS OF PROPHECY

Consider how different prophecy is viewed in the biblical and Greek worlds. In the Greek world, the prophecy is deterministic, and cannot be avoided. *Outcome Y will occur and cannot be avoided.* There is no saving antecedent X. In the biblical world, prophecy can be altered and social intervention can occur. *Consequence Y will occur unless some antecedent X intervenes.* In the book of Jonah, the people of Nineveh will be destroyed—unless they repent. But it is the possibility of the saving antecedent X that gives the Hebrew Bible an inspiring therapeutic vision rather than a tragic one, and this possibility makes the prophet a concerned messenger of God rather than a taunting actuary. If the biblical prophet is successful in his endeavors, then his dire predictions will not come to pass.

Putting Time into the Syllogism

Critical to this difference are the contrasting views of time in the Greek and biblical worlds. Consider the standard Aristotelian syllogism, containing a major premise, a minor premise, and a conclusion.

1. All men are mortal. (Major premise)
2. Socrates is a man. (Minor premise)
3. Therefore, Socrates is mortal. (Conclusion)

Let us apply this Greek syllogistic reasoning to the biblical story of the Israelites coming out of Egypt:

1. No persons who were slaves can enter into the "promised land." (Major premise)
2. All Israelites coming out of Egypt were slaves. (Minor premise)
3. Therefore, no Israelite can enter the "promised land." (Conclusion)

However, according to the biblical account this is not what happened. Or more to the point, this is what happened initially as no persons of the "slave generation" were allowed to enter the "promised land." However, after forty years, descendants coming out of Egypt were considered free enough emotionally and cognitively to be allowed to come into the Promised Land. And it is this awareness of time itself, the passage of time to be exact, that transforms the closed static over-determined Greek syllogism into an open dynamic assertion of freedom and belief in change and development.

A Hebrew conception of the above syllogism can be represented as follows:

1. No persons who have the mentality of slaves can enter into the "promised land." (Major premise)
2. All Israelites coming out of Egypt initially had the mentality of slaves. (Minor premise)
3. Therefore, no Israelite could initially enter into the "promised land" while he has that "slave mentality." (Initial conclusion)
4. However, after 40 years in the desert, a new generation of Israelites were born who did not carry this slave mentality from Egypt. (Adjusted premise)
5. Therefore, after 40 years, the Israelites were allowed to enter into the "promised land." (Adjusted conclusion)

In other words, the Hebrew idea of a syllogism seems to be dynamic. Time is the salvific element missing in the Greek world view, certainly the Platonic one.

Finally, biblical characters do not face the same Hobson's choices that Greek heroes do. They are not presented with riddling sphinxes and oracles that distort their sense of judgment. Even when they do seem to be mired in no-win situations, there is typically a stopper, an opportunity to return to their covenant to deepen their relationship with God. In short, the Bible is not a Greek tragedy.

The Entrapment of the Riddle

A vivid example of how trapped a person can become in a tragic world view has been provided by the senior author in his recently published two-act play *Oedipus in Jerusalem* (Kaplan, 2015). In this play, the biblical prophet Nathan meets the blinded Oedipus near Thebes. Nathan becomes convinced Oedipus is innocent of the crimes of intentional patricide and incest as he didn't know the identity of either his father or mother and actively attempted to avoid committing these crimes. Nathan brings Oedipus for trial at the Sanhedrin in Jerusalem, with the Greek playwright Sophocles serving as accuser and Nathan himself serving as the defender of Oedipus who insists he is guilty. The Sanhedrin acquits Oedipus, concluding he has been done in by "fate" which actually is nothing magical at all but a result of incomplete information, misleading riddles and confusing statements, leaving Oedipus without accurate knowledge of his situation and thus entrapping him.

A dialogue between Nathan and the Oracle of Delphi indicts Greek thinking as representing an abstract geometrical concoction rather than the organic morality inherent in biblical thinking. Oedipus is reprimanded for only one act, destroying his eyes, a prohibited self-mutilation in the Bible and Jewish law. Oedipus, thoroughly indoctrinated by Greek thinking, refuses to accept the verdict of innocence, shouting that he is the "worst of the worst," guilty of the polluting acts of patricide and incest with his mother. As destructive as this world view is, it provides Oedipus with the only meaning structure available to him. Thus, he derives a secondary gain from insisting on his guilt and the impossibility of any redemption.

The very sense of being trapped by the maddening labyrinth of Greek society and its inherent fatalism may lead to the extreme of suicide as the only way out of the trap. For life itself is a riddle and a fatalistic trap in this ancient Greek and Roman world. Indeed, it seems as if the Oracle of Delphi uses the unintelligible riddle as her form of communication, giving no usable information.

In his probing discussion of the non-informative aspect of Apollo's speech, classicist Bruce Heiden (2005) argues that the Greeks actually preferred communication that had no usable life-message. He cites Sophocles fragment 771 in this regard:

> And I thoroughly understand that the god is this way:
> To the wise, always a poser of riddles in divine speech,
> but to the foolish a teacher of lessons, trivial and concise.

Heiden goes on to argue that "the different addressees for whom Apollo's speeches are either lessons or riddles do not exercise different linguistic competencies, but different degrees of wisdom, and the acquisition of the positive meaning of the teaching surprisingly accords with stupidity, while the riddle, whose characteristic is denial of meaning, accords with positive wisdom" (pp. 236–37).

This is an extraordinary statement, leaving poor Oedipus and all people under this life view, and unlike Moses, unable to obtain usable help from others (see chapter 9). The biblical prophet Nathan uses parables to effect change (as he does in his confrontation of King David over his covetousness of Bathsheba, Uriah's wife). The Oracle of Delphi (the Pythia) uses riddles to entrap Oedipus and keep him from avoiding disaster.

PARABLES VERSUS RIDDLES

Consider in more detail the essentially parallel stories of the prophet Nathan's confrontation with King David and that of the blind prophet Teiresias with Oedipus the King. Both David and Oedipus have committed grievous acts. David has knowingly impregnated the wife of one of his most loyal warriors and arranged his death on the battlefield. Oedipus has unknowingly impregnated his mother and killed his father on a road from Corinth into Thebes. Let us examine the roles of Nathan and Teiresias in these stories.

Nathan and David

David has slept with Bathsheba, the wife of Uriah the Hittite, a member of David's elite corps of warriors. She becomes pregnant by David and tells him so. David then asks that Uriah be sent to him from the battlefield and tries to conceal his actions towards Bathsheba by twice urging Uriah to go home and lie with his wife, hoping to deceive Uriah into thinking he is the father of the baby that Bathsheba is carrying. However, Uriah twice refuses to lie with his wife out of loyalty to his men who are encamped in the open field of battle. "My master's servants are encamped in the open field, and shall I then come to my house to eat and to drink and to lie with my wife?" (2 Samuel 11:11).

David responds by writing a letter to Joab and sends it by the hand of Uriah, saying:

"Put Uriah in the face of the fiercest battling and draw back, so that he will be stuck down and die" (ibid., 11:15). Uriah is killed and Joab reports his death back to David. After Bathsheba hears that her husband has died and grieves, David brings her into his house and marries her. And she bears him a son.

Enter the prophet Nathan, sent by the Lord who comes to David with the following parable. Two men lived in the same town, one was rich and the other poor. The rich man had sheep and cattle, in great abundance. And the poor man had nothing save one little ewe that he had bought whom he had nurtured as a daughter from infancy. A wayfarer came to the rich man who used his power to take the poor man's ewe and slaughter it for the meal, rather than slaughter any of his own many sheep and cattle.

David's anger "flared hot against the man," and he said to Nathan, "As the Lord lives, doomed is the man who has done this, and the poor man's ewe he shall pay back fourfold, in as much as he has done this thing, and because he has no pity!" And in one of the most famous lines in all of literature, Nathan says to David: "You are the man!" Nathan uses this parable to drive home the point that David is the rich man, Uriah is the poor man, and Bathsheba is the ewe that David has taken from Uriah, and has gone even further in arranging for Uriah to be killed. To make it worse, David was aware of all that he had done.

When David is made to confront what he has done, he acknowledges his sin, saying "I have offended against the Lord." Nathan replies to David that the Lord has remitted his offense and that he shall not die. But that the newly son born to David and Bathsheba will die, which he does. David grieves and atones, and he and Bathsheba produce another son, Solomon, who will succeed David as King of Israel (ibid., 2 Samuel 12).

Our point here is to highlight the power of a parable to penetrate a person's defenses and help him correct mistakes, even grievous ones, and to grow. Now let us examine the essentially parallel narrative of Oedipus the King and the destructive role of the Greek prophet Teiresias.

Teiresias and Oedipus

Unbeknownst to him, Oedipus has killed his father Laius on the road from Corinth to Thebes, while trying to avoid a prophecy that he is destined to kill his father and marry his mother whom he mistakenly thinks are the King and Queen of Corinth. Oedipus subsequently saves travelers to Thebes from being devoured by the riddling Sphinx. Oedipus solves her riddle and she jumps off a rock to her destruction. Oedipus in turn is rewarded by being presented the widow of the King of Thebes, Laius, as a wife. He impregnates her and begets four children. Unlike David, Oedipus seems unaware of the identity of his biological parents, and has in fact tried his utmost to avoid incest or patricide. Yet he has committed both, and Thebes is now in the throes of a great pestilence. Oedipus believes that this is due to the unsolved murder of Laius and sincerely attempts to find the killer of Laius to remove the pestilence from Thebes. He calls the blind prophet Teiresias, who knows Oedipus is the cause of the pestilence to help him. Rather than provide a parable to Oedipus to help make him aware of his actions and accept them, and perhaps find a solution, Teiresias infuriates Oedipus with his evasive cutting answers. Here are some examples. Teiresias begins his riddling as follows: taunting Oedipus with regard to the total futility of wisdom. "Alas, alas! How dreadful it can be to have wisdom when it brings no benefit to the man possessing it" (Oedipus The King, ll. 374–76). Rather than respond seriously to Oedipus, Teiresias responds maddingly: "You are all ignorant. I will not reveal the troubling things inside" (ibid., ll. 390–92). And when Oedipus, provoked beyond endurance, insults Teiresias regarding his blindness, Teiresias responds as follows with some of the most maddening, vengeful, and chilling lines in all literature. "So I say this to you, since you have chosen to insult my blindness—you have your eyesight, and you do not see how miserable you are, or where you live, or who it is who shares your household (ibid., ll. 410–15). . . . Those eyes of yours which now can see so clearly, will be dark. What harbor will not echo with your cries?" (ibid., ll. 419–20).

Teireisas taunts Oedipus with one vicious riddle after another, entrapping him more and more in an endless labyrinth. If he has something to say to Oedipus, we must ask why does he not say it straight out, or in parable form, rather than entrap him with maddening riddles that do nothing but lead to a tragic ending.

A CALL FOR A BIBLICAL PSYCHOLOGY AND PSYCHOTHERAPY

The Greek understanding of freedom is that it is illusory and can only be obtained by a fight against control by others, and ultimately by suicide.[3] This is based on the assumption that there is an inherent conflict between self and others as expressed in the story of Narcissus in chapter 8. The ultimate freedom is thus escape from others, as expressed in death and suicide itself. "Do you inquire the road to freedom? You shall find it in every vein of your body" (Seneca, *De Ira*, 3.15.3–4).

More generally, mental illness can itself provide an escape from psychic pain, and thus itself provide this secondary gain. Edward Shneidman, the father of the suicide movement in America, has specifically argued that suicide itself serves to reduce what he calls "psychache." And recent work we have cited in chapter 2 has found empirical evidence that a *psychache* scale may be more predictive of suicide than either a *depression* or a *hopelessness* scale (Troister, D'Agata, and Holden, 2015).

We have attempted to show in this book how biblical narratives can be employed to provide people with a hopeful narrative, allowing people to give up the secondary gain implicit in a tragic world view. We have desituated seven biblical narratives (Elijah, Job, David, Jonah, Moses, Rebecca, and Ruth) from their formal theological context and employed them in a psychotherapeutic way to help people overcome an over-determined tragic world view illustrated respectively by seven tragic Greek and Roman counterparts (Ajax, Zeno, Coriolanus, Narcissus, Oedipus, Phaedra, and Antigone), thus promoting life rather than simply preventing suicide. This represents a positive way to promote an individual's capacity to activate and mobilize innate, and perhaps even divinely endowed, domains of resiliency to overcoming major life challenges.

It is important to emphasize that this technique can be used with both religious and secular patients/clients to prevent their suicide and indeed invigorate their lives. What is common to all of these psycho-biblical treatment approaches is the sense that people are not trapped, that change is possible, and life is of intrinsic value. We have offered biblical resolutions to life issues that can help the readers live happier and more fulfilled lives. They represent guides for therapists, counselors, coaches, and people themselves, in how to avoid the psychological traps set up in Greek narratives. Given a biblical world view, people can and do hope, pray, grow, develop, and sometimes even change.

Let us return to the insightful observations of the sociologist, Philip Slater—Western man is nothing but the narcissistic and disloyal Greek leader Alcibiades with a bad conscience, disguised as a plumber (Slater, *The Glory of Hera*, 1968, p. 451). And let us repeat the clarion call of Dr. Eric Wellisch, medical director of Grayford Child Guidance Clinic in England, for a "Biblical psychology," arguing that:

> The very word "psyche" is Greek. The central psychoanalytic concept of the formation of character and neurosis is shaped after the Greek Oedipus myth. It is undoubtedly true that the Greek thinkers possessed an understanding of the human mind which, in some respects, is unsurpassed to the present day, and that the trilogy of Sophocles still presents us with the most challenging problems. But stirring as these problems are, they were not solved in the tragedy of Oedipus. In ancient Greek philosophy, only a heroic fight for the solution but no real solution is possible. Ancient Greek philosophy has not the vision of salvation. . . . There is need for a Biblical psychology. (Wellisch, 1954, p. 115)

Wellisch's clarion call resonates with the contrasting representations of hope versus hopelessness in Greek and biblical writings (Cantz, 2012; 2015; Cantz and Castle, 2013; Kaplan and Schwartz, 2008; Kaplan, 2012; 2013; Kaplan and Anderson, 2013; Kaplan, 2015). Let us repeat our contrast between the role of hope in the story of Pandora and that of Noah. In the Greek account, Zeus sends Pandora, woman, to man (Epimetheus) as punishment for his half-brother Prometheus stealing fire and thus gaining some autonomy. One day, Pandora decides to open the box that Zeus had sent along with her. The box contained all the evils in the world, which fly out. Pandora closes the lid as quickly as she could, but too late; only hope remains locked in the box, and unavailable to people (Hesiod, *Theogony*, ll. 533–615; *Works and Days,* ll. 53–105; Plato, *Protagoras*; 320c–322a).

The Hebrew Scriptures portray hope in a very different way. After the great flood ceases, all living creatures, male and female, come out from the ark built by Noah and repopulate the earth through their sexual union. God places a bow in the heavens as a sign of His covenant with man that he will not send another flood (Genesis 9:13). The bow becomes the very symbol of hope.

Nowhere is this contrast more relevant than in the treatment of suicide. Biblical narratives provide a stopper to suicidal crises unavailable in the tragic Greek myths so ingrained in psychological thinking. They provide a hopeful basis for the modern development of positive psychology (Seligman, 1998; Seligman and Csíkszentmihályi, 2000).

Returning to biblical narratives may represent the strongest antidote to the obsession of "death with dignity" and rational suicide so endemic to Zeno the Stoic, Nazi euthanasia, patient Charlotte (chapter 6), and considerable trends in contemporary bioethics. These latter forces are working to change the default in society from life to death. This must be combated with all our strength, and a biblically-based psychotherapy and ethic in this regard is a good place to start. The question is not whether suicide can be rational but whether rationality can be suicidal! (Kaplan, 2007a).

In the biblical tradition, even a personal and familial experience of helplessness may be overcome by a tradition of hope and efficacy. In the ancient Greek vision, even personal experience of efficacy can be undone by an underlying tragic explanatory style of catastrophizing, and resultant helplessness and hopelessness (c.f., Peterson et al., 1998; Kaplan et al., 2003). In the former, you can't lose for winning, while in the latter you can't win for losing. . . . And your life is on the line.

NOTES

1. See the distinction of the senior author between oscillation between the two clinical polarities of disengagement and enmeshment and healthy development from an immature to a mature interpersonal position (Kaplan, 1988; 1990b; 1998b).

2. See Isaiah Berlin's iconic distinction between positive freedom (freedom toward) and negative freedom (freedom from) in this regard (Berlin, 1969).

3. The authors are indebted to the insights of Kyle Seibert (2016), our student in an online course we teach entitled "A Biblical Approach to Mental Health."

Glossary of Biblical and Graeco-Roman Terms and Figures

Aaron	In the Hebrew Bible, Aaron was the elder brother of Moses and a Prophet of God
Abimelech	King of Israel whose skull is broken by a woman, and then stabs himself with the help of an attendant
Abraham	First of three great patriarchs in Judaism about 1800 B.C.E.
Absalom	Son of King David who rebels against him and then is killed
Achilles	In Greek mythology, Achilles was a Greek hero of the Trojan War and the central character and greatest warrior of Homer's *Iliad*
Adam	First man according to the Hebrew Bible
Admetus	Greek king who asks his wife Alcestis to die for him in tragedy by Euripides
Aeschylus	Great Greek dramatist of the fifth century B.C.E.
Agamemnon	Leader of the Greek expedition against Troy. Father of Electra and Iphigenia
Ahitophel	Biblical figure who strangles himself
Ajax	Greek warrior who falls on his sword in tragedy by Sophocles
Alcestis	Wife of Admetus

Antigone	Daughter and half sister of Oedipus who hangs herself in tragedy by Sophocles
Apollodorus	Compiler of Greek legends, author of *The Library*
Aristotle	Great Greek philosopher of the fourth century B.C.E., student of Plato
Athena	Greek goddess of wisdom
Bathsheba	Uriah's wife coveted by David
Biathanatos	Famous book on suicide by John Donne
Boaz	Husband of Ruth in the Hebrew Bible
Coriolanus (Marcius)	Roman general who provokes his death
Creon	The brother of Jocasta who becomes king of Thebes
Cronus	The son of Uranus and Gaea in Greek mythology
Daineira	The wife of Heracles who stabs herself in tragedy by Sophocles
David, King	The second king of the United Kingdom of Israel and Judah from 1010 to 970 B.C.E.
Delphic Oracle (The Pythia)	Transmitter of messages presumably forecasting the future
Deucalion	Son of Prometheus
Diogenes Laertius	(fl. c. third century C.E.) was a biographer of the Greek philosophers
Earth (Gaea)	The earth goddess in Greek mythology
Electra	The daughter of the Greek warrior Agamemnon and Clytemnestra
Elijah	Biblical prophet whose life is saved by angel bringing food and water
Epimetheus	The half brother of Prometheus and the husband of Pandora
Eteocles	Son of Oedipus who is slain at the Seventh Gate of Thebes by his brother Polyneices in tragedy by Aeschylus
Euripides	Great Greek dramatist of the fifth century B.C.E.
Eurydice	The mother of Haemon who stabs herself in tragedy by Sophocles
Evadne	Jumps into a funeral pyre in tragedy by Euripides

Eve (Chava)	First woman according to the Hebrew Bible
God (Ha-Shem)	The god of the Hebrew Bible
Haemon	The would-be suitor of Antigone who stabs himself in tragedy by Sophocles
Hamlet	Famous character of Shakespeare
Heracles	Great Geek superhero who jumps on a funeral pyre in tragedy by Sophocles
Hermione	An attempted suicide in tragedy by Euripides
Hesiod	Greek author of the *Theogony* and *Works and Days*
Hippocrates	A founder of Greek medicine
Hippolytus	Son of Theseus with whom stepmother Phaedra is infatuated in tragedy by Euripides
Iphigenia	Daughter of Agamemnon and Clytemnestra who acquiesces to stab herself in the throat to bring about good winds for the Greek fleet to sail to Troy in tragedy by Euripides
Isaac	Son of Abraham and Sarah
Jacob	Son of Isaac and Rebecca
Job	Pious man who is tested by God
Jocasta	Mother and wife of Oedipus
Jonah	Reluctant biblical prophet who does not want to go to Nineveh
Jocasta	Mother and wife of Oedipus
Josephus, Flavius	Jewish historian who goes over to the Roman side and records his account of the mass Jewish suicide at Masada in 73 C.E.
Judah	Son of Jacob in the Hebrew Bible
Judas Iscariot	Betrayer of Jesus in the Christian New Testament
Laius	Father of Oedipus who hears from oracle that his son will murder him and marry his wife
Lot	Survivor of destruction of Sodom in the Hebrew Bible who impregnates his daughters
Macaria	The daughter of Heracles who offers herself to be stabbed as sacrifice in tragedy by Euripides
Maimonides	Rabbi and physician in medieval Spain and Turkey

Masada	Scene of purported mass Jewish suicide in 73 C.E.
Merope	Queen of Corinth and adopted mother of Oedipus
Menelaus	Brother of Agamemnon, and husband of Helen of Troy
Menoeceus	Son of Creon who jumps to his death in Euripidean tragedy
Mishna	An important digest of Jewish law composed by Rabbi Judah the Prince and his associates about 200 C.E.
Midrash	A genre of literary works interpreting the books of the Hebrew Bible. Written in the late Roman and early medieval periods
Miriam	Sister of Moses
Moses	Great leader of Israel in the fourteenth century B.C.E. who leads his people out of Egypt
Mount Moriah	Mountain where Abraham takes Isaac to offer him as a sacrifice
Mount Olympus	Abode of the Greek pantheon of gods
Naomi	Mother-in-law of Ruth
Narcissus	Mythical Greek figure who falls in love with his own reflection, with fatal results
Nathan	Famous prophet of Israel who confronts David over his actions toward Uriah
Nessus	A centaur who was killed by Heracles, and whose tainted blood in turn killed Heracles
Noah	Biblical figure who builds the ark
Odysseus	Great Greek hero of the Trojan War, credited with developing the plan to hide the Greek army in the belly of a massive wooden horse which the Trojans brought into their city, leading to the destruction of Troy
Oedipus	Tragic hero of Sophocles and Euripides who unknowingly kills his father and impregnates his mother, while trying to avoid doing this
Ovid	Roman author of Metamorphoses
Pandora	First woman in Greek mythology who unleashes all the evils into the world

Pharaohs	Rulers of Ancient Egypt
Plato	Perhaps the greatest Greek philosopher of the fourth century B.C.E., student of Socrates
Polyneices	Son of Oedipus who is slain at the Seventh Gate of Thebes by his brother Eteocles in a tragedy of Aeschylus
Polyxena	Daughter of Trojan Hecuba who stabs herself in tragedy by Euripides
Procrustes	In the Greek myth, Procrustes owned a bed in which he invited every passerby to spend the night, and where he set to work on them with his smith's hammer, to stretch them to fit. In later tellings, if the guest proved too tall, Procrustes would amputate the excess length; nobody ever fit the bed exactly
Prometheus	Greek god who steals fire for man from Zeus and also the blueprint for an ark after the flood
Pyrrha	In Greek mythology, was the daughter of Epimetheus and Pandora and wife of Deucalion
Rebecca	Wife of Isaac in the Hebrew Bible
Ruth	Biblical figure who is exemplary daughter, mother, and wife, and ancestress of King David
Samson	Biblical strongman who pulls the temple of the Philistines down on them
Sarah	Wife of Abraham and mother of Isaac. Viewed as matriarch of Jewish people
Saul	First ruler of the United Kingdom of Israel and Judah in the eleventh century B.C.E. who falls on his sword after loss in battle with the help of his armor-bearer
Saul's armor-bearer	Falls on own sword after he sees that Saul is dead
Second Temple	The religious center of the Jewish people from 530 B.C.E. until 70 C.E.
Sky (Uranus)	The sky god in Greek mythology
Socrates	Great Greek philosopher of the fifth century B.C.E., 470 to 399 B.C.E., considered to be the epitome of wisdom
Sophocles	Great Greek dramatist of the fifth century B.C.E.

Sphinx	The Greek mythological creature, part woman, part eagle, and part lioness, who terrorizes all who pass below her with her riddles, and devours them when they fail to solve them
Talmud	(Babylonian) The magnum opus of Jewish law and legend
Tamar	The daughter-in-law of Judah whom he unknowingly impregnates
Tanach	The Hebrew Bible (The Old Testament)
Teiresias	Blind Greek seer who "sees" Oedipus's situation clearly
Theseus	The husband of Phaedra and father of Hippolytus in tragedy by Euripides
Uriah	The husband of Bathsheba abandoned by David in the battlefield
Volsci	The enemy of Rome, whom Coriolanus joins after his banishment
Zeno the Stoic (Zeno of Citium)	Founder of the Stoic school of philosophy; said to have held his breath until he died after stubbing his toe
Zeus	The head god in the Greek pantheon
Zimri	Biblical figure; short-lived King of Israel who set fire to his palace, killing himself in defiance being displaced from the throne

References

Abramson, L. Y., Seligman, M. E. P., & Teasdale, J. D. (1978). Learned helplessness: Critique and reformulation. *Journal of Abnormal Psychology, 87*(1), 49–74.

Adam, K., Bouckoms, A., & Streiner, D. (1982). Parental loss and family stability in attempted suicide. *Archives of General Psychiatry, 39*(9) 1081–1085.

Adams, J. 1700. *An essay concerning self-murder.* London, ENG: Privately printed for T. Bennett.

Adelmann, P. K., Antonucci, T. C., Crohan, S. E., & Coleman, L. M. (1989). Empty nest, cohort, and employment in the well-being of midlife women. *Sex Roles, 20*(3–4), 173–189.

Aeschylus. (1938). Prometheus Bound. Translated by Paul Elmore More. In *The Complete Greek Drama: Volume 1* Edited by Whitney J. Oates & Eugene O'Neill, Jr. New York: Random House, 127–166.

Aeschylus. (1938). The Seven Against Thebes. Translated by E.D.A. Moreland. In *The Complete Greek Drama: Volume 1* Edited by Whitney J. Oates & Eugene O'Neill, Jr. New York: Random House, 89–126.

Ainsworth, M. D. S. (1972). Attachment and dependency: A comparison. In *Attachment and Dependency,* ed. J. Gerwitz. Washington, DC: V. H.Winston and Sons.

Alighieri, Dante. (1977). *The Divine Comedy.* Trans. J. Ciardi. New York: W. W. Norton.

Alley, J. C. (1982). Life-threatening indicators among the Indochinese refugees. *Suicide and Life-Threatening Behavior, 12*(1), 46–51.

Alvarez, A. (1970). *The Savage God.* New York: Random House.

Anderson, H. D. (2011). Suicide ideation, depressive symptoms and out-of-home placement among youth in the U. S. Child Welfare System. *Journal of Clinical Child & Adolescent Psychology, 40*(6), 790–796.

Ao, T., Taylor, E., Lankau, E., Sivilli, T. I., Blanton, C., Shetty, S., & Lopes-Cardozo, B. (2012). An investigation into suicides among Bhutanese refugees in the US 2009–2012 stakeholders report. *Center for Disease Control and Prevention.*

Apollodorus. (1976). *The Library.* Trans. M. Simpson. Amherst: University of Massachusetts Press.

Aquinas, T. (1981). *Summa Theologica* (5 vol.) Translated by Fathers of the English Dominican Province, 5.

Aristotle. (1936). *The Poetics.* Ed. and trans. S. H. Butcher. London: Macmillan.

Aristotle. (1976). *The Ethics of Aristotle: The Nichomachean ethics.* Trans. J. A. K. Thomson. New York: Penguin.

Aronson, W. (2014). *Refeathering the Empty Nest: Life after the Children Leave.* Lanham, MD: Rowman & Littlefield.

213

Auerbach, E. (1968). *Mimesis: The Representation of Reality in Western Literature*. Translated from the German by Willard R. Trask. Princeton, NJ: Princeton University Press.

Axelson, L. J. (1960). Personal adjustment in the post parental period. *Marriage and Family Living, 22*, 66–68.

Bakan, D. (1958). *Sigmund Freud and the Jewish Mystical Tradition*. Princeton, NJ: VanNostrand.

Bakan, D. (1966). *The Duality of Human Existence: Isolation and Communion in Western Man*. Boston, MASS: Beacon Press.

Barker, R. G., & Wright, H. F. (1955). *Midwest and Its Children: The Psychological Ecology of an American Town*. Oxford: Row, Peterson.

Bart, P. B. (1971). Depression in middle-aged women. In V. Gornick and B. K. Moran (Eds.), *Woman in Sexist Society*. New York: The New American Library, 99–117.

Barter, J. T., Swaback, D. O., & Todd, D. (1968). Adolescent suicide attempts: A follow-up study of hospitalized patients. *Archives of General Psychiatry, 19*, 523–527.

Battin, M. P. (1996). *The Death Debate: Ethical Issues in Suicide*. New York: Prentice Hall.

Beck, A. T. (1963). Thinking and depression. I. Idiosyncratic content and cognitive distortions. *Archives of General Psychiatry, 9*, 324–335.

Beck, A. T. (1967). *Depression: Clinical, Experimental and Theoretical Aspects*. New York: Harper & Row.

Beck, A. T. (1996). Hopelessness as a predictor of eventual suicide. *Annals of the New York Academy of Sciences, 487*, 90–96.

Beck, A.T., Brown, G., Berchick, R. J., Stewart, B. L., & Steer, R. A. (1990). Relationship between hopelessness and ultimate suicide: A replication with psychiatric outpatients. *The American Journal of Psychiatry, 147*, 190–195.

Beck, A. T., Resnik, H. L. P., & Lettieri, D. (Eds.). (1974). *The Prediction of Suicide*. Bowie, MD: Charles Press.

Beck, A. T., Steer, R. A., & Carbin, M. G. (1988). Psychometric properties of the Beck Depression Inventory. Twenty-five years of evaluation. *Clinical Psychology Review, 8*, 77–100.

Bedrosian, R. C., & Beck, A .T. (1979). Cognitive aspects of suicidal behavior. *Suicide and Life-Threatening Behavior, 9*(2), 87–96.

Ben Gurion, J. (1956). *Sefer Yosippon. Jerusalem. Hotstaat Hominer*.

Ben-Shahar, T. (2014). *Choose the Life You Want: The Mindful Way to Happiness*. New York: The Experiment LLC.

Benson, R. A., & Brodie, D. C. (1975). Suicide by overdoses of medicines among the aged. *Journal of the American Geriatrics Society, 23*(7), 304–308.

Berardo, F. M. (1968). Widowhood status in the United States: Perspective on a neglected aspect of the family life-cycle. *The Family Coordinator, 17*, 191–203.

Berardo, F. M. (1970). Survivor and social isolation: The case of the aged widower. *The Family Coordinator, 19*, 11–25.

Berlin, I. (1969). Tso concepts of liberty. In *Four Essays on Liberty*. Oxford: Clarendon Press, 121–154, 169–172.

Berlin, I. N. (1987). Suicide among American Indian adolescents: An overview. *Suicide and Life-Threatening Behavior, 17*(3), 218–232.

Bernard, J. S. (1974). *The Future of Motherhood*. New York: Dial Press.

Bidder, J. (2005). Learning to cope with the empty nest syndrome. *Times (The United Kingdom)*, August 18, Student Guide 9.

Biller, O. A. (1977). Suicide related to the assassination of President John F. Kennedy. *Suicide and Life-Threatening Behavior, 7*(1), 40–44.

Bock, E. W., & Webber, I. L. (1972). Suicide among the elderly: Isolating widowhood and mitigating alternatives. *Journal of Marriage and the Family, 34*, 24–31.

Bohannan, P. (1960). *African Homicide and Suicide*. Princeton, NJ: Princeton University Press.

Boman, T. (1960). *Hebrew Thought Compared with Greek*. Philadelphia, PA: Westminster Press.

Borowsky, I. W., Ireland, M., & Resnick, M. D. (2001). Adolescent suicide attempts: Risks and protectors. *Pediatrics, 107*(3), 485–493.

Boszormenyi-Nagy, I., & Spark, G. M. (1973). *Invisible Loyalties: Reciprocity in Intergenerational Family Therapy.* New York: Harper & Row.

Bowlby, J. (1969). *Attachment.* New York: Basic Books.

Bowlby, J. (1973). *Separation: Anxiety and Anger.* New York: Basic Books.

Bowlby, J. (1977). The making and breaking of affectional bonds: Etiology and psychopathology in the light of attachment theory. *British Journal of Psychiatry, 130*: 201–210.

Brandt, R. B. (1975). The rationality of suicide. From "The morality and rationality of suicide." In S. Perlin (Ed.), *A Handbook for the Study of Suicide.* Oxford: Oxford University Press.

Brockington, I. (2001). Suicide in women. *International Journal Psychopharmacology, 16*(2), S7–S19.

Brown, G. K., Beck, A. T., Steer, R. A., & Grisham, J. R. (2000). Risk factors for suicide in psychiatric outpatients: A 20 year prospective study. *Journal of Consulting and Clinical Psychology, 68*, 371–377.

Brown, J. P. (1994). Yahweh, Zeus, Jupiter: The high God and the elements. *Zeitschrift fu¨r die Alttestamentliche Wissenschaft, 106*, 175–197.

Buber, M. (1938, 1963). Plato and Isaiah. In *Israel and the World New York 1963*, 111–112.

Calear, A. L., Batterham, P. J., & Christensen, H. (2014). Predictors of help-seeking for suicidal ideation in the community: Risks and opportunities for public suicide prevention campaigns. *Psychiatry Research, 219*(3), 525–530.

Calhoun, G., & Morse, W. C. (1977). Self-concept and self-esteem: Another perspective. *Psychology in the Schools, 14*(3), 318–322.

Campbell, A. (1975). The American way of mating; Marriage yes, children only maybe. *Psychology Today, 8*, 37–43.

Campbell, A., Converse, P. E., & Rodgers, W. L. (1976). *The Quality of American Life: Perceptions, Evaluations, and Satisfactions: Perceptions, Evaluations, and Satisfactions.* New York: Russell Sage Foundation.

Campbell, J. (1969). *The Masks of God: Primitive Mythology.* New York: Viking Press.

Camus, A. (1955). *The Myth of Sisyphus and Other Essays.* New York: Alfred A. Knopf.

Cantz, P. (2012). Towards a biblical psychoanalysis: A second look at the first book. *Mental Health, Religion & Culture, 15*, 779–797.

Cantz, P. (2015). Suspicious circumcisions: A psychoanalytic exploration of the connection between misogyny and antisemitism. *Mental Health, Religion & Culture, 18*, 354–367.

Cantz, P. & Castle, M. (2013). A psycho-biblical response to death anxiety: Separation and individuation dynamics in the Babel narrative. *Journal of Psychology & Theology, 41*, 327–339.

Cantz, P. & Kaplan, K. J. (2013). Cross cultural reflections on the feminine "other": Hebraism and Hellenism redux. *Pastoral Psychology, 62*, 485–496.

Carballo, M., & Nerukar, A. (2001). Migration, refugees, and health risks. *Emerging Infectious Diseases, 7*(3 Suppl), 556–560.

Caspi, Y. (2011) *Inquiring of God: Foundations of Talmudic and Biblical Psychology.* Michael Kohane and Betsy Rosenberg (Translators). Amazon Digital Services LLC.

Catanzaro, D. (1995). Reproductive status, family interactions, and suicidal ideation: Surveys of the general public and high-risk groups. *Ethology and Sociobiology, 16*(5), 385–394.

Cheng, T. A., Chen, T. H. H., Chen, C. C., & Jenkins, R. (2000). Psychosocial and psychiatric risk factors for suicide Case—control psychological autopsy study. *The British Journal of Psychiatry, 177*(4), 360–365; DOI: 10.1192/bjp.177.4.360

Chia, B. H. (1979). Suicide of the young in Singapore. *Annals of the Academy of Medicine, Singapore, 8*(3), 262–268.

Choron, J. (1972). *Suicide.* New York: Scribner.

Cicero. (1914). *De finibus bonorum et malorum.* Trans. H. Rackham. New York: Macmillan.

Cicero. (1945). *Tusculan disputations.* Trans. J. E. King. Cambridge, MA: Harvard University Press. (Loeb Classical Library).

Clines, D. J. (1995). *Interested Parties: The Ideology of Writers and Readers of the Hebrew Bible (Vol. 1).* Sheffield: Sheffield Academic Press.

Cohen, J. (2008). Safe in our hands? A study of suicide and self-harm in asylum seekers. *Journal of Forensic and Legal Medicine, 15*(4), 235–244.

Cohen, S. J. D. (1982). Masada, literature, tradition, archaeological remains, and the credibility of Josephus. *Journal of Jewish Studies, 33*, 385–405.

Conon. (1798). *Narrationes Quinquaginta et Parthenii Narrationes Amatoriae,* Gottingae, GER: J. C. Dietrich.

Conwell, Y. (1996). Relationships of age and Axis I diagnoses in victims of completed suicide: A psychological autopsy study. *American Journal of Psychiatry, 153*, 1001–1008.

Corder, B. F., Page, P. V., & Corder, R. F. (1974). Parental history, family communication and interaction patterns in adolescent suicide. *Family Therapy, 1*, 285–290.

Cowley, C. (2006). Suicide is neither rational nor irrational. *Ethical Theory and Moral Practice, 9* (5), 495–504.

Coyl, D., & Van Dulmen, M. (2000). Adopted adolescents' overrepresentation in mental health counseling: Adoptees' problems or parents' lower threshold for referral? *Journal of the American Academy of Child And Adolescent Psychiatry, 39* (12), 1504–1511.

Cumming, E., & Henry, W. E. (1961). *Growing Old, the Process of Disengagement.* New York: Basic Books.

Curlee, J. (1969). Alcoholism and the empty-nest. *Bulletin of the Menninger Clinic, 33,* 165–171.

Cyrulnik, B. (2011). *Resilience: How Your Inner Strength Can Set You Free from the Past.* New York: Jeremy B. Tarcher/ Penguin.

da Costa Nunez, R. (1994). *Hopes, Dreams & Promise: The Future of Homeless Children in America.* New York: Institute for Children and Poverty, Homes for the Homeless.

Darbonne, A. R. (1969). Suicide and age: A suicide note analysis. *Journal of Consulting and Clinical Psychology, 33*(1), 46.

De Silva, P. (1995). What you can change and what you can't—The complete guide to successful self-improvement: Martin E.P. Seligman: Alfred A. Knopf, New York (1994)

De Tocqueville, A. (1863). *Democracy in America,* Vol. 1. Translated by Henry Reeve, Esq. Third Edition, Cambridge, England: Sever and Francis. .

Deutscher, I. (1964). The quality of postparental life: Definitions of the situation. *Journal of Marriage and the Family, 26*, 52–59.

Deykin, E., Jacobson, S., Klerman, G. & Solomon, M. (1966). The empty nest: Psychosocial aspects of conflict between depressed women and their grown children. *American Journal of Psychiatry, 122*, 1422–1426.

d'Holbach, P. H. T. [1770] [1821]. *Système de la nature.* Paris: Etienne Ledoux.

Diogenes Laertius. (1972). *Lives of Eminent Philosophers.* Robert D. Hicks (Trans.). Cambridge, MA: Harvard University Press: Loeb Classical, 1972.

Dodds, E. R. (1966). On misunderstanding the "Oedipus Rex." *Greece & Rome, Second Series (1)*, 37–49.

Donne, J. (1608, 1984). *Biathanatos.* Ernest W. Sullivan II. (Ed.) Cranbury, NJ: Associated University Press.

Dorpat, T. L. (1973). Suicide, loss, and mourning. *Suicide and Life-Threatening Behavior, 3*(3), 213–224.

Dorpat, T. L., & Ripley, H. S. (1967). The relationship between attempted suicide and committed suicide. *Comprehensive Psychiatry, 8*(2), 74–79.

Douglas, J. D. (1967). *The Social Meanings of Suicide.* Princeton, NJ: Princeton University Press.

Droge, A. J., & Tabor, J. D. (1992). *A Noble Death: Suicide and Martyrdom among Christians and Jews in Antiquity.* San Francisco: Harper: San Francisco.

Dublin, L. I. (1963). *Suicide: A Sociological and Statistical Study.* New York: Ronald Press.

Dublin, L. I., & Bunzel, B. (1933). *To Be, or Not To Be: A Study of Suicide.* New York: Smith and Haas.

Durkheim, E. (1897/1951). *Suicide.* J. A. Spaulding and G. Simpson (Trans.). Glencoe, IL: Free Press.

Dutton, D. G., & Yamini, S. (1995). Adolescent parricide: An integration of social cognitive theory and clinical views of projective-introjective cycling. *American Journal of Orthopsychiatry, 65*(1), 39.

Dwivedi, K. N. (ed.). (1993). *Group Work with Children and Adolescents: A Handbook*. London: Jessica Kingsley Publishers.

Eagle, M. (2003). Clinical implications of attachment theory. *Psychoanalytic Inquiry, 23*(1), 27–53.

Edelstein, L. (1943). *The Hippocratic Oath, text, translation and interpretation*. Baltimore: Johns Hopkins Press.

Eisenberg, D., Gollust, S. E., Golberstein, E., & Hefner, J. L. (2007). Prevalence and correlates of depression, anxiety, and suicidality among university students. *American Journal of Orthopsychiatry, 77*(4), 534–542.

Ellis, T. E., Rufino, K. A., Allen, J. G., Fowler, J. C., & Jobes, D. A. (2015). Impact of a suicide-specific intervention within inpatient psychiatric care: The collaborative assessment and management of suicidality. *Suicide and Life-Threatening Behavior, 45*(5), 556–566.

Elwin, V. (1943). *Muria Murder and Suicide*. London: Oxford University Press.

Epictetus. (1885). *The Discourses of Epictetus: With the Enchiridion and Fragments*. Translated by George Long. London, UK: G. Bell and Sons.

Epstein, Y. M. (undated). *Aruch HaShulchan, Yoreh Deah*. New York: Friedman.

Euripides. (1938). Alcestis. Translated by Richard Aldington. In *The Complete Greek Drama: Volume II*, edited by Whitney J. Oates and Eugene O'Neill Jr., 677–722. New York: Random House.

Euripides. (1938). Andromache. Translated by E. P. Coleridge. In *The Complete Greek Drama: Volume I*, edited by Whitney J. Oates and Eugene O'Neill Jr., 847–884 New York: Random House.

Euripides. (1938). The Bacchae. Translated by G. Murray. In Whitney J. Oates and Eugene O'Neill Jr. (Eds.), *The Complete Greek Drama: Volume II*. New York: Random House, 227–288.

Euripides. (1938). Hecuba. Translated by F. M. Stawall. In *The Complete Greek Drama: Volume I*, edited by Whitney J. Oates and Eugene O'Neill Jr., 807–846. New York: Random House.

Euripides. (1938). The Heracleidae. Translated by E. P. Coleridge. In Whitney J. Oates and Eugene O'Neill Jr. (Eds.), *The Complete Greek Drama: Volume I*. New York: Random House, 763–806.

Euripides. (1938). Hippolytus. Translated by E. P. Coleridge. In Whitney J. Oates and Eugene O'Neill Jr. (Eds.), *The Complete Greek Drama: Volume I*. New York: Random House, 763–806.

Euripides. (1938). Iphigenia in Aulis. Translated by F. M. Stawall. In Whitney J. Oates and Eugene O'Neill Jr. (Eds.), *The Complete Greek Drama: Volume II*. New York: Random House, 289–350.

Euripides. (1938). The Phoenissae. Translated by E. P. Coleridge. In *The Complete Greek Drama: Volume II*, edited by Whitney J. Oates and Eugene O'Neill Jr., 171–226. New York: Random House.

Euripides. (1938). The Suppliants. Translated by E. P. Coleridge. In *The Complete Greek Drama: Volume I*, edited by Whitney J. Oates and Eugene O'Neill Jr., 919–958. New York: Random House.

Exline, J. J., Kaplan, K. J., & Grubbs, J. B. (2012). Anger, exit, and assertion: Do people see protest toward God as morally acceptable? *Psychology of Religion and Spirituality, 4*(4), 264.

Faber, M. (1970). *Suicide and Greek Tragedy*. New York: Sphinx.

Fabes, R., & Eisenberg, N. (1992). Young children's coping with interpersonal anger. *Child Development, 63*, 116–128.

Fedden, H. R. (1938). *Suicide: A Social and Historical Study*. London: Peter Davies.

Feigleman, W. (2001). Comparing adolescents in diverging family structures: Investigating whether adoptees are more prone to problems than their nonadopted peers. *Adoption Quarterly, 5*, 5–37.

Feigleman, W. (2005). Are adoptees at increased risk for attempting suicide. *Suicide and Life-Threatening Behavior, 35*(2), 206–216.

Ferrada-Noli, M. (1997). A cross-cultural breakdown of Swedish suicide. *Acta Psychiatrica Scandinavica, 96*(2), 108–116.

Ferrada-Noli, M. (2014). Suicide among immigrants increases. *Lakartidningen, 111*(8), 326.

Festinger, L. (1957). *A Theory of Cognitive Dissonance.* Stanford, CA: Stanford University Press.

Finch, S. M., & Poznanski, E. O. (1971). *Adolescent Suicide.* Springfield, IL: Charles C. Thomas Publishers.

Fine, L., Rodrigue, A., Aron, & Zipperstein, S. (eds). (2003). *Physician of the Soul, Healer of the Cosmos: Isaac Luria and His Kabbalistic Fellowship.* Stanford, CA: Stanford University Press. p. 48.

Finley, M. I. (1959). *The World of Odysseus.* New York: Meridian.

Finley, M. I. (1966). Review of "Enter Plato." *New York Review of Books, VII,* August, *18,* 27–29.

Foster, T., Gillespie, K., McClelland, R., & Patterson, C. (1999). Risk factors for suicide independent of DSM-III-R Axis I disorder. Case-control psychological autopsy study in Northern Ireland, 175 (2), 175–179; DOI: 10.1192/bjp.175.2.175

Frankfort, H., Frankfort, H. A. G., Wilson, J. A., & Jacobsen, T. (1964). *Before Philosophy.* Harmondsworth: Penguin.

Frankl, V. E. (1962). *Man's Search for Meaning.* Boston, MA: Beacon Press.

Freud, S. (1914). On narcissism: An introduction. In J. Strachey (Ed. and Trans.), *The Standard Edition of the Complete Works of Sigmund Freud,* (Vol. 14: 73–102). London: Hogarth Press.

Freud, S. (1923a). The ego and the id. In J. Strachey (Ed. and Trans.), *The Standard Edition of the Complete Psychological Works of Sigmund Freud* (Vol. 19, pp. 3–66). London: Hogarth Press.

Freud, S. (1923b). The infantile genital organizations: An interpolation into the theory of sexuality. In J. Strachey (Ed. and Trans.), *The Standard Edition of the Complete Psychological Works of Sigmund Freud* (Vol. 19, pp. 141–48). London: Hogarth Press.

Freud, S. (1924). The dissolution of the Oedipus complex. In J. Strachey (Ed. and Trans.), *The Standard Edition of the Complete Psychological Works of Sigmund Freud* (Vol. 19, pp. 173–79). London: Hogarth Press.

Freud, S. (1927). The future of an illusion. In J. Strachey (Ed. and Trans.), *The Standard Edition of the Complete Psychological Works of Sigmund Freud* (Vol. 21, 1–56). London: Hogarth Press.

Freud, S. & Breuer, J. (1895). Studies on hysteria, 306. In J. Strachey (Ed. and Trans.), *The Standard Edition of the Complete Psychological Works of Sigmund Freud* (Vol. 2, pp. 21–319). London: Hogarth Press.

Fromm, E. (1950.) *Psychoanalysis and Religion.* New Haven: Yale University Press.

Ganzini, L., Johnston, W. W., McFarland, B. H., Toll, S. W., & Lee, M. A. (1998). Attitudes of parents with amyotrophic lateral sclerosis and their care givers toward assisted suicide. *The New England Journal of Medicine, 339 (14)*, 967–973.

Garfinkle, D., Froese, A., & Hood, J. (1982). Suicide attempts in children and adolescents. *Group, 76*(36.5), 12.

Gay, P. (1987). *A Godless Jew: Freud, Atheism and the Making of Psychoanalysis.* New Haven, CT: Yale University Press.

Giddens, A. (1971). Durkheim's political sociology. *The Sociological Review, 19*(4), 477–519.

Glenn, J. (1977). Pandora and Eve: Sex as the root of all evil. *The Classical World, 71,* 179–185.

Goethe, J. W. V. (1774). *The Sorrows of Young Werther.* Tran. Burton Pike. New York: Modern Library, 2005, 176.

Golden, W. W. (1900). Maimonides' Prayer for Physicians. *Transactions of the Medical Society of West Virginia, 33,* 414–415.

Goldney, R. D. (1981). Attempted suicide in young women: Correlates of lethality. *British Journal of Psychiaty, 139,* 382–390.

Gordon, C. (1965). *The Common Background of Greek and Hebrew Civilizations.* New York: Norton Library.

Gorsuch, N. M. (2006). *The Future of Assisted Suicide and Euthanasia.* Princeton, NJ: Princeton University Press.

Gould, M. S., Fisher, P., Parides, M., Flory, M., & Shaffer, D. (1996). Psychosocial Risk Factors of Child and Adolescent Completed Suicide. *Arch Gen Psychiatry,* (53–12):1155–1162. doi:10.1001/archpsyc.1996.01830120095016

Gouldner, A. (1965). *Enter Plato.* New York: Basic Books.

Gutmann, D. (1975). Parenthood: A key to the comparative study of the life cycle. In N. Datan & L. Ginsberg (Eds.), *Life-span Developmental Psychology: Normative Life Crises.* New York: Academic Press, 167–184.

Haasse, H. S. (1994). *In A Dark Wood Wandering.* Translated from the Dutch by Lewis C. Kaplan. Chicago: Academy Chicago Publishers.

Hadda, J. (2012). *Passionate Women, Passive Men: Suicide in Yiddish Literature.* Albany: State University of New York Press.

Hagaman, A. K., Sivilli, T. I., Ao, T., Blanton, C., Ellis, H., Cardozo, B. L., & Shetty, S. (2016). An investigation into suicides among Bhutanese refugees resettled in the United States between 2008 and 2011. *Journal of Immigrant and Minority Health,* 1–9.

Haight, B. K., & Hendrix, S. A. (1998). Suicidal intent/life satisfaction: Comparing the life stories of older women. *Suicide and Life-Threatening Behavior, 28*(3), 272–284.

Halevy, S. C., & Kaplan, K. J. (1998). Moses and Oedipus: Psychological perspectives on their life stories. *Journal of Psychology and Judaism, 22,* 7–20.

Hankoff, L. D. (1979). Judaic origins of the suicide prohibition. In L. D. Hankoff (Ed.), *Suicide: Theory and clinical aspects.* Littleton, MA: PSG.

Harden, B. (2004). Safety and stability in foster care: A developmental perspective. *The Future of Children, 14*(1), 31–48.

Harrow, M., Jobe, T., & Faull, B. (2012). Do all schizophrenia patients need antipsychotic treatment continuously throughout their lifetime? A twenty year longitudinal study. *Psychological Medicine, 42,* 2145–2155.

Harrow, M., Jobe. T., & Faull, R. (2014). Does treatment of schizophrenia with antipsychotic medications eliminate or reduce psychosis? A twenty year multi-follow-up study. *Psychological Medicine, 44,* 3007–3016.

Harwood, D., Hawton, K., Hope, T., & Jacoby, R. (2001). Psychiatric disorder and personality factors associated with suicide in older people: A descriptive and case-control study. *International Journal of Geriatric Psychiatry, 16*(2), 155–165.

Hazony, Y. (2012). *The Philosophy of Hebrew Scripture.* New York: Cambridge University Press.

Heiden, B. (2005). Eavesdropping on Apollo: Sophocles' *Oedipus the King. Literary Imagination: The Review of the Association of Literary Scholars and Critics* (7.2), 233–57.

Heikkinen, M., Aro, H., & Lonnqvist, J. (1993). Life events and social support in suicide. *Suicide and Life-Threatening Behavior, 23 (4),* 343–358.

Heisel, M. J., Neufeld, E., & Flett, G. L. (2015). Reasons for living, meaning in life, and suicide ideation: Investigating the roles of key positive psychological factors in reducing suicide risk in community-residing older adults. *Aging & Mental Health,* 1–13.

Hendin, H. C. (1994). Seduced by death: Doctors, patients and the Dutch cure: *Issues in Law and Medicine, 10*(2), 123–168.

Hendin, H. C. (1995). Assisted suicide, euthanasia and suicide prevention: The implication of the Dutch experience. *Suicide and Life-Threatening Behavior, 25,* 193–204.

Hendin, H. C. (1998). *Seduced by Death: Doctors, Patients and Assisted Suicide.* New York: W. W. Norton and Company.

Hendin, H., Foley, K., & White, M. (1998). Physician-assisted suicide: Reflections on Oregon's first case. *Issues in Law and Medicine, 14,* 243.

Henriksson, M. M., Aro, H. M., Marttunen, M. J., Heikkinen, M. E., Isometsa, E. T., Kuoppasalmi, K. E. E. A., & Lonnqvist, J. K. (1993). Mental disorders and comorbidity in suicide. *American Journal of Psychiatry, 150,* 935–935.

Hesiod, (1991). *The Works and Days, Theogony, The Shield of Heracles.* Translated by Richmond Lattimore. Ann Arbor, MI: Ann Arbor Paperbacks: The University of Michigan Press.

Hill, M. N. (1970). Suicidal behavior in adolescents and its relationship to the lack of personal empathy. *Dissertation Abstracts International, 31,* 472.

Hobdy, J., Hayslip, B., Jr., Kaminski, P. L., Crowley, B. J., Riggs, S. and York, C. (2007). The role of attachment style in coping with job loss and the empty nest in adulthood. *International Journal of Aging and Human Development, 65*(4), 335–371.

Holy Scriptures, The, According to the Masoretic Text (Volumes 1 and 2). (1985). Philadelphia, PA: The Jewish Publication Society of America.

Huizinga, J. (1955). *Homo Ludens.* Boston: Beacon Press.

Hume, D. (1894). *An Essay on Suicide.* With a historical and critical introduction by G. W. Foote. London: R. Forder.

Hunter, V. J. (1971). Thucydides and the historical fact. *The Classical Journal, 67*(1), 14–19.

Hunter, V. J. (1982). *Past and Process in Herodotus and Thucydides.* Princeton, NJ: Princeton University Press, 102–103.

Illfeid, F. W. (1977). Current social stressors and symptoms of depression. *American Journal of Psychiatry, 134,* 11–166.

Inskip, H. M., Harris, E. C., & Barraclough, B. (1998). Lifetime risk of suicide for affective disorder, alcoholism and schizophrenia. *The British Journal of Psychiatry, 172*(1), 35–37.

Ionesco, E. (1967). *Exit the King.* Translated from French by Donald Watson. Grove Press.

Joiner, T. E., Jr. (2005). *Why People Die by Suicide.* Cambridge, MA: Harvard University Press.

Joiner, T. E., Jr., Hollar, D. & Van Orden, K. A. (2006). On Buckeyes, Gators, Super Bowl Sunday, and the Miracle on Ice; "Pulling together" is associated with lower suicide rates. *Journal of Social and Clinical Psychology, 25,* 179–195.

Joiner, T. E., Jr., Pettit, J. W., Walker, R. L., & Voelz, Z. R. (2002). Perceived burdensomeness and suicidality: Two studies on the suicide notes of those attempting and those completing suicide. *Journal of Social and Clinical Psychology, 21*(5), 531.

Joiner, T. E., Jr., Van Orden, K. A., Witte, T. K., & Rudd, M. D. (2009). *The interpersonal theory of suicide: Guidance for working with suicidal clients.* Washington, D. C.: American Psychological Association

Joiner, T. E., Jr., Pettit, J. W., Walker, R. L., Voelz, Z. R., Cruz, J., Rudd, M. D., & Lester, D. (2002). Perceived burdensomeness and suicidality: Two studies on the suicide notes of those attempting and those completing suicide. *Journal of Social and Clinical Psychology, 21,* 531–545.

Josephus, F. (1873). *The Works of Flavius Josephus.* New York: Routledge.

Kagan, J. (2009). Why the arts matter: Six good reasons for advocating the importance of arts in school. In Barbara Rich and Johanna Goldberg (Eds.), *Neuroeducation Learning Arts and the Brain,* 29–36. New York: Dana Press.

Kant, I. (1788). *Grundlegung zur Metaphysik der Sitten.* Riga: J. F. Hartknoch.

Kaplan, E. S. (1995). *Russian Nightmares, American Dreams.* New York: The Solomon Press.

Kaplan, K. J. (1987). Jonah and Narcissus: Self-integration versus self-destruction in human development. *Studies in Formative Spirituality, 8:* 33–54.

Kaplan, K. J. (1988). TILT: Teaching individuals to live together. *Transactional Analysis Journal, 18*(3), 220–230.

Kaplan, K. J. (1990a). Isaac and Oedipus: A reexamination of the father-son relationship. *Judaism, 39,* 73–81.

Kaplan, K. J. (1990b). TILT for couples: Helping couples grow together. *Transactional Analysis Journal, 20,* 229–41.

Kaplan, K. J. (1991–1992). Suicide and suicide prevention: Greek versus Biblical Perspectives. *Omega, 24,* 227–39.

Kaplan, K. J. (1998a). Jonah versus Narcissus. In Kalman J. Kaplan and Matthew B. Schwartz (Eds.), *Jewish Approaches to Suicide, Martyrdom and Euthanasia.* Northvale, NJ: Jason Aronson, Inc., 186–196.

Kaplan, K. J. (1998b). Shneidman's definition of suicide and Jewish law: A brief note. In K. J. Kaplan and M. B. Schwartz (Eds.), *Jewish Approaches to Suicide, Martyrdom and Euthanasia,* 78–79. Northvale, NJ: Jason Aronson Inc.

Kaplan, K. J. (1998c) *TILT: Teaching Individuals to Live Together.* Philadelphia, PA: Brunner/ Mazel.

Kaplan, K. J. (1999–2000) *Right to Die versus Sacredness of Life,* Amityville, NY: Baywood Publishing Company. (Published simultaneously as a special issue of *Omega: Journal of Death and Dying, 40*(1), 1999–2000).

Kaplan, K. J. (2002). Isaac versus Oedipus: An alternative view. *Journal of the American Academy of Psychoanalysis, 30*(4): 707–717.

Kaplan, K. J. (2007a). Job, Zeno and Martha Wichorek: A case study in the irrationality of "rational suicide." Presented at Bar Ilan Conference on Rational or Irrational: Psychiatric Disorders and Suicide, Bar Ilan University, Bar-Ilan, ISRAEL, July 5, 2007

Kaplan, K. J. (2007b). Zeno, Job and Terry Schiavo: The Right to Die versus the Right to Life. *Ethics & Medicine, 23*(2), 95.

Kaplan, K. J. (2009). Towards a biblical psychology: Ten commandments for mental health. *Filsosofia Oggi , XXXII –N.128-E-14 (Oct.-Dec.),* 279–303.

Kaplan, K. J. (2012). *Living Biblically: Ten Guides for Fulfillment and Happiness.* Eugene,OR: WIPF and STOCK Publishers

Kaplan, K. J. (2013). Hope unbound: Using biblical narratives to affirm life and prevent suicide. *The Military Chaplain, 87*(2), 23–27.

Kaplan, K. J. (2014). Martha Wichorek's Death. *First Things, October, 246,* 17–19.

Kaplan, K. J. (2015). Oedipus in Jerusalem: A Play in Two Acts. Eugene, OR: WIPF and STOCK Publishers.

Kaplan, K. J. (2016). Towards a biblical psychology for modern Israel: Ten guides for healthy living., *Israel Affairs,* 22 (2), 291–317. Online publication. *(doi:10.1080/ 13537121.2016.1140349)*

Kaplan, K. J., & Anderson, J. W. (2013). Freud, Greek narratives, and Biblical counter-narratives: A dialogue. *Clio's Psyche, 20*(1), 101–111.

Kaplan, K. J., Dodge, N., Wallrabenstein, I., Thiel, K., Ficker, L., Laird, P., Folk, M., Smith, J., Goodman, L., & Shchesyuk, M. (2008). Zenoism, depression & attitudes toward suicide and physician-assisted suicide: The moderating effects of religiosity and gender. *Ethics and Medicine, 24*(3), 167–187.

Kaplan, K. J., Ficker, L., Dodge, N., Thiel, K., Wallrabenstein, I., Laird, P., & Folk, M. (2007–2008). Why does Zeno the Stoic hold his breath? "Zenoism as a new variable for studying suicide. *Omega: The Journal of Death and Dying, 56*(4), 369–400.

Kaplan, K. J., & Harrow, M. (1996). Positive and negative symptoms as risk factors for later suicidal activity in schizophrenics versus depressives. *Suicide and Life-Threatening Behavior, 26*(2), 105–121.

Kaplan, K. J., & Harrow, M. (1999). Psychosis and functioning as risk factors for later suicidal activity among schizophrenia and schizoaffective patients: An interactive model. *Suicide and Life-Threatening Behavior, 29*(1), 10–24.

Kaplan, K. J., Harrow, M., & Clews, K. (2016). The twenty-year trajectory of suicidal activity among post-hospital psychiatric men and women with mood disorders and schizophrenia. *Archives of Suicide Research, 20*(3), 336–348.

Kaplan, K. J., Harrow, M. & Faull, R. B. (2012) Are there gender-specific risk factors for Suicidal activity among patients with schizophrenia and depression? *Suicide and Life- Threatening Behavior, 42*(6), 614–627.

Kaplan, K. J., Harrow, M., & Schneiderhan, M. (2002). Suicide, physician-assisted suicide and euthanasia in men versus women around the world: The degree of physician control. *Ethics and Medicine, 18*(1), 33–48.

Kaplan. K. J., & Leonhardi. M. (2000). Kevorkian, Martha Wichorek and us: A personal account. In K. J. Kaplan (Ed.), *Right to Die versus Sacredness of Life,* 267–270. Amityville, NY: Baywood Publishing Company. (Published simultaneously in a special issue of *Omega: Journal of Death and Dying, 40*(1), 1999–2000: 267–270.

Kaplan, K. J., & Maldaver, M. (1993). Parental marital style and completed adolescent suicide. *Omega: Journal of Death and Dying, 27*(2), 131–154.

Kaplan, K. J., & Markus-Kaplan, M. (1979). Covenant versus contract as two modes of rela-tionship-orientation: On reconciling possibility and necessity. *Journal of Psychology and Judaism, 4,* 100–116.

Kaplan, K. J., & O'Connor, N. A. (1993). From mistrust to trust: Through a stage vertically. In S. I. Greenspan and G. H. Pollock (Eds.), *The Course of Life,* vol. 6, pp. 153–98. New York: International Universities Press.

Kaplan, K. J., & Ross, L. T. (1995). Life ownership orientation and attitudes toward abortion, suicide and capital punishment. *Journal of Psychology and Judaism, 19*(1), 177–193.

Kaplan, K. J., & Schwartz. M. W. (Ed.) (1998). *Jewish Approaches to Suicide, Martyrdom and Euthanasia.* Northvale, NJ: Jason Aronson.

Kaplan, K. J., & Schwartz, M. W. (2006, 2008). *The Seven Habits of the Good Life: How the Biblical Virtues Free Us from the Seven Deadly Sins.* Lanham, MD: Rowman and Littlefield Publishing Group.

Kaplan, K. J., & Schwartz, M. B. (2008). *A Psychology of Hope: A Biblical Response to Tragedy and Suicide.* Grand Rapids, MI: Wm. B. Eerdmans Publisher, 2008.

Kaplan, K. J., Schwartz, M. B., & Jones, E. R. (2010). A biblical view of health, sickness and healing: Overcoming the traditional Greek view of medicine. In J. H. Ellens (Ed.) *The Healing Power of Spirituality, How Religion Helps Humans Thrive,* 3 vols., Westport, CT: Praeger, Vol. 3, 230–242.

Kaplan, K. J., Schwartz, M. B., & Markus-Kaplan. M. (1984). *The Family: Biblical and Psychological Foundations.* New York: Human Sciences Press.

Kaplan, K. J., & Worth, S. (1993). Individuation-attachment and suicide trajectory: A develop-mental guide for the clinician. *Omega: Journal of Death and Dying, 27,* 297–237.

Katz, J. (1968). *No Time for Youth.* San Francisco: Jossey-Bass.

Kidd, S. A. (2007). Youth homelessness and social stigma. *Journal of Youth Adolescence, 36,* 291–299.

Kissane, D. W., Street, A., & Nitchske, P. (1998). Seven deaths in Darwin:Case studies undr the Rights of the Terminally Ill Act, Northern Territory in Australia, *The Lancet, 353,* 1097–1102.

Kleiman, E. M., & Beaver, J. K. (2013). A meaningful life is worth living: Meaning in life as a suicide resiliency factor. *Psychiatry Research, 210*(3), 934–939.

Knox, K. L. (2003). Risk of suicide and related adverse outcomes after exposure to a suicide prevention programme in the US Air Force: cohort study. *The BMJ, 327,* 1376–0.

Kobler, A. L., & Stotland, E. (1964). *The End of Hope.* Free Press of Glencoe.

Koch, H. J. (2005). Suicides and suicide ideation in the Bible: an empirical survey. *Acta Psychiatrica Scandinavica, 112*(3), 167–172.

Koenig, H. G. (2005). *Faith and Mental Health: Religious Resources for Healing.* West Con-shohocken, PA: Templeton Foundation Press.

Kohut, H. (1971). *The Analysis of the Self: The Psychoanalytic Study of the Child.* Monograph No. 4. New York: International Universities Press.

Kosky, R. (1983). Childhood suicidal behaviour. *Journal of Child Psychology and Psychiatry, 24*(3), 457–468.

Lafuze, J. E., Perkins, D. V., & Avirappatt, G. A. (2004). Pastors' perceptions of mental disorders. *Psychiatric Services, 53–7,* 900–901.

Lange, A., De Beurs, E., Dolan, C., Lachnit, T., Sjollema, S., & Hanewald, G. (1999). Long-term effects of childhood sexual abuse: Objective and subjective characteristics of the abuse and psychopathology in later life. *The Journal of Nervous and Mental Disease, 187*(3), 150–158.

Lattimore, R. A. (Ed.). (1951). *The Iliad of Homer.* Chicago: University of Chicago Press.

Lattimore, R. A. (Ed.). (1967). *The Odyssey of Homer.* New York: Harper & Row.

Lawton, M. P. (1980). *Social and Medical Services in Housing for the Aged.* Dept. of Health and Human Services, Public Health Service, Alcohol, Drug Abuse, and Mental Health Administration.

Lebacqz, K., & Englehardt, H. T., Jr. (1977). Suicide and covenant. In D. J. Horam and D. Mall (Eds.), *Death and Dying and Euthenasia.* Washington, DC: University. Publications of America.

Ledgerwood, D. M. (1999). Suicide and attachment: Fear of abandonment and isolation from a developmental perspective. *Journal of Contemporary Psychotherapy, 29*(1), 65–73.

Lee, E. E. (1978). Suicide and youth. *Personnel & Guidance Journal, 57*(4), 200–204.

Lemon, B. W., Bengtson, V. L., & Peterson, J. A. (1972). An exploration of the activity theory of aging: Activity types and life satisfaction among in-movers to a retirement community. *Journal of Gerontology, 27*(4), 511–523.

Lerner, M. J., & Miller, D. T. (1978). Just world hypothesis and the attribution process: Looking forward and ahead. *Psychological Bulletin, 85*(5), 1030–1051.

Lester, D. (2003). Adolescent suicide from an international perspective. *The American Behavioral Scientist, 46*(9), 1157–1170.

Lester, D., Saito, Y., & Ben Park, B. C. (2011). Suicide among foreign residents of Japan. *Psychological Reports, 108*(1), 139–140.

Lester. G., & Lester, D. (1971). *Suicide: The Gamble with Death.* Englewood Cliffs, NJ: Prentice Hall.

Lester, J., & Pinkney, J. (1987). *The Tales of Uncle Remus: The Adventures of Brer Rabbit* (Vol. 1). New York: Dial Books.

Levi-Strauss, C. (1970). *The Raw and the Cooked.* John and Doreen Weightman (Translators). New York: Harper and Row.

Lifton, R. J. (1986). *The Nazi Doctors: A Study of the Psychology of Evil.* London, ENG: Macmillan.

Lindell, K. (1973). Stories of suicide in ancient China. *Acta Orientalia, 35*, 167–239.

Litman, R. E., & Tabachnick, N. D. (1968). Psychoanalytic theories of suicide. In *Suicidal Behaviors, Diagnosis, and Management.* Boston: Little, Brown & Co, 73–81.

Lowenthal, M. F., & Chiriboga, D. (1972). Transition to the empty nest: Crisis, challenge, or relief?. *Archives of General Psychiatry, 26*(1), 8–14.

MacMahon, B., & Pugh, T. F. (1965). Suicide in the widowed. *American Journal of Epidemiology, 81*(1), 23–31.

Main, M., Kaplan, N., & Cassidy. J. (1985). Security in infancy, childhood, and adulthood: A move to the level of representation. In *Growing Points of Attachment Theory and Research, Monographs of the Society for Research in Child Development, 50*(1/2), 66–104 Published by: Wiley on behalf of the Society for Research in Child Development.

Mann, T. (1925). *Death in Venice.* Trans L. Kenneth Burke. New York: Knopf.

Margolin, N. L., & Teicher, J. D. (1968). Thirteen adolescent male suicide attempts: Dynamic considerations. *Journal of the American Academy of Child Psychiatry, 7*(2), 296–315.

Maris, R. W. (1969). *Social Forces in Urban Suicide.* Homewood, IL: Dorsey Press.

Maris, R. W. (1971). Deviance as therapy: The paradox of the self-destructive female. *Journal of Health and Social Behavior, 12*, 113–124.

Maris, R. W. (1981). Social relations of suicide: Isolation, negative interaction, and sexual deviance. In R. W. Maris (Ed.), *Pathways to Suicide.* Baltimore, MD: Johns Hopkins University Press, 100–134.

Maris, R. W. (1982). Rational suicide: An impoverished self-transformation. *Suicide and Life-Threatening Behavior* 12: 4–16.

Maris, R. W. (1985) The3 adolescent suicide problem. *Suicide and Life-Threatening Behavior, 15*(2), 91–109.

Markus-Kaplan, M., & Kaplan, K. J. (1979). The typology, diagnosis, pathologies and treatment-intervention of Hellenic versus Hebraic personality styles: A proposal on the psychology of interpersonal distancing. *Journal of Psychology and Judaism, 3*, 153–167.

Martin, G., Rozanes, P., Pearce, C., & Allison, S. (1995). Adolescent suicide, depression and family dysfunction. *Acta Psychiatrica Scandinavica, 92*(5), 336–344.

Martin, W. T. (1968). Theories of variation in the suicide rate. *Suicide.* New York: Harper & Row.

McFadyen, J. E. (1904). Hellenism and Hebraism. *The American Journal of Theology, 8*, 30–47.

McIntire, M. S., & Angle, C. R. (1973). Psychological "biopsy" in self-poisoning of children & adolescents. *Archives of Pediatrics & Adolescent Medicine, 126*(1), 42.

McKenry, P. C., Tishler, C. L., & Kelley, C. (1982). Adolescent suicide: A comparison of attempters and nonattempters in an emergency room population. *Clinical pediatrics, 21*(5), 266–270.

Miller, B. C., Fan, X., Christensen, M., Grotevant, H. D., & Van Dulmen, M. (2000). Comparisons of adopted and nonadopted adolescents in a large, nationally representative sample. *Child Development, 71*(5), 1458–1473.

Miller, B. C., Fan, X., Grotevant, H. D., Christensen, M., Coyl, D., & Van Dulmen, M. (2000). Adopted adolescents' overrepresentation in mental health counseling: Adoptees' problems or parents' lower threshold for referral? *Journal of the American Academy of Child & Adolescent Psychiatry, 39*(12), 1504–1511.

Miller, M. (1979). *Suicide after Sixty: The Final Alternative.* New York: Springer.

Minuchin, S. (1974). *Families and Family Therapy.* Cambridge, MA: Harvard University Press.

Mitchell, B. (1999–2000). Of euphemisms and euthanasia. The language games of the Nazi doctors and some implications for the modern euthanasia movement. *Omega, 40*(1), 255–265.

Modrcin–McCarthy, M. A., Pullen, L., Barnes, A. F., & Alpert, J. (1998.) Childhood anger: So common, yet so misunderstood. *Journal of Child and Adolescent Psychiatric Nursing, 11*(2), 69–77.

Moilanen, J., Haapea, M., Mietunen, J., Jaaskelainen, E., Veijola, J., Isohanni, M., & Koponen, H. (2013). Characteristics of subjects with schizophrenia spectrum disorder with and without antipsychotic medications: A ten year followup of the Northern Finland 1966 Birth Cohort Study. *European Psychiatry, 28,* 53–58.

Moustakas, C. E. (1961). *Loneliness.* Englewood Cliffs, NJ: Prentice-Hall.

Muntner, S. (1977). Medicine in ancient Israel. In F. Rosner (Ed.), *Medicine in the Bible and the Talmud.* Hoboken, NJ: KTAV, 3–20.

NASB Interlinear Greek-English New Testament. (1984). Grand Rapids, MI: Zondervan.

Neugarten, B. L. (1968). *Middle Age and Aging: A Reader in Social Psychology.* Chicago, IL: University of Chicago Press.

Newton, R. R., Litrownik, A. J., & Landsverk, J. A. (2000). Children and youth in foster care: Disentangling the relationship between problem behaviors and number of placements. *Child Abuse & Neglect, 24*(10), 1363–1374.

Nyman, A. K., & Jonsson, H. (1986). Patterns of self-destructive behaviour in schizophrenia. *Acta Psychiatrica Scandinavica, 73*(3), 252–262.

Oates, R. K. (2004). Sexual abuse and suicidal behavior. *Child Abuse and Neglect, 28*(5), 487–489.

Oates, W. J., & O'Neill, E., Jr. (1938). *The Complete Greek Drama: Volumes 1 and 2.* Translated and Edited by Whitney J. Oates and Eugene O'Neill, Jr. New York: Random House, 1938.

Ohara, K. (1961). A study of main causes of suicide. *Psychiatric Neurology of Japan, 63,* 107–166.

Ovid, *Metamorphoses,* Translated by Charles Boer. Dallas, TX: Spring Publications, 1989.

Oyama, H., Koida, J., Sakashita, T., & Kudo, K. (2004). Community-based prevention for suicide in elderly by depression screening and follow-up. *Community Mental Health Journal, 40*(3), 249–263.

Palmer, B. A., Pankratz, V. S., & Bostwick, J. M. (2005). The lifetime risk of suicide in schizophrenia: A reexamination. *Archives of General Psychiatry, 62*(3), 247–253.

Pargament, K. I. (1997). *The Psychology of Religious Coping.* New York: Guilford.

Pargament, K. I., & Mahoney, A. (2002). Spirituality: Discovering and conserving the sacred. In C. R. Snyder (Ed.), *Handbook of Positive Psychology* (pp. 646–675). Washington, DC: American Psychological Association.

Parnitzke, C., & Regel, H. (1973). Self-destruction of minors caused by social disintegration. *Psychiatrie, Neurologie und Medizinische Psychologie. 25,* 606–614.

Paul, H. (1995). *When Kids Are Mad, Not Bad.* New York: Berkeley.

Pearson, J. L., & Conwell, Y. (Eds). (1996). *Suicide and Aging: International Perspectives.* New York: Springer Publishers.

Pearlin, & Lieberman, M. (1977) Social sources of emotional distress. In R. Simmons (Ed.), *Research in Community and Mental Health*. Greenwich, CT: JAI Press.

Peterson, C., & Seligman, M. E. P. (1984). Causal explanations as a risk factor for depression. Theory and evidence. *Psychological Review, 91*, 347–374.

Peterson, C., Seligman, M. E. P., Yurko, K. H., Martin, L. R., & Friedman, H. S. (1998). Catastrophizing and untimely death. *Psychological Science, 9*(2), 127–130.

Pfeffer, C. R. (1981). Parental suicide: An organizing event in the development of latency age children. *Suicide and Life-Threatening Behavior, 11*(1), 43–50.

Phipps, W. E. (1988). Eve and Pandora contrasted. *Theology Today, 45*, 34–48.

Pirke Aboth-The Ethics of the Talmud: Sayings of the Father. (1962). New York: Schocken Books.

Plato, (1999). Laws. Translated by A. E. Taylor. In *Plato, The Collected Dialogues, Including the Letters*. 1225–1513. Edited by Edith Hamilton and Huntington Cairns. Bollingen Series LXXI, Princeton, NJ: Princeton University Press.

Plato, (1999). Protagora. Translated by W. K. C. Guthrie. In *Plato, The Collected Dialogues, Including the Letters*. 308–352. Edited by Edith Hamilton and Huntington Cairns. Bollingen Series LXXI, Princeton, NJ: Princeton University Press.

Plato, (1999). Republic. Translated by P. Shorrey. In *Plato, The Collected Dialogues, Including the Letters*. 575–844. Edited by Edith Hamilton and Huntington Cairns. Bollingen Series LXXI, Princeton, NJ: Princeton University Press.

Plato, (1999). Socrates' Defense (Apology). Translated by P. Shorrey. In *Plato, The Collected Dialogues, Including the Letters*. 3–26. Edited by Edith Hamilton and Huntington Cairns. Bollingen Series LXXI, Princeton, NJ: Princeton University Press.

Pliny the Elder. (1857). *The Natural History of Plinius Secundus*, vol. 6. Trans. J. Bostock and H. T. Riley. London: Henry G. Bohn.

Plotinus. (1918). *Complete works*. Trans. K. S. Guthrie. London: George Bell and Son.

Plunkett, A. M., O'Toole, B., Swanston, H. I., Oates R. K., Shrimpton, S., & Parkinson, S. (2001). Suicide risk following child sexual abuse. *Ambulatory Pediatric, 1*, 262–266.

Plutarch (1909). *Lives of Themistocles, Pericles, Aristides, Alcibiades and Coriolanus, Demosthenes and Cicero, Caesar and Antony*. The Harvard Classics, Edited by Charles N. Eliot. In the translation called Dryden's Corrected and Revised by Arthur Hugh Clough. New York: P. F. Collier and Sons.

Plutarch. (1932). *The Lives of the Noble Grecians and Romans*. New York: Modern Library.

Ponizovsky, A. M., Ritsner, M. S., & Modai, I. (1999). Suicidal ideation and suicide attempts among immigrant adolescents from the former Soviet Union to Israel. *Journal of the American Academy of Child and Adolescent Psychiatry, 38*(11), 1433–1441.

Pretzel, P. W. (1972). *Understanding and Counseling the Suicidal Person*. Nashville, TN: Abingdon.

Preuss, J. (1978). *Biblical and Talmudic Medicine* F. Rosner (Tr. and Ed.). Northvale, NJ: Jason Aronson, Inc.

Radloff, L. S. (1980). Depression and the empty nest. *Sex Roles, 6* (6), 775–781. Ralbag on 2 Sam. 1:14.

Rahman, A., & Hafeez, A. (2003). Suicidal feelings run high among mothers in refugee camps: A cross-sectional survey. *Acta Psychiatrica Scandinavica, 108*(5), 392–393.

Reik, T. (1948). *Listening with the Third Ear: The Inner Experience of a Psychoanalyst*. New York: Farrar, Strauss and Giroux.

Reik, T. (1961). *The Temptation*. New York: George Brazilier.

Rew, L., Thomas, N., Horner, S. D., Resnick, M. D., & Beuhring, T. (2001). Correlates of recent suicide attempts in a triethnic group of adolescents. *Journal of Nursing Scholarship, 33*(4), 361–367.

Rich, C. L., Young, D., & Fowler, R. C. (1986). San Diego suicide study: I. Young vs. old subjects. *Archives of General Psychiatry, 43*(6), 577.

Richman, J. (1978). Symbiosis, empathy, suicidal behavior, and the family. *Suicide and Life-Threatening Behavior, 8*(3), 139–149.

Richman, J. (1981). Suicide and the family: Affective disturbances and their implications for understanding, diagnosis, and treatment. *Family Therapy and Major Psychopathology*, 145–160.

Richman, J. (1986). *Family Therapy for Suicidal People*. New York: Springer.

Rin, H. (1975). Suicide in Taiwan. In N. Farberow (Ed.), *Suicide in Different Cultures*. Baltimore: University Park Press.

Ringel, E. 1981. Suicide prevention and the value of human life. In M. P. Battin and D. J. Mayo (Eds.), *Suicide: The Philosophical Issues*. London: Peter Owen.

Rojzcewicz, S. J. (1971). War and suicide. *Suicide and Life-Threatening Behavior, 1*, 46–54.

Rollins, R. C., & Feldman, H. (1970). Marital satisfaction over the family life cycle. *Journal of Marriage and the Family, 32*, 20–28.

Rojzcewicz, S. J. (1971). War and suicide. *Suicide and Life-Threatening Behavior, 1*, 46–54.

Rolnik, E. (2007). *Freud in Zion: History of Psychoanalysis in Jewish Palestine/Israel 1918–1948*, Tel-Aviv: ISRAEL: Am Oved.

Rosenzweig, F. (1971, 1985). *The Star of Redemption*, translated by William W. Hallo. Notre Dame, IN: Notre Dame Press.

Rosner, F. (1970). Suicide in biblical, Talmudic, and rabbinic writ zweiings. *Tradition, 11*, 25–40.

Rosner, F. R. (1998). Suicide in Jewish law. In K. J. Kaplan and M. B. Schwartz (Eds.), *Jewish Approaches to Suicide, Martyrdom and Euthanasia*, 61–77. Northvale, NJ: Jason Aronson Inc.

Ross, L. T., & Kaplan, K. J. (1993–1994). Life ownership orientation and attitudes toward abortion, suicide, doctor-assisted suicide and capital punishment. *Omega: The Journal of Death and Dying, 28*, 17–30.

Rossau, C. D., & Mortensen, P. B. (1997). Risk factors for suicide in patients with schizophrenia: Nested case-control study. *The British Journal of Psychiatry, 171*(4), 355–359.

Rossi, P. H. (1980). *Why Families Move*. Beverly Hills, CA: Sage Publications, Inc.

Rotenberg, M. (1993). *Dialogue with Deviance: The Hasidic Ethic and the Theory of Social Contraction.* Lanham, MD: University Press of America.

Rotenberg, M. (2004a). *Hasidic Psychology: Making Space for Others*. With a new introduction by the author. New Brunswick, NJ: Transaction Publishers.

Rotenberg, M. (2004b). *Rewriting the Self: Psychotherapy and Midrash (1st Edition).* Transaction Publishers. New Brunswick, NJ: Transaction Publishers.

Rotenberg, M. (2005). *Between Rationality and Irrationality: The Jewish Psychotherapeutic System.* With a new introduction and appendix by the author. New Brunswick: Transaction Publishers.

Rotenberg, M. (2016). *The Psychology of Tzimtzum: Self, Other and God.* Jerusalem Israel: Koren Publishers Jerusalem.

Roth, C. (1970). *A History of the Jews: From Earliest Times through the Six Day War*. New York: Schocken.

Rousseau, J. J. [1761] (1925). *La Nouvelle Héloise.* Paris: Hachette.

Rubin, D. M., Allesandrini, E. A., Feudtner, C., Mandell, D. S., Localio, A.R., & Hadley, T. (2004). Placement stability and mental health costs for children in foster care. *Pediatrics, 113*(5), 1336–1341.

Rubin, D. M., O'Reilly, A. L. R., Luan, X., & Localio, A. R. (2007). The impact of placement stability on behavioral well-being for children in foster care. *Pediatrics, 119*(2), 336–344.

Rygenstad, T. K. (1982). A prospective study of social and psychiatric aspects of self-poisoned patients. *Acta Psychiatrica Scandinavica, 66*, 139–153.

Sainsbury, P. (1986). *The Epidemiology of Suicide*. Baltimore, MD: Williams and Wilkins.

Sarwer-Foner, G. J. (1969). Depression and suicide. On some particularly high risk suicidal patients. *Diseases of the Nervous System, 30*(2), Suppl–104.

Sathyavathi, K. (1975). Suicide among children in Bangalore. *The Indian Journal of Pediatrics, 42*(6), 149–157.

Schneer, H. I., Perlstein, A., & Brozovsky, M. (1975). Hospitalized suicidal adolescents: Two generations. *Journal of the American Academy of Child Psychiatry, 14*(2), 268–280.

Schwartz, M. W., & Kaplan, K. J. (2004). *Biblical Stories for Psychotherapy: A Sourcebook.* Binghamton. NY: The Haworth Press.

Schwartz, M. W., & Kaplan, K. J. (2007). *The Fruit of Her Hands: A Psychology of Biblical Woman.* Grand Rapids, MI: Wm B. Eerdmans.

Schwartz, M. W., & Kaplan, K. J. (2013). *Politics in the Hebrew Bible: God, Man and Government.* Lanham, MD: Jason Aronson. Rowman and Littlefield Publishing Group.

Scioli, A. & Biller, H. B. (2009). *Hope in the Age of Anxiety.* New York: Oxford University Press.

Seligman, M. E. (1975, 1992). *Helplessness: On Depression, Development and Death.* With a new introduction by the author. New York: SWH Freeman/Times Books/Henry Holt & Co.

Seligman, M. E. P. (1998). *Learned Optimism.* New York: Free Press.

Seligman, M. E. P. (2002). *Authentic Happiness: Using the New Positive Psychology to Realize Your Potential for Lasting Fulfillment* New York: Free Press.

Seligman, M. E. P. (2011). *Learned Optimism: How to Change Your Mind and Your Life.* New York: Vintage.

Seligman, M. E. P., & Csíkszentmihályi, M. (2000). Positive Psychology: An Introduction. *American Psychologist, 2000, 55,* 5–14.

Selinger, S. S. (1998). Moses: "Kill Me I Pray." In Kalman J. Kaplan & Matthew B. Schwartz (Eds.), *Jewish Approaches to Suicide, Martyrdom and Euthanasia.* Northvale, NJ: Jason Aronson, Inc., 176–185.

Semahot 2: 2 *Tanakh: The Holy Scriptures.* (1985). Philadelphia, PA and Jerusalem, Israel: The Jewish Publication Society.

Seneca (2010). Lucius Annaeus. *De Ira* (Anger, Mercy, Revenge) Translated by Robert A. Kaster & Martha C. Nussbaum Chicago, IL and London, England: University of Chicago Press.

Seneca the Elder (1974). *Oratorum et rhetorum sententiae divisiones, colores.* Trans. M. Winterbottom. Cambridge, MA: Harvard University Press.

Seneca the Younger. (1918). *Ad lucilium epistulae morales.* 3 vols. Trans. R. M. Gummere. London: W. Heinemann.

Seneca the Younger (1979). *Seneca.* Cambridge, MA: Harvard University Press.

Seneca (2010). Lucius Annaeus. *De Ira* (Anger, Mercy, Revenge) Translated by Robert A. Kaster and Martha C. Nussbaum Chicago, IL and London, England: University of Chicago Press.

Shaffer, D. (1974). Suicide in childhood and early adolescence. *Journal of Child Psychology and Psychiatry, 15*(4), 275–291.

Shagle, S. C., & Barber, B. K. (1993). Effects of family, marital, and parent-child conflict on adolescent self-derogation and suicidal ideation. *Journal of Marriage and the Family,* 964–974.

Shakespeare, W. (2014). Coriolanus. In *The Complete Works of William Shakespeare.* San Diego, CAL: Canterbury Classics, 1061–1105.

Shakespeare, W. (2014). Hamlet. In *The Complete Works of William Shakespeare.* San Diego, CA: Canterbury Classics, 735–1105.

Sharansky, N. (1998). *Fear No Evil: The Classic Memoir of One Man's Triumph over a Police State.* Translated by Stefani Hoffman. New York: Public Affairs.

Shedler, J. (2010). The efficacy of psychodynamic therapy. *American Psychologist, 65,* 98–109.

Shedler, J. (2015). Where is the evidence for "evidence-based" therapy? *The Journal of Psychological Therapies in Primary Care, 4,* 47–59.

Shemesh, Y. (2009). Suicide in the Bible. *Jewish Bible Quarterly, 37*(3), 157.

Shestov, L. (1966). *Athens and Jerusalem.* B. Martin (Trans.). New York: Simon and Schuster.

Shneidman, E. S. (1985). *Definition of Suicide.* New York: John Wiley and Sons.

Shneidman, E. S., & Farberow, N. L. (1957). The logic of suicide. In E. S. Shneidman and N. L. Farberow (Eds.), *Clues to Suicide.* New York: McGraw-Hill.

Shoham, S. G. (2011). *Genesis of Genesis: The Mytho-Empiricism of Creation.* Newcastle Upon Tyne, England: Cambridge Scholars Publishing.

Silove, D., Austin, P., & Steel, Z. (2007). No refuge from terror: The impact of detention on the mental health of trauma-affected refugees seeking asylum in Australia. *Transcultural Psychiatry, 44*(3), 359–393.

Simon, B. (1978). *Mind and Madness in Ancient Greece: The Classical Roots of Modern Psychiatry.* Ithaca, NY: Cornell University Press.

Skodlar., B., & Parnas, J. (2010). Self-disorder and subjective dimensions of suicidality in schizophrenia. *Comprehensive Psychiatry, 51,* 363–366.

Skodlar, B., Tomori, M., & Parnas, J. (2008). Subjective experience and suicidal ideation in schizophrenia. *Comprehensive Psychiatry, 49*(5), 482–488.

Slap, G., Goodman, E., & Huang, M. (2001). Adoption as a risk factor for attempted suicide During adolescensce, *Pediatrics, 108,* 1–8.

Slater, P. E. (1968). *The Glory of Hera: Greek Mythology and the Greek Family.* Boston, MA: Beacon Press.

Slater, J., & Depue, R. A. (1981). The contribution of environmental events and social support to serious suicide attempts in primary depressive disorder. *Journal of Abnormal Psychology, 40,* 275–285.

Smyth, C. L., & MacLachlan, M. (2004). The context of suicide: An examination of life circumstances thought to be understandable precursors to youth suicide. *Journal of Mental Health, 13*(1), 83–92.

Snell, B. (1953). *Discovery of the Mind: The Greek Origins of European Thought.* New York: Dover.

Sophocles. (1938). Ajax Translated by R. C. Trevelyan. In Whitney J. Oates and Eugene O'Neill, Jr. (Eds.), *The Complete Greek Drama: Volume 1.* New York: Random House, 315–368.

Sophocles. (1938). Antigone. Translated by R. C. Jebb. In Whitney J. Oates and Eugene O'Neill, Jr. (Eds.), *The Complete Greek Drama: Volume 1.* New York: Random House, 423–460.

Sophocles. (1938). Oedipus at Colonus. Translated by R. C. Jebb. In Whitney J. Oates and Eugene O'Neill, Jr. (Eds.), *The Complete Greek Drama: Volume 1.* New York: Random House, 613–670.

Sophocles. (1938). Oedipus the King. Translated by R. C. Jebb. In Whitney J. Oates and Eugene O'Neill, Jr. (Eds.), *The Complete Greek Drama: Volume 1.* New York: Random House, 369–422.

Sophocles. (1938). The Trachinae. Translated by R. C. Jebb. In *The Complete Greek Drama: Volume 1,* edited by Whitney J. Oates and Eugene O'Neill Jr. , 465–504. New York: Random House.

Stael, A. L. De. (1796). *Sur L'influence des passions.* Paris: Charpentier.

Stael, A. L. De. (1814). *Réflexions sur le suicide.* Paris: Charpentier.

Stengel, E. (1964). *Suicide and Attempted Suicide.* Baltimore: Penguin Books.

Szasz, T. (1962). *The Myth of Mental Illness: Foundations of a Theory of Personal Conduct.* London: Secker and Warburg.

Szasz, T. (1971). The ethics of suicide. *Antioch Review, 31*(1).

Talmud, Babylonian. *Babylonian Talmud.* 1975. Vilna edition. Jerusalem.

Tatai, K., & Kato, M. (Eds.). (1974). *Thinking of Suicide in Japan.* Tokyo: Igaka-Shoiu.

Taussig, H., Clyman, R., & Landsverk, J. (2001). Children who return home from foster care: A 6-year prospective study of behavioral health outcomes in adolescence. *Pediatrics, 108* (1), E10.

Tavernise, S. (2016). Sweeping pain as suicides hit a 30-year high. *New York Times,* April 22, A1.

Thakur, Y. (1963). *The history of suicide in India.* Delhi: Musnshiram Manoharlal.

Titus Livius (Livy) (1960). *The Early History of Rome. Books I-V of the History of Rome from its Foundation.* Translated by Aubrey De Selincourt. Baltimore, MD: Penguin Classics.

Tolstoy, L. (2000). *Anna Karenina.* Leonard J. Kent AEL Nina Berbrova (Editors), Constance Garnett (Translator). Mona Simpson (Introduction) New York: Modern Library Classics.

Topol, P.,& Resnikoff, M. (1982). Perceived peer and family relationships, hopelessness and locus of control as factors in adolescent suicide attempts. *Suicide and life-Threatening Behavior, 12,* 141–150.

Troister, T., D'Agata, M. T., & Holden, R. R. (2015). Suicide risk screening: Comparing the Beck Depression Inventory-II, Beck Hopelessness Scale, and Psychache Scale in undergraduates. *Psychological Assessment, 27,* 1500–1506.

Trout, D. L. (1980). The role of social isolation in suicide. *Suicide and Life-Threatening Behavior, 10* (1), 10–23.

Tuke, Rev. (1613). *A Discourse on Death.* London: n.p.

Vaillant, G. E. (1977). *Adaptation to Life.* Boston, MA: Little, Brown.

Van Orden, K. A., Lynam, M. E., Hollar, D., & Joiner, T. E., Jr. (2006). Perceived burdensomeness as an indicator of suicidal symptoms. *Cognitive Therapy and Research, 30*(4), 457–467.

Voltaire, F. M. A. (1764, 1924). *The Philosophical Dictionary.* Selected and Translated by H.I. Woolf. New York: Knopf.

Voltaire, F. M. A. (1733, 1973). *The Selected Letters of Voltaire.* Ed. and trans. R. A. Brookes. New York: New York University Press.

Wagner, B. M., Silverman, M. A. C., & Martin, C. E. (2003). Family factors in youth suicidal behaviors. *American Behavioral Scientist,* 1171–1191.

Wahoush, E. O. (2009). Reaching a hard-to-reach population such as asylum seekers and resettled refugees in Canada. *Bull World Health Organization,* August, *87 (8),* 568.

Waldvogel, J. L., Rueter, M., & Oberg, C. N. (2008). Adolescent suicide: Risk factors and prevention strategies. *Current Problems in Pediatric and Adolescent Health Care, 38*(4), 110–125.

Warren, L. W., & Tomlinson-Keasey, C. (1987). The context of suicide. *American Journal of Orthopsychiatry, 57,* 41–48.

Weaver, Andrew J. (1995). Has there been a failure to prepare and support parish-based clergy in their role as frontline community mental health workers: A review. *Journal of Pastoral Care, 49–2,* 129–14.

Weininger, O. (2005). *Sex and Character: An Investigation of Fundamental Principles.* Bloomington: Indiana University Press.

Weiss, A. (2000). *Rabbis as Mental Health Professionals*: A Major Metropolitan Study. Lanham, MD: University Press of America.

Wellisch, E. (1954). *Isaac and Oedipus: Studies in Biblical Psychology of the Sacrifice of Isaac.* London: Routledge and Kegan Paul, 1954.

Wenz, F. V. (1978). Economic status, family anomie, and adolescent suicide potential. *The Journal of Psychology, 98*(1), 45–47.

Wenz, F. V. (1979). Family constellation factors, depression and parent suicidal potential. *American Journal of Orthopsychiatry, 49,* 164–167.

Whitaker, R. (2010). *Anatomy of an Epidemic: Magic Bullets, Psychiatric Drugs and the Astonishing Rise of Mental Illness.* New York: Broadway Paperbacks.

Whitaker, R. (2010). *Mad in America: Bad Science, Bad Medicine and the Enduring Mistreatment of the Mentally Ill.* New York: Basic Books.

Wiersma, D., Nienhuis, F. J., Slooff, C. J., & Giel, R. (1998). Natural course of schizophrenic disorders: A 15-year follow-up of a Dutch incidence cohort. *Schizophrenia: Bulletin, 24*(1), 75–85.

Willis, G. C. (1950). *St. Augustine and the Donatist Controversy.* London: S.P.C.K.

Wold, C. I. (1968). Some syndromes among suicidal people: The problem of suicide potentiality. Presented at the Annual Meeting of the American Psychological Association. August, San Francisco, CA.

Wold, C. I. (1970). Characteristics of 20,000 suicide-prevention center patients. *Bulletin of Suicidology, 6,* 24–28.

Wunderink, L., Nieboer, R. M., Wiersma, D., Sytema, S., & Nienhuis, F. J. (2013). Recovery in remitted first-episode psychosis at seven years of follow-up of an early dose reduction/discontinuation or maintenance treatment strategy: Long term follow-up of a two-year randomized clinical trial recovery in remitted first episode psychosis. *JAMA Psychiatry*, 7, 913–920.

Xenophon. (1854). *The Anabasis, or Expedition of Cyrus, and the Memorabilia of So Rates.* Trans. J. S. Watson. London: Henry G. Bohn.

Xenophon. (1857). *Minor Works [including the Apology of Socrates].* Trans. Rev. J. S. Watson. London: Henry G. Bohn.

Yap, Pow-Meng. (1958). *Suicide in Hong Kong, with Special Reference to Attempted Suicide.* Foreword by Martin Roth. Hong Kong: Hong Kong University Press.

Yerushalmi, Y. H. (1991). *Freud's Moses: Judaism Terminable and Interminable.* New Haven, CT: Yale University Press.

Zeller, E. (1962). *The Stoics, Epicureans, and Sceptics.* Trans. O. J. Reichel. New York: Russell and Russell.

Ziffer, E. (2006). *All the People of the Bible.* Tel Aviv: Havav Publishers.

Zubin, J., & Spring, B. (1977). Vulnerability—A new view of schizophrenia. *Journal of Abnormal Psychology, 86*(2), 103–126.

Index

About the Authors

Kalman J. Kaplan, PhD, is professor of clinical psychology and director of the Center for Religion, Spirituality and Mental Health in the Department of Psychiatry and the Department of Medical Education at the University of Illinois at Chicago College of Medicine and adjunct professor of psychology and Judaism at Spertus Institute for Jewish Learning and Leadership. He is also a licensed clinical psychologist in Illinois and Michigan.

Dr. Kaplan has retired as professor of psychology at Wayne State University and held visiting positions at a number of universities, including the University of California, Davis, Harvard University, Boston University, Northwestern University Medical School, and Tel Aviv University. He has been editor of the *Journal of Psychology and Judaism* and on the editorial board of *Omega*. Dr. Kaplan has published widely in the area of interpersonal and international relations, social psychology, personality theory, political psychology, schizophrenia and suicide/suicide prevention, and the emerging field of biblical psychology. Dr. Kaplan is a fellow in the American Psychological Association, was the co-recipient of the 1998 Alexander Gralnick Award for outstanding original research in suicide and schizophrenia, and was a 2006–2007 and 2011–2012 Fulbright Fellow at Tel Aviv University. Dr. Kaplan has published 15 books, many book chapters, and close to 100 published articles. He has also given over 150 presentations, both nationally and internationally.

Dr. Kaplan has had a number of grants in the past, including several from the National Science Foundation and the National Institute of Mental Health. In 2007–2010, Dr. Kaplan was awarded a start-up grant from the John Templeton Foundation to develop an online program in Religion, Spirituality and Mental Health at the University of Illinois College of Medicine. Over the last 10 years, his program in biblical psychology has enrolled over 200 students from all over the world, including therapists, clergy, nurses, and chaplains. He has also developed a Hebrew-subtitled version. He argues that modern psychology and psychiatry have been implicitly based on classical Greek rather than biblical narratives and thinking, and suggests that a biblical psychology would produce a more positive hopeful perspective. Dr. Kaplan is also a member of the ongoing Faith Communities Task Force of the National Action Alliance for Suicide Prevention.

Among Dr. Kaplan's books are *The Family: Biblical and Psychological Foundations* (1984), *Living with Schizophrenia* (1997), *TILT: Teaching Individuals to Live Together* (1998), *Jewish Approaches to Suicide, Martyrdom and Euthanasia* (1998), *Right to Die versus Sacredness of Life* (2000), *Biblical Stories for Psychotherapy and Counseling: A Sourcebook* (2004), *The Seven Habits of the Good Life: How the Biblical Virtues Free Us from the Seven Deadly Sins* (2006, 2008), *The Fruit of Her Hands: A Psychology of Biblical Woman* (2007), *A Psychology of Hope: A Biblical Response to Tragedy and Suicide* (2008), *Living Biblically: Ten Guides for Fulfillment and Happiness* (2012), *In the Beginning: Biblical Sparks for a Child's Week* (2013), and *Politics in the Hebrew Bible: God, Man and Government* (2013). He has recently published a two-act play entitled *Oedipus in Jerusalem* (2015), exploring the conflict between biblical and Greek thinking set in a courtroom drama.

Paul Cantz, PsyD, ABPP, is a licensed, board certified clinical psychologist and associate director of Training and associate professor at Adler University—Chicago; clinical assistant professor, Department of Psychiatry at the University of Illinois at Chicago College of Medicine; coordinator for the UIC Program in Religion, Spirituality and Mental Health and an adjunct faculty member at the Spertus Institute for Jewish Learning and Leadership.

Dr. Cantz concurrently works as the supervising psychologist at Hartgrove Hospital's Inpatient Unit for the therapy/advanced training program. Dr. Cantz maintains a therapy caseload in private practice.

Dr. Cantz has published and presented original scholarship on the topics of the intellectual foundations of psychiatry, the psychology of religious conversion, death anxiety, cross cultural concepts of femininity, psychodynamics of music, the historical uniqueness of baseball, the connection between misogyny and Antisemitism, the bio-ethical ramifications of the anti-aging movement, and most recently on the existential considerations in rise in popularity of dystopian myths, particularly zombie media.

Made in the USA
Coppell, TX
04 July 2020